ADVISING STUDENT ATHLETES

THROUGH THE

COLLEGE RECRUITMENT PROCESS

ADVISING STUDENT ATHLETES

THROUGH THE

COLLEGE RECRUITMENT PROCESS

A Complete Guide for Counselors, Coaches and Parents

MICHAEL D. KOEHLER

PRENTICE HALL

Library of Congress Cataloging-in-Publication Data

Koehler, Michael D.
    Advising student athletes through the college recruitment process: a complete guide
for counselors, coaches, and parents / Michael D. Koehler.
        p. cm.
    ISBN 0-13-311564-X : Spiral   ISBN 0-13-541343-5 : Paper
    1. High school athletes—Recruiting—United States. 2. High school athletes—
Counseling of—United States. 3. Students—Scholarships, fellowships, etc.—United
States. I. Title.
GV350.5.K64   1996   95-24275
796.071'173—dc20   CIP

Printed in the United States of America
10 9 8 7 6 5 4 3 2 1 (S)   10 9 8 7 6 5 4 3 2 1 (P)

ISBN 0-13-311564-X (S)   ISBN 0-13-541343-5 (P)

Prentice-Hall International (UK) Limited, *London*
Prentice-Hall of Australia Pty. Limited, *Sydney*
Prentice-Hall Canada Inc., *Toronto*
Prentice-Hall Hispanoamericana, S.A., *Mexico*
Prentice-Hall of India Private Limited, *New Delhi*
Prentice-Hall of Japan, Inc., *Tokyo*
Simon & Schuster Asia Pte. Ltd., *Singapore*
Editora Prentice-Hall do Brasil, Ltda., *Rio de Janeiro*

DEDICATION

To Pat, because I owe her so much.
To Kathleen, Carrie, and Peggy, for sharing their love.
To Eric and Cassie, for blessing my life.

ACKNOWLEDGMENTS

The author would like to thank several people for contributing their time and knowledge to the completion of this book. The book literally would have been impossible without their help. Thanks to my good friend Lou Adler for all his help with many of the reproducibles and for being such a willing and available sounding board. Thanks as well to Marybeth Kravets for Figure 10-1. It may be copyrighted in my name for purposes of this book, but the information is all hers. The same is true of Figure 9-1, which is the brainchild of Joe Russo, the Director of Financial Aid at the University of Notre Dame. Joe is perhaps the most knowledgeable person in the country regarding financial aid, and, fortunately, he's a good friend.

Thanks also to Tim Albers, the athletic director at Libertyville High School in Illinois, for his assistance with the information regarding student athletes, and to Roger Grooters, the Director of Academic Advisement at Florida State University, for his help with Section 10. Thanks to Lorna Straus for her help with the section on regulatory organizations, to Connie Kallback for her growing friendship and her continuing professional approach to publishing, to Win Huppuch for his belief in this project, to Bill Warren for taking such pains to review the materials, and, as always, to my wife Pat for reading, reviewing, and just being there. Finally, a big thanks to George Kelly, a true legend at the University of Notre Dame for being such a genuine representative of what a coach should be.

ABOUT THE AUTHOR

Mike Koehler played fullback for Marquette University and the University of Nebraska, coached high school football for 31 years, counseled high school students for 25, and has been an adjunct professor of educational administration and supervision since 1974. Currently, he is devoting all his time to writing, teaching at the university level, speaking at conventions, and consulting with schools on teacher supervision and on the eligibility and recruitment of student athletes. Mike is the author of scores of articles for professional journals, a nationally syndicated radio show, a newspaper column, and the videotape, *The ABCs of Eligibility for the College-Bound Student Athlete,* which is being marketed by the College Board. It currently is in its second edition.

In addition to *Advising Student Athletes Through the College Recruitment Process,* Mike has written 10 other books, the three most recent being *Building the Total Athlete, The Department Head's Survival Guide,* and *The Football Coach's Survival Guide,* all with Prentice Hall. He currently is in the planning stages for more books, at least one videotape, and a variety of speaking engagements in and around metropolitan Chicago.

Mike has been married to wife Pat since 1962, has three delightful daughters, Kathleen, Carrie, and Peggy, two fine sons-in-law: Bruce and Dwight, and enjoys time spent with his two grandchildren, Eric Michael and Cassie Jean.

For additional information or to contact Mike, write or call:

Mike Koehler
Ideation, Inc.
1281 Banbury Rd.
Mundelein, IL 60060
708-949-8451

ABOUT THIS RESOURCE

Imagine a Saturday afternoon in early November, a bright blue sky, gusting winds, and swirls of yellow and red leaves on the common between College Avenue and Sicard Street in New Brunswick, New Jersey. Students from Princeton and Rutgers are sizing each other up before the start of a game that is little more than a swarm of bodies and an anarchy of rules. Two teams of twenty-five players alternately kick the ball, their opponents, and each other until merciful darkness sends everyone home. History will recognize it as college football's first game. The year is 1869.

The players use pocket money for budgets, layered clothing for protective equipment, and captains-elect for coaches. The dimensions of the field are make shift, and the fifty players on it stage a game that is more a combination of English rugby and soccer than American football, but it marks the beginning of an autumn tradition that still brightens most college campuses and reaches into millions of American homes.

In 1874, just five years after that first game, James McCash, the President of Princeton University, said, "It's a nice question whether evils may not arise from sports in no way under control of the college authorities." His concern was expressed well before women played college basketball's first game in 1896. The observation, however, was prophetic for all of sport and would be echoed several years later when Amos Alonzo Stagg, in his book *Touchdown* (1927), explained the captain's authority, "He chose the team and was not above playing favorites. Once elected, he was answerable to no one."

"Answerable to no one" has remained the best way to describe the continuing relationship between athletic departments and university officials for one hundred years. Once a glorified pickup game to establish the pecking order among local universities, football has become a multimillion-dollar giant that now reaches boldly into the homes of promising athletes to guarantee them everything from big-time competition to bigger-time bucks. And football is not the only sport so involved.

A member of both the basketball and football halls of fame, Stagg provides another quote that can be applied to most college sports: "Most of the evils that have beset the game from time to time have been the direct result of student and alumni management, but the blame lies *on the faculty doorstep.*" [italics mine] Fortunately, within the past several years, groups like the NCAA and the Knight Commission have intervened.

In response to reports that fully one-half of the nation's 106 Division 1-A football schools received sanctions from the NCAA in the 1980s, the Knight Commission, in March of 1991, after two years of study, recommended that university presidents assume complete control of their schools' academic *and* athletic departments. They also made specific suggestions regarding academic integrity, financial integrity, and accountability through certification.

This "One-Plus-Three" model was a timely complement to the NCAA's legislative changes regarding player eligibility. Proposition 48 in the mid-1980s established minimum scores for the ACT and SAT and a core of academic courses to determine the eligibility of high school athletes who wanted to play in college. Controversial for several reasons, the most prominent being its alleged discrimination against the disadvantaged, Prop 48 survived its critics and has, in fact, increased the academic awareness of high school athletes.

In addition, the national focus on student athletes not only curbed abuses but influenced such factors as recruiting practices, numbers of scholarships, and the length of practice sessions in and out of season. It also highlighted the importance of high school coaches and counselors and their early involvement in balancing the athletic and academic interests of high school athletes.

My thirty years in high school athletics have taught me that for every "abused" college athlete, there's a high school coach somewhere who didn't do his or her job. High school athletes, therefore, need the assistance of their coaches and counselors. Recent attempts to secure such involvement have revealed that the coaches, counselors, and parents need help. Most are unfamiliar with NCAA rules, recruiting restrictions, and processes that assure a balance between the athletic and academic interests of student athletes.

Advising Student Athletes Through the College Recruiting Process provides such help. The first section looks briefly at the evolution of college sports and provides an important perspective for assisting student athletes with the recruiting and college selection processes. The second section explains the purposes and procedures of the NCAA, its relevant committees and legislative processes, and such specifics as bylaw 14.3, recruiting requirements, and contact periods.

Section 3 discusses the "real world" of athletic scholarships. It focuses on the fact that only 1% to 3% of high school athletes receive scholarships to play in college. It also explains that another percentage use their athletic ability to gain admission to highly selective colleges and universities—schools that normally might not admit them. Section 4 discusses recruiting and college selection from a parental perspective and highlights parents' role in the process.

Section 5 outlines the coach's role in the process, focusing on his or her pre-season, in-season, and post-season responsibilities, including the development of highlight tapes and processes for maintaining communication with college personnel. Section 6 discusses the responsibilities of counselors, athletic directors, and college consultants, if a college consultant is available in your school. This section focuses on the need to monitor compliance with NCAA requirements, to sustain a focus on the importance of academics, and to assure career exploration and an appropriate college selection process.

Section 7 outlines the responsibilities of the athlete. Parents, coaches, counselors, athletic directors, and college consultants should be available to assist student athletes with the transition to college, but the primary responsibility belongs to the student. Section 8 outlines the specifics of a coalition that combines the student athletes, their parents, coaches, counselors, and others to guarantee continuing communication among all parties. It begins with a discussion of activities during the student's freshman year and concludes with the particulars of meetings during the college selection process.

Section 9 reviews the whole question of financial aid: the particulars of the actual scholarship, the additional aid that is available to athletes, the processes for securing such aid, and the responsibilities of the college and the student after the athlete matriculates. Section 10 provides information about colleges that offer academic advisement for athletes. Increasing numbers of major universities have such programs to assure not only player eligibility but ongoing compliance with NCAA requirements. A few representative programs will be mentioned: those of Notre Dame, Nebraska, and others.

Finally, Section 11, the concluding section, considers the question "Sports for what?" It discusses the ethics of the recruiting process, from a college as well as a high school perspective, and affirms the value of athletic participation for its own sake. This section reemphasizes that our work with student athletes involves more than helping them to achieve a balance between athletics and academics, and to find an appropriate college.

We also affirm the value of fair play and sport for its own sake. Winning may be the fundamental purpose of any game, but it isn't the only purpose. The job of coaches, counselors, and parents is also to guarantee that young athletes achieve a balance between striving to win and enjoying the satisfactions derived from individual and team effort.

At the end of each section you'll find a variety of useful forms, letters, memos, and passouts for large- and small-group meetings—all of which are reproducible. The task of advising student athletes and promoting educational equilibrium is indeed difficult and it is becoming more difficult each year. *Advising Student Athletes Through the College Recruitment Process* may not resolve *all* your problems, but it provides the processes and materials that will make the task much easier for you and your student athletes, who are, after all, the most important people in this book.

CONTENTS

Section
TWO

THE NCAA AND OTHER
GOVERNING BODIES • 15

Section Two Figures

Section

THREE

THE REAL WORLD
OF ATHLETIC SCHOLARSHIPS • 43

Section Three Figures

Section

FOUR

THE HIGHLY RECRUITED
STUDENT ATHLETE • *85*

DEFINING A "BLUE-CHIPPER" (86) • On Being a Blue-chipper (87) • On Being a Parent of a Blue-chipper (88) • The Blue-chipper and the High School Coach (89) • WHAT IS THE COUNSELOR'S ROLE? (91) • Important Steps to Take (91) • DEALING WITH COLLEGE RECRUITERS (93) • ASKING THE RIGHT QUESTIONS DURING THE COLLEGE VISIT (95) • Ask Recruiters (95) • Ask Players at the School (95) • Ask the School's Nonathletes (96) • Ask School Officials and Admissions Officers (96) • QUESTIONS TO ASK AFTER THE CAMPUS VISIT (96) • A FINAL WORD ABOUT BOOSTERS (97) • LET'S WRAP IT UP (98)

Section Four Figures

Section

FIVE

STUDENT ATHLETES AND THE HIGH SCHOOL COACH • *111*

THE JOB OF THE HIGH SCHOOL COACH (112) • IN UNITY, THERE IS STRENGTH (113) • WHO HAS THE *REAL* POWER? (114) • The High School Coach and the Pre–High School Athlete (114) • THE RELATIONSHIP BETWEEN COACH AND PLAYER (115) • THE ATHLETE AND PARENT PLEDGE (117) • THE COACH'S RESPONSIBILITIES (117) • The Coach's Pre-season Responsibilities (118) • The Coach's In-season Responsibilities (118) • The Coach's Post-season Responsibilities (120) • A CLOSER LOOK AT THE FIRST MEETING (122) • Looking at Such Meetings from the Parents' Perspective (123) • KEEPING RECORDS (124) • ALERTING COLLEGE RECRUITERS TO THE UNDERPUBLICIZED ATHLETE (124) • WHEN SOMEONE OTHER THAN THE COACH IS NEEDED (126) • MEETING THE NEEDS OF FEMALE ATHLETES (127) • Helping Young Women with the Recruiting Process (127) • DIALOGUING WITH COLLEGE COACHES (128) • FOLLOWING UP WHEN THE ATHLETE GOES TO COLLEGE (131) • LET'S WRAP IT UP (131)

Section Five Figures

Section

SIX

STUDENT ATHLETES AND THE HIGH SCHOOL'S SUPPORT SERVICES • *147*

WHAT IS THE COUNSELOR'S ROLE REGARDING STUDENT ATHLETES? (148) • Finding a Solution (148) • STUDENT ATHLETES AND THE SCHOOL'S ATHLETIC DIRECTOR (149) • SPEAKING THE SAME LANGUAGE: A GLOSSARY OF SPORTS TERMS (151) • THE COUNSELOR'S RESPONSIBILITIES (151) • The Counselor's Pre-season Responsibilities (151) • The Counselor's In-season Responsibilities (152) • The Counselor's Post-season Responsibilities (153) • STUDENT ATHLETES AND THE COLLEGE CONSULTANT (154) • RECOGNIZING THE JUNIOR COLLEGE AS A REALISTIC ALTERNATIVE TO FOUR-YEAR SCHOOLS (155) • HELPING STUDENT ATHLETES FIND THE RIGHT INFORMATION (155) • STUDENT ATHLETES AND COMMERCIAL "SCHOLARSHIP FINDERS" (156) • ACCOMMODATING THE NEEDS OF STUDENTS WITH LEARNING DISABILITIES (157) • COLLEGE COACHES AND HIGH SCHOOL PERSONNEL (158) • LET'S WRAP IT UP (159)

Section Six Figures

Section

SEVEN

THE RESPONSIBILITIES OF STUDENT ATHLETES AND PARENTS • *167*

THE FUTURE, LIKE CHARITY, BEGINS AT HOME (168) •
THE FAMILY'S PRE-SEASON RESPONSIBILITIES (168) •
Looking into Careers (169) • THE FAMILY'S IN-SEASON
RESPONSIBILITIES (169) • Maintaining Academic
Achievement (170) • THE FAMILY'S POST-SEASON
RESPONSIBILITIES (171) • Parent Involvement in the
Recruiting Process (171) • ORGANIZING FOR SUCCESS (172)
• LEAVING THE RIGHT IMPRESSION (173) • KEEPING
ALL THE DOORS OPEN (174) • REVIEWING THE NEEDS
OF THE FEMALE ATHLETE (175) • SELECTING THE RIGHT
COLLEGE OR UNIVERSITY (177) • WHAT TO DO AFTER
DECIDING ON A COLLEGE (179) • LET'S WRAP IT UP (179)

Section Seven Figures

Section

EIGHT

DEVELOPING COALITIONS OF ATHLETES, PARENTS, COACHES, AND COUNSELORS • *189*

Section Eight Figures

Section

NINE

FINANCING THE STUDENT ATHLETE'S COLLEGE EDUCATION • *205*

Section
TEN
ACADEMIC ADVISEMENT IN COLLEGE • *217*

Section
ELEVEN
"SPORTS FOR WHAT?" • *227*

Appendix

A

LOOKING FOR AN ATHLETIC SCHOLARSHIP TO COLLEGE?

If you are a highly recruited high school athlete, you need this booklet!

A–1

Appendix

B

LOOKING FOR AN ATHLETIC SCHOLARSHIP TO COLLEGE?

If you need to sell yourself to college recruiters you need this booklet!

B–1

Appendix

C

LOOKING FOR AN ATHLETIC SCHOLARSHIP TO COLLEGE?

If you are a female high school athlete, you need this booklet!

C–1

Appendix

D

LOOKING FOR AN ATHLETIC SCHOLARSHIP TO COLLEGE?

If you are currently a high school underclassman, you need this booklet!

D–1

ADVISING STUDENT ATHLETES

THROUGH THE

COLLEGE RECRUITMENT PROCESS

ONE

COLLEGE ATHLETICS
Past, Present, and Future

First, a quick story. One of history's great football coaches once said: "The day boys play football with one eye on the university and the other on professional futures, the sport will become a moral liability to the colleges." The coach was Amos Alonzo Stagg, and he made the comment in 1927, only six or seven years after the founding of the NFL. One of history's most outspoken proponents of amateur athletics, Stagg at the time was the head coach of the University of Chicago, one of the charter members of the Western Conference, the forerunner of the Big Ten.

One of the nation's first football coaches, Stagg started at the University of Chicago in 1892 and was paid the very generous salary of $2,500.00. Interestingly, he also found the time to *play* for his team, even against the two high school teams that were on their schedule. He had been an All-American end at Yale in 1889 and, during his first few years with the maroon and yellow, apparently decided that his win/loss record would be enhanced by his own experienced involvement on the field as well as the sidelines. He was twenty-eight at the time.

People who first hear this story are often shocked by Stagg's apparent duplicity, his surprising disregard for the most basic rules of amateurism. Has history been so kind to the Grand Old Man of Football to overlook such indiscretions, which, after all, resulted more from enthusiasm than greed? Not likely; more appropriately, history had to acknowledge that he wasn't cheating. The rules at the time did not prohibit coaches from donning the pads and showing the youngsters a thing or two about the game. Those of

1

us who enjoy sports history, therefore, can be assured that Stagg, and many others like him, did, in fact, practice what they preached.

He was also prophetic. Stagg could just as easily have said, "The day youngsters play sports with one eye on the high school and the other on athletic scholarships, athletics will become a moral liability to the schools." For our purposes, "moral liability" may be a bit strong; "educational liability" seems more appropriate. Whatever the focus for young athletes, college or pros, such a liability inhibits their total personal development and aims instead at the skills and behaviors that promote athletic performance.

Those among us who have vested interests in athletics sometimes become unwitting accomplices to the failure of these youngsters to develop completely as young adults. We may close our eyes to abuses or rationalize our own unwillingness or inability to meet the real needs of kids. At that point, just a moment of introspection enables us to realize how easy it is to succumb to subtle temptations and, in effect, to perpetuate the student athlete "problem."

In spite of the range of such temptations, we must never forget that honesty and integrity are the hallmarks of most coaches and players, no matter what their sport or how far back we go in the history books. Athletics in this country has had its share of cheaters, but, as witnessed in today's media, their departure from the norm, not their obedience to it, has made them newsworthy. This is true of the entire story of sport in this country, from the earliest to the most current coaches and players.

INTRODUCTION

It has been a fascinating story. Although glamorized by characters and accomplishments of legendary proportions, it nonetheless has had a very predictable plot. It is a story that has satisfied our need for drama—more, however, from the uniqueness and larger-than-life accomplishments of the characters than from any surprising twists of plot. In fact, the authors of American sport have created a very consistent story line. It involves winning games and making money—and, for the most part, they have been very honest about their motives.

Some of the characters have been less honest about theirs. Many have been equally interested in money. Fortunately, most athletes have made a commitment more to their sport than to any money it promised. This is not to say that early players didn't find ways to make a few easy dollars. Baseball organized on a professional level almost from the moment Alexander Cartwright standardized the dimensions of the diamond and discovered that intercity rivalries provoked combative but entertaining fun in the sun.

The game was earning its own way in Cincinnati, Ohio, in 1869 with its first professional team, the Red Stockings, who earned a net profit their first year of $1.39. The amount may have been uninspiring to the growing legion of post–Civil War investors, but "pay for play" was an interesting philosophy to many young athletes.

With the advent of professional baseball, college players and probably a wide range of gifted high schoolers, discovered an exciting way to pick up a few bucks during the summer. In fact, "summer baseball" became an annual irritation to America's guardians of "gentlemanly amateurism." Committed to a code that reflected social status and personal behavior as well as money, they regarded summer baseball as a disease that was insidiously destroying the otherwise healthy values of young athletes.

Summer baseball was not the only problem. "Cheating," according to contemporary standards, has been eating away at the philosophies of sports officials in this country for more than a century—in a variety of sports. While baseball, the blue-collar worker of American sports, was struggling to support itself on the streets and vacant lots of urban America, football was being nursed through the Halls of Ivy by enterprising young athletes who enjoyed battling each other for campus bragging rights.

Many of them furthered their causes by hiring itinerant players who had no association with the school other than sharing a common desire to win "the big game." Many of these "ringers" played for different schools on alternating weekends, their loyalty inspired more by easy money than by school colors. To reiterate the comment made in 1874 by James McCash, then President of Princeton University: "It's a nice question whether evils may not arise from sports in no way under the control of the college authorities."

His comment was made just five years after history's first college football game between Princeton and Rutgers. McCash was concerned more with the impropriety than the illegality of hiring ringers, but his comment suggested a future potential for abuse. Unfortunately, some of his fears have been realized. Just a glimpse at the reasons documented by the *Chronicle of Higher Education* for colleges and universities being put on NCAA probation reveals a wide range of recurring violations:

- "Ineligible athletes permitted to compete"
- "Providing improper inducements to prospective athletes"
- "Improper certification of a men's basketball player"
- "Female track athletes improperly admitted and allowed to compete"
- "Booster gifts to players at coach's urging"
- "Payment for a prospective athlete to attend a junior college"
- "Extra benefits and cash given to players"

Let's look more carefully at these issues by borrowing from a recent article I wrote for the College Board *Review*.

A WORLD OF VESTED INTERESTS

Plagued by such problems since the late 1800s, college sports experiences are precious for most young athletes, but they also carry the potential for significant abuse. In essence, college sports is a diamond flawed by vested interests. Valuable for millions of young athletes and inspired by occasional brilliance, the challenge of playing a sport in college is complicated by the needs of several important "others."

Among these, the coach is foremost. Aside from current pressures to focus on academics, the pressure for coaches to win is as pronounced today as at any time in our history. University administrators may use the National Collegiate Athletic Association (NCAA) as a bullhorn to shout their demands for academic integrity in the nation's colleges and universities, but they're still firing losing coaches—less dramatically but every bit as conclusively.

Many university administrators still find themselves battling the demands of alumni pressure groups to develop and maintain winning programs. The NCAA has successfully restricted boosters (the supporters of university athletics programs) from recruiting practices, but they have no way to restrict the subtle but convincing influence of booster donations to university programs.

The boosters themselves have a range of vested interests. Most obviously, they want to see their alma maters or favorite schools in the local or national spotlight. Almost as obvious, they realize the economic implications of national recognition. Consider the local businessman from Lincoln, Nebraska, who, in the early 1900s suggested that a winning Cornhusker football team would be"good for the local economy."

In a recent year, almost 40 million spectators watched football games at just under 700 four-year colleges. Some major universities, with just six or seven home football games, boost the local economy by as much as $20 million a year. College athletics programs themselves may, in fact, be losing money, but the surrounding communities are cashing in on the thrill of competition.

So are the colleges themselves. A director of admissions at a prominent midwestern university indicated to me recently that his school raised admissions standards because of the significant increase in their applicant pool. A school with a wide range of excellent academic programs, they had always enjoyed a large pool of applicants. A current year, however, was particularly good; they had just won a major bowl game.

Finally, and perhaps most significantly, the athletes have vested interests. At one time satisfied with an all-expenses-paid trip to academia, many young athletes now tolerate college as a sometimes frustrating hiatus between high school and the pros. The problem has become so pronounced that a recent survey conducted by The Center for the Study of Sport in Society (CSSS) at Northeastern University revealed that more than 40% of the nation's inner-city black high school athletes expect to play a professional sport. Many will not even graduate from high school.

That sports is seen as a meal ticket by many young athletes is nothing new. Young athletes did it back in the ancient Olympics; Jim Thorpe did it back in 1909; I did it in 1956; and some youngster from inner-city Chicago will do it tomorrow. As long as someone is willing to pay a youngster to dunk a basketball or spend Sunday afternoons running into other players, professional sports will continue to be the quickest way to cash in on abilities or to break the grip of poverty.

JIM THORPE:
TURN-OF-THE-CENTURY STUDENT ATHLETE

Perhaps my grandfather, Jim Thorpe, even though he played more than eighty years ago, is the prototype of today's student athlete. Jim was an athlete who used, and was used by, the system. In 1909, having made third team All-American in football the previous year, he signed out of the Carlisle Indian School to play semiprofessional baseball for the Rocky Mount Railroaders in the Carolina League.

With dollar signs as well as stars in his eyes, he entertained visions of joining Chief Bender, another Carlisle standout and a future Hall of Famer with the Philadelphia Athletics, in order to cash in on his athletic ability. Clearly, he knew what he was doing at the time. Because he had no intentions of returning to Carlisle, he used his own name on the team roster, a fact that would resurface years later and result in the loss of his records and Olympics medals.

Unfortunately, Jim's brief semiprofessional baseball career was unspectacular. After his first year, his pitching record was 9 wins and 10 losses, and his batting average was .235—respectable but uninspiring to major league scouts. Shocked by the reality of his limitations, Jim accepted Pop Warner's invitation to return to Carlisle for the 1911 football season. Because Carlisle had suffered through an 8–6 record in 1910 without Jim, his return was hailed by coaches and teammates alike.

As with most coaches and players, they enjoyed a symbiotic relationship; Pop needed a left halfback, and Jim needed Pop's generous athletic budget. History is very clear regarding Pop's knowledge of Jim's apparent violations of the amateur code. Both he and Moses Friedman, the Superintendent of The Carlisle Indian School, knew that Jim had played baseball but were willing to allow their need for a left halfback to obscure their knowledge of Jim's "professionalism."

Booster and other illegal dollars have induced young athletes to attend certain schools for decades; Jim was promised a clothing allowance and spending money at Carlisle to tie his future to Pop Warner's dreams of football and Olympic glory. Nowhere in this stage of Jim's life does anyone mention the value of an education. Even though a favorite of his English teacher, American poet Marianne Moore, and the winner of an essay contest on campus, Jim, not unlike many of today's student athletes, allowed his academic talents to take a back seat to sports.

Jim never graduated from Carlisle. He was twenty-five when he left to play baseball with the New York Giants and equipped with only a few vocational skills to make his way in white society. Again his situation is similar to that of today's student athletes. According to the NFL Players' Association, in any given year approximately two-thirds of college players fail to graduate from college. In recent years, the graduation rates of college basketball players have been as low as 27%. One school, according to the CSSS, in the NCAA's Final Four a few years ago was alleged not to have graduated a black player in more than a decade.

The school's dreams of basketball glory, however, were realized. So were Pop Warner's. Jim became a first-team All-American in both 1911 and 1912, scored 198 points in a single season (a record broken only recently), and won two gold medals in the 1912 Olympics in Stockholm, Sweden. He received a congratulatory letter from the President of the United States and returned home to a ticker tape parade and the adulation of Americans everywhere.

A year later, his records were erased from the books and his medals taken away because the AAU and, later, the International Olympic Committee had found him in violation of amateur standards. This is where Jim's story diverges somewhat from the circumstances of today's student athletes. Today's young Olympic athletes have few amateur standards. The desire for money has plagued amateurism for so many years and altered its appearance so imperceptibly that its death has gone virtually unnoticed in this country. No athlete in this country, whether involved in intercollegiate or international competition, has ever been subject to definitions of amateurism like those of turn-of-the-century America.

Consider the following excerpt from *A Sporting Pilgrimage,* the definitive turn-of-the-century book on American sports, written by the "Dean of American Sportswriters," Caspar Whitney:

> Why there should be such constant strife to bring together in sport the two divergent elements in society that never by chance meet elsewhere on even terms is quite incomprehensible, and it is altogether the sole cause of all our athletic woe.... The laboring class are all right in their way; let them go their way in peace, and have their athletics in whatsoever manner best suits their inclinations.... Let us have our sport among the more refined elements.

Reflecting not only the economic but the racial characteristics of class distinction, Whitney also wrote:

> It sounds quite as senseless and impracticable as the theory of the other Utopian philanthropist who fondly expects the Negro, lifted suddenly out of generations of bondage to fraternize and favorably compare with the race whose individuals have always been the refined and cultured members of the civilized world.

Undoubtedly, the "sportsmen" of the early 1900s, Whitney in particular, were influenced by the social philosophies that started in England decades earlier, as exemplified in the quote from the Amateur Rowing Association of London in the late 1860s: A professional is anyone who "... is or has been a mechanic, artisan, or laborer." Approximately ten years later, in July of 1872, the *Sporting Gazette* reported:

> Sports nominally open to gentleman amateurs must be confined to those who have a real right to that title, and men of class considerably lower must be given to understand that the facts of their being well-conducted and civil and never having run for money—are not sufficient to make a man a gentleman as well an amateur.

As late as 1948, shades of the same philosophy were reflected in a quote from Avery Brundage, then the President of the United States Olympic Committee:

> If in certain countries there are people who are too poor to play ... let the government raise their standard of living until they have some leisure time instead of asking us to lower our amateur standards.

Jim Thorpe didn't stand a chance. The loss of his records and trophies resulted as much from such social philosophies as the few dollars he accepted by playing semipro baseball. These same social philosophies provoked a reaction from professional sports. The reaction to "gentlemanly amateurism" was that players like Ty Cobb climbed into the stands to pound lumps on hecklers. Much of baseball, therefore, was anything but "refined," so again it became an option for Jim.

He was now a drawing card. Just as for many young athletes before him and millions since, the adoring arms of professional sport embraced him, creating for him a heroic image and protecting him from household budgets, a middle-class career, and life's inevitable demands that he "grow up." Jim's life, like that of some of the young athletes today, was an extended adolescence, a succession of bar fights, drinking sprees, and fishing trips with his retinue of good old boys.

When he coached the Oorang Indians in LaRue, Ohio, in what has become the smallest franchise in NFL history, he established a somewhat less heroic image. He won only two or three games in two years and gathered an assortment of Indian athletes boasting names like Wrinkle Meat and Bear Behind. They were so seamy in behavior and appearance that—arriving for a game in most NFL towns—they were frisked by the local sheriff for guns and knives before being allowed to get off the train!

Unfortunately, the extended adolescence of today's college and professional athletes provokes similar kinds of behaviors—few involving guns and knives but many involving fights, rapes, and drug convictions. Such incidents have been widely documented in recent years by the media.

In a recent discussion with an official from the Center for the Study of Sport in Society, I discovered that, according to the most recent data from the NFL Players' Association, 41% of professional football players admit to financial problems when they retire from the game and 33% are divorced. The center would not confirm the widespread allegation that the average life expectancy of pro football players is fifty-six, but they did indicate that the figure "had been around" for several years.

Such statistics help strip away some of the veneer from a "surface analysis" of professional sport. Who can deny the intrigue of a multimillion-dollar contract that also guarantees a generous, if unhealthy, dose of international recognition? How many kids even care that a pro career lasts only three or four years—certainly not the 13-year-old scuffing his Nikes on black-topped basketball courts in downtown Chicago? Give him the hint of a pro career, and his motivation to practice will leave his classroom teachers slack jawed. Certainly, Jim Thorpe would not have cared about such statistics, even though when he finally retired from professional sports at the age of forty-three, he, too, was financially troubled, divorced, and fated to have his first heart attack at age fifty-five.

During his athletic career, he and his first wife (my grandmother) had traveled extensively, compelled to leave their three daughters in Indian boarding schools. My mother, his middle daughter, even admitted once that he was often unavailable as a parent, reflecting that he may not even have known her name. Like her sisters, however, she was devoted to him, even to the point of sublimating herself in a lifelong struggle to restore his records, his Olympic medals, and especially his good name. Fortunately, she was successful; Jim's Olympic medals were presented to his family members at the Biltmore Hotel in Los Angeles in 1983.

At the close of his career, my grandfather was the embodiment of the problems of many American athletes. The recipient of two Olympic gold medals, the first president of what was to become the NFL, a three-time All-American, the coach of the World Champion Canton Bulldogs, and the leading scorer in college football history, Jim walked away from professional sports with a glorious past and a very dim future. He had two more heart attacks and at age sixty-six, living with his third wife in a trailer court in Lomita, California, Jim Thorpe died.

To sympathize with him because he was "a simple Indian schoolboy" (his own phrase used in a 1913 letter to Olympic officials), who committed what history has described as a slight indiscretion, is simplistic. More profoundly, Jim Thorpe was a highly publicized test case exploited by the AAU to prevent college athletes from accepting money to play summer baseball.

He was an example as well for elitist Olympic officials whose decision to take away his medals was influenced almost as much by his lower-class status as an Indian as by his professionalism. Jim Thorpe's tragedy, one that persisted until his death in 1953, did not result from a "slight indiscretion" but from a social philosophy that continues to exploit some young athletes, many of whom are culturally and economically disadvantaged and are used, like Jim, to satisfy the vested interests of the sporting world.

Fortunately, this situation doesn't affect all athletes—not even most of them. In many instances, the media fail to remind us that most college and high school coaches are in the business because they enjoy working with youngsters in an activity that involves excitement and mutual commitment. We must never forget, however, that abuse, whether it be intended or unintended, is just around the corner. When winning becomes an end in itself, even the well-intentioned coach begins to turn that corner—and when the desire for money or prestige becomes more important than the enjoyment of participation, players do the same thing.

As high school students, many young athletes seek not only scholarships to college but professional futures guaranteeing fame and fortune. Jim Thorpe was lucky. Although his professional earnings paled before the multimillions earned by some of today's athletes, he earned good money for his day and enjoyed the world's recognition. By contrast, one in a hundred high school senior athletes today can expect a scholarship to college, and only eight one-thousandths of one per cent can expect professional careers.

Although their athletic accomplishments may never parallel those of Jim Thorpe, many of these young athletes have more in common with him than they realize. They are being drawn into a world that often promises much more than it delivers. They share the same excitements, the same expectations for easy money, and the same potential for personal tragedy. And they require that enlightened advice regarding the world after sports that my grandfather was denied so many years ago.

TRYING TO FIND SOLUTIONS

The quality of the advice they receive is a function of how well each of us has defined the problem. Certainly, we understand that a preoccupation with money and winning can lead to some form of abuse, and we want to do everything in our power to emphasize the importance of participation for its own sake. But the issue is so abundant in conflicting opinion that the search for solutions seems more difficult every day.

Perhaps the difficulty involves a poor definition of the problem. If we define a problem as the measurable or observable discrepancy between "what is" and "what should be," we can begin to give dimension to the student athlete situation in this country. Fortunately, there is a wide range of opinion and fact to draw from. Perhaps the best place to start is with "what is."

"What Is"

Anyone considering the student athlete situation in this country must acknowledge initially that the majority of young athletes are good students. Said *ChicagoTribune* staff writers Barry Tempkin and Ed Sherman in a recent special report on athletics and academics in college: "Most athletes are solid students, a fact regularly obscured by the scandals that scar college sports."

They went on, however, to indicate that

- The graduation rates for football and basketball players at most major universities are lower than the rates for all students at the same schools.

- At a recent summer basketball camp, half of the 123 high school players tested below grade level in reading; about 20% of them were reading at the 3d- and 5th-grade levels.

- Major colleges routinely admit athletes with grades and test scores that are well below the average of those of other incoming students to improve the school's chances to win.

- Athletes put in incredible amounts of time, especially during the in-season. Many athletes refer to their sports as "jobs."

Just a few years ago, the General Accounting Office indicated that a third of the colleges and universities with major basketball programs graduate fewer than one in five players. Every month, significant numbers of major colleges are put on probation because they have violated NCAA standards, yet the president of Stanford University once indicated, "The evil in current football rests not on the hired men, but in academic lying and in the falsification of our standards as associations of scholars and of honest men." This particular comment was made in 1905—almost a century ago.

Certainly, the situation has improved, but many of the same problems persist. A consideration of "what is," therefore, must acknowledge that abuses in American sports change periodically more by degree than by type. The rule changes introduced by the NCAA, for example, have not provoked a corresponding change in attitudes. The potential for abuse, therefore, is an ever-present reality within even the most upstanding university program.

"What Should Be"

How, then, do we define "what should be"? When we try, we experience similar problems. Consider, for example, the opinions of different segments of our society:

- "Some athletes generate ten to twenty times as much income as their scholarship is worth to a school.... Why not pay them their worth?" Ken Denlinger, the author of *Athletes for Sale*.

- "Millions of dollars just went to Notre Dame and Michigan last Saturday. It's a shame to think that the only ones who weren't paid were the players." A comment from an amateur sports official during a recent conversation.

- "The reasonable response to the apparently inevitable professionalization of big-time college sports clearly is to accept professionalism. Pay the athletes a decent salary and provide them with adequate fringe benefits...." Allen Guttmann, a professor from Amherst College, writing in the *Chronicle of Higher Education*.

By contrast, consider the earlier comments of prominent sports figures and organizations:

- "... the abolishment of the so-called 'athletic scholarship' indicates an awakening conscience to a much-needed reform." Amos Alonzo Stagg, in his book *Touchdown,* written in 1927.

- "There is no valid reason why even the most worthy athlete should receive any consideration that is not available to the general body of undergraduates." From a study conducted by the Carnegie Foundation in 1929.

More recently, groups like the Knight Commission have brought together people like Father Hesburgh from the University of Notre Dame; Dick Schultz, the Executive Director of the NCAA; Harvey Schiller from the United States Olympic Committee; and coaches like Joe Paterno from Penn State and Mike Krzyzewski from Duke to recommend a course of action for intercollegiate athletics in this country. Much of their thinking is abstracted in an early quote from their report, issued in March of 1991: "Student athletes should compete successfully in the classroom as well as on the playing field and, insofar as possible, should be indistinguishable from other undergraduates."

A year later, the Commission issued another report, this time stating: "The task for academic and athletics administrators is to keep their eyes on the main prize: a structure for intercollegiate sports embodying the standards and values befitting higher education."

At approximately the same time, prominent author Norman Cousins was writing in the *Christian Science Monitor*: "The basic purpose of education is not to provide a convenient springboard to lucrative contracts in the NFL or the NBA, but to teach people how to think ... how to enable people to come into possession of all their powers."

The Problem Persists

Defining "what should be," therefore, is virtually impossible in the face of such conflicting opinion. Without a clear definition of "what should be," the characteristics of any problem are obscured. It's no wonder that the debate over intercollegiate athletics has been raging for more than a century. Aside from the frustration caused by a poorly defined problem, the issue is complicated further by a circumstance best described by Voltaire, when he said, "In a long dispute, both parties are wrong."

The wide range of vested interests described earlier in this section suggests that, to varying degrees, *all* parties engaged in this dispute are wrong. From the moment football and basketball found their way onto university campuses, *some* players, coaches, alumni, university officials, and professional teams have been concerned only with their self-interests.

Consider the transition from college to the pros. Basketball and football were born in college and have continued to use college as a training ground for professional sports. Both sports have grown so significantly within the past few decades that many colleges have become the setting not only for traditional rivalries but for lucrative professional contracts. Therein lies much of the problem.

Baseball developed its own minor league program, which continues to operate independently of colleges and universities. From 1965 to 1976, for example, major league baseball drafted more high school than college players. Even as recently as 1988, 515 high school players (not the most in history) were drafted by major league baseball, compared with the 625 from the college ranks.

Contrast these statistics with the NFL and NBA practices, which allow no high school draft. Football and basketball, therefore, remain almost completely dependent on colleges for the training and the recruitment of professional prospects. With the introduction of the NCAA's Proposition 48, poorly educated athletes, many of whom are socially and economically disadvantaged, are unable to secure the exposure they need to play such sports on the professional level.

Although Proposition 48 is well intentioned and current statistics indicate that it seems to have provoked a better-qualified high school student athlete, it nonetheless holds the potential to deprive some student athletes of the opportunity to play a sport in college and ultimately to attract the attention of professional scouts. We must all be diligent, therefore, to guard against the possibility that Caspar Whitney's desire "to have our sport among the more refined elements" does not come true.

LOOKING AT BOTH SIDES OF THE ISSUE

This section has already emphasized that most young athletes will not receive college scholarships; significantly fewer of them will have professional careers. High school coaches, counselors, and parents, however, must work hard for each of them to guarantee even the remotest possibility of continuing a sport on the college or professional level. We have, therefore, a multifold responsibility: to emphasize the importance of academics, to inform youngsters of the unlikelihood of college or professional sports futures, but to keep their athletic dreams alive—particularly for those who have the ability to play a sport beyond high school.

These appear to be contradictory responsibilities. They are, in fact, the delicately interrelated elements that constitute the essence of working with young athletes. We want them, first of all, to acknowledge the importance of an education. Then we want to help them develop as realistic a vision of their athletic futures as possible—without destroying their dreams. We may have to transform those dreams, but we don't want to destroy them. We must help young athletes learn from their unfolding experiences with sport that their dreams are realized more through associations than through performances.

Not everyone can be a Michael Jordan or a Jim Thorpe, but we can all share the accumulated sensations associated with the sports we love. I coached football for thirty-one years and, frankly, never tried to become an Ara Parseghian. Instead, I wrestled with the same strategic and motivational issues that plagued Ara between game days. And I stopped every so often to let the sounds of popping pads and the smells of new-mown grass and analgesic balm create lasting memories for me.

Look at it this way. I'm the first to admit that I wasn't the world's best coach, but I sure did enjoy sharing the stage with Ara. We both walked the sidelines and established warm and lasting relationships with players and other coaches. We both learned to love the anticipation of the season's first scrimmage and the letdown of the final game. He may stand taller in the nation's annals of football, but he derived from the game not one jot more enjoyment than I did.

The associations I established have proven to be far more important to me than my performance. Certainly, I wanted to do the best job I could, but I didn't admit failure because I fell short of legendary status at Notre Dame. Can we allow our young athletes to be any less fair to themselves? Certainly, what they do on game day is important, but what they contribute to the team on a daily basis and the associations they derive from the experience are even more important.

SO WHERE ARE THE SOLUTIONS?

If a preoccupation with money and winning has provoked some of the problems on the college level, we must necessarily look to the high schools for at least some of the solutions. I have spoken for many years at conferences and conventions across the country. During the first few years, I found myself talking about changes in NCAA legislation and the growing focus on intercollegiate athletics.

As the NCAA and groups like the Knight Commission watched university officials exert greater leadership over college athletics, it became increasingly apparent to me that the battle to protect the integrity of amateur athletics must shift to a different front. I decided, for example, that for every "abused" college athlete, there is a high school coach and, maybe, a counselor somewhere who didn't do his or her job—perhaps because he or she didn't have the information to do it.

Let's put it this way. During my entire coaching career, I never met a college coach who was interested in recruiting an electrical engineer. Fortunately, I have worked with a great many who wanted to help young athletes realize such a career goal, but all were interested primarily in recruiting a fullback, a tackle, or a middle linebacker. They wanted kids who were bright enough to be electrical engineers, but they were most interested in signing youngsters with good growth potential who derived some strange satisfaction from running into other players.

The job of high school coaches, counselors, athletic directors, and parents, therefore, is to guarantee that the university gets a good athlete and that the athlete gets a good university. If we don't offer such assurances, they sometimes won't be made—and when we do, we must acknowledge and use the significant power we possess. Certainly, college coaches have the authority to recruit young athletes, but high school personnel have the ultimate power to influence the decisions of these athletes regarding their selection of schools.

Colleges recruit blue-chippers; high schools make them. If high school personnel steer kids toward upstanding university programs, those programs will get bigger and better. Conversely, if we steer them away from abusive programs, we have the power to destroy the programs, to make even the most vigorous NCAA sanction seem like a slap on the hand.

Such are the purposes of this book. Sports are forever interwoven within the fabric of college life. Contrary to the suggestions and opinions of some writers and college officials, that fact isn't going to change. The vested interests and sheer love of sports on both sides of the college administrator's door guarantee the long and, yes, prosperous life of intercollegiate athletics.

The job of parents and high school personnel is to protect the interests of young athletes. We do that by promoting academics, a realistic assessment of each player's abilities, the joy of sport for its own sake, the self-confidence that comes from discipline and commitment, and a decision-making process that plans carefully for life after high school. The materials and ideas in this book should do much to make these tasks easier.

LET'S WRAP IT UP

As emphasized recurrently throughout this section, most of the athletes and coaches in intercollegiate sports are honest. Enough people abuse the system, however, to make intercollegiate athletics a continuing national concern. They do it for a variety of reasons. Some of them cheat because the stakes are too high. Such stakes, whether they involve national recognition or money, seem to be growing every year.

Others cheat when excessive pressure causes them to do things they normally might not do, or when the punishment isn't a sufficient deterrent. Still others are inclined to cheat simply because they know they can get away with it, because they have flimsy value systems, or because their wants are larger than their needs. Some head coaches, for example, won't fly to games by commercial jet; many charter private planes, further exacerbating the unnecessary drains on the school's athletic funds.

Finally, it is essential that each of us acknowledge that the "system" is the primary problem. I've been teaching educational supervision for more than twenty years. Each year, I work long and hard to convince aspiring administrators that the first thing they must do when they bump into teacher resistance is look at themselves and their systems to find causes. Regarding the student athlete "problem," therefore, each of us must find the nearest mirror and ask ourselves, "What am *I* doing wrong that's causing this problem?"

As indicated earlier in this section, vested interests are perpetuating a wide range of inconsistencies and abuses in intercollegiate athletics. To a much lesser extent, these same kinds of vested interests provoke problems in interscholastic sports programs. Money may be less an issue, but winning can be as all-consuming in high school as in college. To the extent that each of these obscures for coaches and players the simple joy of participation, they are problems.

There's an old saying: "When you're up to your rear end in alligators, it's hard to remember that your original goal was to clean the swamp!" Alligators are snapping everywhere in the world of athletics: young athletes going to college for the wrong reasons, scores of universities receiving NCAA sanctions, elementary students being "recruited" by high school coaches, illiterate high school athletes being recruited by major universities, reports of increased alcohol and other drug use by young athletes, and a whole range of similar abuses.

Like all those alligators in the swamp, these issues warrant our immediate attention. In the meantime, however, we must not lose sight of the fact that if we clean the swamp, we'll also eliminate many of the alligators. In essence, we must address the symptoms of our problems but not allow them to obscure the problems themselves. Much easier said than done? Maybe so, but this resource will help.

It focuses on ways not just to respond to the processes, procedures, and requirements mandated by the NCAA and other regulatory organizations but to emphasize academics as the ultimate goal of schools and to reaffirm sport for its own sake. These are the problems. In many instances, academics has taken a back seat to athletics, and sport has become a means to an end instead of a source of enjoyment for its own sake. The NCAA, the Knight Commission, and similar agencies have taken steps in the right direction to resolve these issues, but more needs to be done at the high school level.

Certainly, we will not eliminate the corrupting influence of money, which affects sports in college as well as the pros, but we can help redirect the energies of young athletes. In the process, we can influence the attitudes of those college coaches who use young athletes as means to their own ends. Look at it this way: College coaches have a great deal of authority; many are loaded with charisma. They are often as impressive to high school coaches as they are to young athletes and their parents.

Most are able to dangle seemingly irresistible incentives in front of impressionable youngsters—legitimate incentives ranging from scholarships to professional careers, others not so legitimate. The problems in intercollegiate and interscholastic athletics wouldn't be so pronounced if these incentives were less tempting. The charisma of the coaches and the strength of their temptations, however, can be effectively compromised if high school coaches, counselors, and parents keep one fact in mind.

We have the power. We have the power, first of all, to promote athletic competition for its own sake, to help young athletes find the deep personal satisfaction that comes from hard work and team effort. We have the power to sustain their focus on academics, sometimes simply by sharing information with them about college scholarships and the unlikelihood of professional careers. We have the power to use their athletic ability to gain admission for them to some of the best colleges and universities in the nation.

We have the power to influence the college decisions of our young athletes, to steer them toward upstanding programs. To the extent that we use this power, we weaken the influence of abusive programs. To exercise the full strength of that power, we must make it coalesce. Those of us involved with young athletes, therefore—coaches, counselors, teachers, and parents—must work together to assure a wholesome and productive college experience for each of our young athletes.

Until field hockey and soccer players take the field together and coordinate their individual efforts, they are *potential* power. They become *actual* power only when they work together to achieve a common goal, to advance the causes of the team as well as of individual players. Such effort requires strategy. That's what this book is about—proven strategies that counteract the vested interests so evident in American sport, and that meet the real needs of young athletes.

Section

TWO

THE NCAA
AND OTHER
GOVERNING BODIES

First, a quick story. During the mid-1950s in South Chicago, had there been a Proposition 48 when I was scraping my elbows on the dust bowls we called football fields, I would have missed out on college. "Academic integrity," a phrase that looms large in NCAA history, was gaining a foothold in the nation's colleges and universities, but it was still struggling to promote eligibility standards for high school athletes. Young athletes like me, therefore, who wasted precious academic time in high school were finding renewed opportunities in many universities.

Fortunately, during the first year of such opportunities, we were ineligible to compete. The free time introduced us to a wide range of educational opportunities. I was especially fortunate because I had coaches who "encouraged" me to grasp such opportunities *before* I heard *someone's* knock on the door. Many schools nationwide prohibited freshmen from playing varsity sports. Several conferences were formed because of the freshman eligibility question. The Atlantic Coast Conference (ACC) is an example.

Charter members of the ACC originally were members of the old Southern Conference. In 1953, however, seeking to affirm the value of academic integrity, Duke, North Carolina, Wake Forest, and several others formed a conference that disallowed freshmen participation. At that point, the new ACC joined established conferences like the Big Ten, the Big Eight, and the Ivy League, all of whom found their origins in the freshman eligibility rule.

It was a rule that worked for me. Like several friends who formerly had only passed through the classroom en route to the football field, I found that ineligibility during my first year in college gave me the time to focus on my coursework and to realize that tomorrow's game days were dependent on today's classes. I even went on to major in English, a subject during high school that appealed to me about as much as homework, lawn mowers, and alarm clocks.

THE RISE OF ATHLETIC PARITY

A quick look at the history of intercollegiate sports in this country reveals a coin with "academic integrity" on one side, "athletic parity" on the other. Small schools needed their freshmen to compete with larger schools, and young athletes wanted to play for schools that enabled them to compete the first year. Under such circumstances, academic integrity suffered, particularly during the 1950s and 1960s in the absence of a national policy.

Over the years, many larger schools have responded by developing freshman programs that were less stressful and time-consuming than varsity programs but that permitted competition. The expense of such programs, however, and the perseverance of many officials seeking academic integrity resulted in NCAA legislation in 1964 that required all freshmen receiving scholarships to predict a 1.6 grade point average in college. Interestingly, this legislation had much the same effect as today's Proposition 48 (bylaw 14.3).

It was even more stringent. As with Prop 48, standardized test scores and high school grade point average were used to determine eligibility. As indicated in a future section, Proposition 48 requires a student with a 700 combined score on the SAT to have a 2.5 GPA in high school. In 1964, the same student needed a 3.0 GPA in high school to predict a 1.6 in college. Such legislation was not particularly new. As far back as 1906, Amherst and Wesleyan had restricted freshman participation if the student's entrance requirements were "deficient."

The NCAA's decision was nonetheless criticized. Minority groups claimed that tests like the SAT are discriminatory, and conferences like the Ivy League argued that the NCAA should not be able to dictate the entrance requirements and financial aid decisions of individual schools. Prop 48 has revived such criticisms. Neither Prop 48 nor the 1.6 prediction, however, affected the question of freshman eligibility. In fact, the 1.6 prediction policy eventually was forced to coexist with a 1968 NCAA decision that declared freshmen eligible in every sport but football and basketball, and in 1972 freshmen were declared eligible even in those sports.

During the same year, the 1.6 rule was voted out by the member schools of the NCAA. Advocates of its elimination claimed that the pool of qualified athletes had grown too small and that more legislative flexibility in NCAA rules was needed to assure the availability of more athletes. A year later, the minimum requirement for high school athletes to receive athletic scholarships to college became a 2.0 grade point average, regardless of the courses taken.

Nothing much changed until 1983, when the NCAA Convention in San Diego debated what was to become Proposition 48, now bylaw 14.3. Still controversial, bylaw

14.3 continues to evolve, perhaps ultimately to address the question of freshman eligibility; perhaps not. Proponents of the legislation are convinced that bylaw 14.3 is already the best of all worlds, assuring the academic qualifications of entering freshmen, yet allowing them to compete.

Thus assured that the needs for academic integrity and athletic parity have been satisfied, such proponents seek only the refinement of bylaw 14.3 and forgo any consideration of additional legislation to restrict freshman eligibility. The issue of freshman eligibility, however, remains a focus of attention for many high school and college personnel but, like the many other recommendations regarding the student athlete situation in this country, will not become national policy until the NCAA decides to pass legislation.

WHAT IS THE NATIONAL COLLEGIATE ATHLETIC ASSOCIATION (NCAA)?

The NCAA is the most powerful governing body in this country for intercollegiate athletics. It actually started in the winter of 1905, when Chancellor Henry MacCracken of New York University convened a group of thirteen schools to bring about reforms in college football. The increasing violence of the game had caused 33 deaths and 246 debilitating injuries that fall, resulting primarily from "mass formations" like the Flying Wedge that dominated the game.

President Theodore Roosevelt responded by gathering the Big Three—Harvard, Yale, and Princeton—and telling them "to clean up their act" if they wanted to save the sport. One result was significant rules changes, including an emphasis on the forward pass; another was the development of the Intercollegiate Athletic Association of the United States, boasting sixty-two new members. In 1910, the organization changed its name to the National Collegiate Athletic Association, and shortly after World War II, voted itself legislative and executive powers, making itself the primary guardian of intercollegiate athletics in this country.

Several factors caused the decision. An earlier set of guidelines called the *Sanity Code* had failed to deter continuing abuses of student athletes. Unregulated television coverage of athletic events was threatening college attendance figures, and post-season football games were increasing. In addition, the growth of the association's membership required full-time professional coordination.

In 1952, a national headquarters was developed in Kansas City, Missouri, and shortly thereafter the association established procedures to govern televised football games and to control post-season football. In 1973, the NCAA membership separated into three divisions, and eight years later the 75th Convention voted to include women's athletic programs.

How Does the NCAA Operate?

This evolution of the NCAA represents the enlightened reaction of thousands of college and university personnel to the intercollegiate abuses and emerging needs that hold the potential to compromise athletic as well as academic standards in this country. Each year, a convention is held in January to discuss and act on legislation. This convention represents the NCAA's ultimate authority. Each qualified member has one vote to influence the convention's issues.

Committee activity is the heart and soul of the NCAA. Approximately seventy committees perform responsibilities ranging from rule making to overseeing the national convention and various tournament activities. In addition, ad hoc committees are often created by the executive committee to perform special functions. Following are the three primary committees of the NCAA:

- The NCAA Council coordinates activities and policy between conventions. The council consists of forty-six members, including a president and a secretary-treasurer, and forty-four representatives from the three divisions.

- The NCAA Executive Committee, which is composed of the president, secretary-treasurer, and twelve other members representing the three divisions, coordinates championships and financial issues.

- The third major committee, one that receives considerable media attention, is the NCAA President's Commission. Members of this commission are elected by the chief executive officers of member institutions and are responsible for studying issues affecting intercollegiate athletics and proposing legislation for each annual convention.

That the NCAA is an association governed by its members is evident in its purposes and operation. Contrary to at least one popular misconception, the NCAA is not a cadre of geezers sitting in smoke-filled backrooms struggling their way to middle-aged fulfillment by hamstringing coaches with irrelevant rules and regulations. It is not a behind-the-scenes force that imposes irrelevant rules and regulations on unsuspecting coaches, kids, and colleges and universities. It *is* the colleges and universities.

The NCAA's Influence on Colleges and Universities

Such self-governance involves a wide range of advantages to member institutions. For example, some of the services provided by the NCAA include

- represent intercollegiate athletics regarding legislation and regulation on the state and federal levels
- enhance national communication through the *NCAA News* and other publications
- maintain and distribute statistics on regular-season activities in football and basketball and on championship records in all sports
- conduct a variety of research activities regarding academics, recruiting, injuries, cost factors, and a range of issues involving student athletes
- maintain a service that answers questions about NCAA issues
- administer community service programs

The NCAA administers approximately 80 championship events in which some 21,000 men and women compete for national titles. It also provides a mechanism for enforcing all NCAA legislation—a big job, given the scope of athletics in this country. An interim report by the Knight Commission, however, indicated only a few years ago that fully half the Division 1a colleges in this country received sanctions of varying severity for violations of NCAA legislation in the 1980s.

Recently, an official of the NCAA explained in conversation that most of these sanctions resulted from "self-reports" and that many involved minor infractions. The fact remains, the NCAA is a powerful force in this country and has gotten the attention of most, if not all, of its member institutions. The process it uses to investigate suspected violations involves the institution in question almost immediately.

Suspected problems are referred to the association's investigative staff to determine the appropriateness of an official inquiry. The problem is then referred to the NCAA Committee on Infractions, and the school in question is notified immediately in the event it wants to appear before the committee. If a penalty results, it is reported to the university, which may appeal to the NCAA Council for further study. The council may then uphold the committee's recommendation, rule in favor of the institution, or declare its own recommendation based on its interpretation of the findings.

How the NCAA Affects High Schools

A friend once told me that television is called a medium because it is neither rare nor well done. Well, I'm not sure of either, but I do know that the media attention given to schools receiving NCAA sanctions raises the eyebrows of most university and high school officials in this country. Why wouldn't it? Violations of NCAA legislation can result in sanctions that immobilize winning programs and that deprive youngsters of promising athletic futures.

This does not make the NCAA evil. To the contrary, it affirms the need of organizations like the NCAA to safeguard standards of fair play and, in its own words, "to maintain intercollegiate athletics as an integral part of the educational program and the athlete as an integral part of the student body." To do this, the NCAA legislates rules and regulations that govern the participation of both high school and college athletes.

High school coaches, athletes, counselors, athletic directors, and parents, therefore, must be familiar with the particulars of this legislation whenever a young athlete expresses an interest in intercollegiate athletics. For most young athletes, particularly those living in homes that value education and that promote academic challenges to prepare their children for the rigors of college, NCAA legislation governing academic eligibility is not a problem.

The NCAA Grant-in-Aid

The NCAA grant-in-aid is the most obvious influence on high school athletes. Financially, it provides

- the costs of tuition and fees
- room and board costs, as outlined in the school's catalogue
- the cost of books as required by the student athlete's course load
- other forms of financial aid if student athletes qualify

Financial aid is not the only consideration for young athletes. The grant-in-aid affirms the student athlete's place in the high school's pecking order and fortifies a developing self-image. It also opens the door to a world of excitement that may or may not lead to professional sports. Because colleges and universities are traditionally the only pathway to the pros, especially in football and basketball, rigorous NCAA eligibility requirements may have a profound influence on the culturally and educationally disadvantaged youngsters in our society. This is one of its most significant influences on high schools.

The Culturally Disadvantaged High School Athlete and the NCAA

That colleges and universities perpetuate class distinctions seems historically obvious. They have always been cultural membranes that screen out the less fortunate and the academically less able. This is not to say that their essential purpose is to further deprive the culturally deprived. College admissions officers are not the bad guys in America's struggle for social equality; they seek only the most capable students to further the cause of knowledge and to realize for their students and our society its personal and social advantages.

Whenever colleges and universities accommodate the academically and culturally able student, however, they necessarily affirm the distinctions that separate segments of our society. Colleges do not create the class distinctions, but they do risk making them each time admissions decisions are made. A result is that college remains beyond the reach of most disadvantaged young adults. In Section 1 of this book, I quoted Caspar Whitney's desire to keep the lower classes "in their place." Well, times have changed since then, but the problem persists, particularly as it relates to college athletics.

In this regard, neither is the NCAA the bad guy. Recent legislation was not designed to further complicate the lives of the disadvantaged. It was established to validate the academic experiences of high school students and to emphasize the fact that colleges train minds, not professional prospects. Just before the 1989 NCAA Convention, when the Southeast Conference recommended legislation that would deny scholarships to Prop 48 partial qualifiers, SEC Commissioner Harvey Schiller said, "What we hope is that it will force the high schools to do a better job of preparing students so they can do a better job in college."

His intentions were good, if a bit misguided. Depriving academically unqualified students, many of whom are disadvantaged, of athletic scholarships in the hope that their punishment will provoke social or educational redesign is applying the ruler to the wrong hind end! I know of several high schools in this country that should be feeling the business end of education's yardstick. Their coaches and counselors are unfamiliar with NCAA eligibility requirements, and some of them spend more time trying to help kids beat the system than to prepare for college.

Many of these youngsters are intellectually capable, but they are products of systems that somehow lose sight of education's fundamental purposes. Our failure to educate them—because they're not educated—magnifies their disadvantaged status and disregards society's responsibility to them. This book will not resolve such a problem, but it can help, especially if coaches and counselors share information like that provided in Figure 2-1. The relationship between lifetime earnings and education does much to affirm the good intentions of organizations like the NCAA.

THE SPECIFICS OF BYLAW 14.3
(PROPOSITION 48)

The NCAA affects high schools in other ways as well. Certainly, one of the most pronounced influences involves the legislation that may be enacted each year following its annual convention. Such legislation is extensive, as evidenced in the *NCAA Manual*, a document that is well over 500 pages and can be as complex as any university textbook. The piece of legislation that has received the most media attention within the past few years, however, involves bylaw 14.3, originally called Proposition 48. It involves the eligibility requirements for freshmen to play a sport in college.

Bylaw 14.3 involves three primary requirements. The first two stipulate the following:

- High school student athletes must graduate from high school.
- They must maintain an appropriate grade point average and receive equivalent composite scores on the ACT or the SAT as specified on a sliding scale, which is provided for young athletes, coaches, and counselors in the *NCAA Guide for the College-Bound Student Athlete.*

Note: NCAA Division II colleges and universities have many of the same requirements, including graduation from high school and a core of thirteen academic units. Division II schools, however, do *not* use a sliding scale and require only a 2.0 grade point average on a 4.0 scale. Because all these requirements are subject to annual change, coaches and counselors are encouraged to secure a copy of the *NCAA Guide for the College-Bound Student Athlete* each year to have access to updated information.

The third requirement of bylaw 14.3 is that student athletes must show evidence on their high school transcripts of having maintained a core curriculum of a required number of academic units, consisting of English, math, science, social studies, and other approved courses.

NCAA Division III colleges and universities are not subject to the requirements of bylaw 14.3. Coaches and counselors, therefore, are encouraged to contact the individual schools to determine eligibility requirements, many of which are more rigorous than those of bylaw 14.3 due to the relative selectivity of Division III schools.

The requirements are mentioned only generally in this book because they are subject to change each year at the NCAA Convention. The reproducible provided in Figure 2-2 is also open-ended so that it can be used each time a school meets with student athletes and their parents individually or collectively to discuss the NCAA's eligibility requirements. The format provides two important advantages:

1. Coaches, counselors, and athletic directors will be able to use the same form every year without having to design a new one each time the NCAA modifies its eligibility requirements.
2. The form instructs your young athletes to *write down* the requirements as they are discussed in the meeting. If current learning research is valid, students will be more inclined to remember the requirements if they deal with them visually, auditorily, and tactilely.

The reproducibles in Figure 2-3 will get you started. They outline the eligibility requirements as of August, 1995, as well as the changes that will go into effect after

August of 1996. The reproducibles can be used to make transparencies for meetings with athletes and their parents. Distribute the handout beforehand and instruct the students to write down the information that is appropriate for them. Again, this information is likely to change, so be sure to secure updated NCAA legislation and modify the information in the transparencies accordingly.

MAINTAINING CURRENT NCAA INFORMATION

Interestingly, legislative changes constitute one of the NCAA's biggest influences on high schools. Though a factor in college recruiting and selection for well over a decade and a half, bylaw 14.3 has yet to receive the widespread attention it deserves in high schools. Changes in the legislation have been so frequent that high school personnel feel unable, sometimes unwilling, to keep up with them. They may read about them in newspapers and hear about them on radio and TV, but the almost predictable adjustments made in them each year leave high school personnel frustrated in their attempts to keep up.

One result is the failure of many young athletes to understand the general importance or specific requirements of their academic programs. Certainly, this is not primarily the fault of the NCAA. Information is distributed by them to high schools each year, explaining current changes in legislation and encouraging young athletes to focus on academics in high school in order to prepare themselves for a worthwhile college experience.

Neither is it the fault of many coaches and counselors. Often, the information fails to reach them, and if it does, it is not often discussed at length in departmental or coaches' meetings. For that matter, rarely have high schools devised processes and procedures that systematically distribute information to all parties involved and engage them in ongoing planning activities to assure compliance with NCAA requirements.

Athletic directors are well advised, therefore, to use the reproducible in Figure 2-4, "An NCAA Update," to share updated regulatory information with coaches, counselors, and others in the building who assist young athletes with college planning and selection. The form is easily revised each time the legislation changes, and it provides for coaches and counselors easy reference to important information to use with young athletes and their parents during planning activities.

No one likes to appear ignorant of vital information, particularly when it is publicized so broadly in the media. That's why most coaches and counselors will read the *NCAA Update*; it is interesting and provides information relevant to their jobs. More important, it is concise enough to keep on hand for quick reference each time they assist a young athlete with program planning and college selection. Finally, it is yet another suggestion that the athletic director is doing his or her job.

COMPLIANCE AND THE NCAA

It's important to recognize that the NCAA provides compliance services to member institutions to help university officials complete their self-studies, financial audits, and disclosures of graduation rates. Many of these materials are available to high school personnel to use as guides when helping young athletes find appropriate college experiences. The information involving graduation rates is particularly helpful. Compliance services provide resource materials explaining financial aid, eligibility, and recruiting; they also work with universities and colleges that have been penalized to improve conditions that resulted in rules violations.

Compliance and the High School: A Look at the NCAA's Clearinghouse

The NCAA initiated the Clearinghouse a couple of years ago to evaluate the transcripts of high school athletes who want to continue playing their sports in college. Simply stated, the Clearinghouse guarantees that young athletes meet the academic requirements of bylaw 14.3 before they can be recruited or offered an athletic scholarship. It's safe to say—and this may be the single most obvious understatement in this book—that colleges and universities over the years have looked at high school transcripts differently.

Many have looked at the same course differently, one accepting it as an academic course, the other denying it. Some have overlooked the absence of high school graduation or university admissions requirements; others have even falsified transcripts to secure the admission of athletically gifted but academically deficient young athletes.

The Clearinghouse, a program administered by the American College Testing program (ACT), was created to eliminate such abuses by standardizing the recruitment and admissions processes. As reflected in figure 2-5, the process is relatively simple. Use the reproducible to develop a transparency that illustrates the process, then explain it:

- Early in each school year, high schools send form *48-H* to the Clearinghouse. The form contains the titles of all the school's academic courses that satisfy the requirements of the NCAA's bylaw 14.3. If the Clearinghouse disagrees with the school on one or more courses or requires additional information, they will contact the school to communicate their concerns. Dialogue between the school and the Clearinghouse continues until form 48-H has been approved by the Clearinghouse. The Clearinghouse will then send one copy back to the high school and retain another in its library for future reference.

- Early in the senior year, student athletes are expected to fill out the "Student Release Form," a copy of which is included in Figure 2-6. The students mail the white copy on the form to the Clearinghouse and give the pink and yellow copies to the designated person in the school who will process his or her academic information. This person usually is the high school counselor. The counselor forwards the yellow copy of the form, along with an official copy of the student's transcript, including test scores and proof of graduation, to the Clearinghouse. The counselor keeps the pink copy of the form for his or her records.

- The Clearinghouse then compares the academic information it has received with the student's file and the form *48-H* to determine eligibility and notifies the student of its decision. Any discrepancies are corrected by additional dialogue as needed.

- Finally, NCAA Division I and II schools can request eligibility information about prospective student athletes from the Clearinghouse for purposes of initial recruitment or after enrollment, generally for walk-ons. When the Clearinghouse receives the lists from each school, it will search its files for each student listed and, if given permission from the student on the student release form, will share the information with the school(s).

If a student has not given permission on the student release form for his or her information to be shared with any school that requests it, the Clearinghouse will contact the student to get permission for its release to the school or schools that ask for it. The information will either be released or denied to the university based on the student's response.

Notice that the student release form asks the student to check either of two options, to release information to any school that requests it or to just the five listed on the form. Obviously, students who are seeking an athletic scholarship to college and who may not be heavily recruited will want to check option 1. Heavily recruited "blue-chippers" may want to check option 2. Advise your young athletes accordingly.

THE NCAA'S SCHOLARSHIP PROGRAMS

Finally, the NCAA provides a wide range of additional programs that may not receive the media attention of bylaw 14.3 and the Clearinghouse but that assist student athletes in dramatic ways. The NCAA provides opportunities to assist current and former athletes by recognizing their contributions to the world of sport:

- The NCAA Honors Program recognizes and rewards significant accomplishments by current and former college athletes. The "Teddy," named after President Theodore Roosevelt and initiated in 1967, is its biggest honor and is presented annually at the NCAA convention. It is given to a varsity letter winner who has distinguished himself or herself as a highly visible representative of the ideals of amateur athletics.

- The *College Athletics Top XII Awards* honor Today's Top Six senior student athletes and the Silver Anniversary Top Six, six former student athletes who have distinguished themselves since their graduation from college twenty-five years earlier.

- One hundred twenty-five postgraduate scholarships are also awarded each year to academically successful student athletes who are nominated by representatives of their schools and ultimately selected by the NCAA Postgraduate Scholarship Committee.

- *The Walter Byers Postgraduate Scholarship Program,* named for the former executive director of the NCAA, annually awards a basic stipend of $10,000 to one male and one female student athlete who has demonstrated significant academic accomplishment in the classroom. The initial requirement is that the students earn a minimum grade point average of 3.5 on a 4.0 scale.

- The NCAA also awards *Degree-completion Grants* to student athletes who are close to graduation and have exhausted their eligibility for financial aid; it offers two programs—a *Women's Enhancement Program* and an *Ethnic Minority Enhancement Program*—that award postgraduate scholarships and internships in the NCAA national office to qualified female and minority athletes to enhance their future involvement in sports as coaches or administrators.

MAINTAINING CONTACT WITH THE NCAA

Coaches, counselors, athletic directors—even students and parents—are encouraged by the NCAA to contact them to secure answers to questions regarding rules, regulations, and processes. Many high school personnel forgo such contacts because the NCAA seems to them an unapproachable giant of the sports world, alternately serving and slapping the hands of universities and currying the favor of government officials and other VIPs.

The NCAA may be all these things, but it also works hard to respond to the concerns of high school personnel, including students and parents. Whenever you have questions involving a specific situation, therefore, you are encouraged to contact the NCAA for detailed answers. Obviously, many questions can be answered by referring to the materials provided by the NCAA and contained in the *NCAA Manual,* a copy of which can be purchased from NCAA Publications.

When a specific situation, however, requires clarification, give them a call or write a letter seeking additional information.

The phone number is:

913-339-1906

The address is:

The National Collegiate Athletic Association
6201 College Blvd.
Overland Park, Kansas 66211-2422

Most questions regarding rules and regulations can be answered by a member of the legislative services. Simply ask for one of them whenever you or one of your students calls. The NCAA is quick to indicate that they also talk to students and their parents.

UNDERSTANDING THE NATIONAL ASSOCIATION OF INTERCOLLEGIATE ATHLETICS (NAIA)

Since its inception in 1937 as the "National Small College Basketball Tournament," the NAIA has served up to 500 colleges and universities, most of which during recent years have continued to be relatively small schools. The organization is divided into thirty-two districts representing the fifty states, and it sponsors district and national championships in a variety of sports, including baseball, basketball, cross country, football, golf, soccer, swimming, tennis, track, and wrestling.

As explained by Al Duer, the NAIA executive secretary-treasurer, during a district meeting in 1960, "The central aim of the National Association of Intercollegiate Athletics is for collegiate athletics to be an integral part of the total educational program of the institution, with emphasis upon instilling high ethical and moral character, health and leadership traits in youth." Consistent with this philosophy, the NAIA honored more than 700 student athletes by naming them All-America Scholar-Athletes. Representing some 225 member institutions, each of the honorees qualified by earning at least a 3.5 grade point average on a 4.0 scale.

Like the NCAA, the NAIA awards full or partial scholarships if students meet eligibility requirements. Scholarships consist of the following:

- tuition costs for that particular institution
- mandatory fees, books, and supplies required for courses in which the student is enrolled
- room and board costs, as specified in the university's catalogue

The NAIA makes no provisions for travel to and from the university as does the NCAA.

Entering student athletes are expected by the NAIA to meet *two* of the following three eligibility requirements:

- graduate in the upper half of the high school graduating class
- earn a composite score of 18 on the ACT and/or a 740 on the SAT
- Earn a cumulative high school grade point average of 2.0 on a 4.0 scale

Both the NCAA and the NAIA require that student athletes meet additional eligibility requirements while in college. Each must be enrolled in a minimum number of courses, must remain in good academic standing, and must be making appropriate progress toward graduation. Coaches and counselors are encouraged to share such information with high school student athletes to prepare them for college expectations. A reproducible is provided in Figure 2-7. Also included are the phone numbers and addresses of the NCAA and the NAIA. To reach the NAIA, write (or call):

The National Association of Intercollegiate Athletics
6120 S. Yale Avenue
Suite 1450
Tulsa, Oklahoma 74136
918-494-8828

THE NATIONAL JUNIOR COLLEGE
ATHLETIC ASSOCIATION (NJCAA)

In 1937, a small group of Jaycees met in Fresno, California, to organize what was to become the National Junior College Athletic Association. The 13 original California schools that were the charter members of the association grew to well over 500 schools, organized into three divisions, by the early 1990s. Like the NCAA, Division I schools in the NJCAA award full or partial scholarships in a variety of sports. They include

- tuition

- room and board

- books and fees

- transportation costs one time per academic year to and from the university by direct route

Division II schools are allowed to award scholarships consisting only of tuition, books, and fees. Division III schools may not award athletic scholarships, although they may compete with Division I and II schools.

Over the years, the NJCAA has maintained close affiliation with a number of other regulatory organizations in the United States. In 1957, they allied with the National Federation of State High School Athletic Associations (NFSHSAA) and the NAIA to cooperate on issues of mutual concern, initially to establish common codes in playing rules for several major sports. In 1963, the NJCAA became a member of the United States Olympic Committee and a representative on several NCAA rules committees. The NJCAA is also a member of most of the United States sports federations.

These affiliations and the broad athletic and academic offerings of junior colleges make them unique opportunities for some high school students. Available to any student interested in intercollegiate athletics, junior colleges are particularly appropriate for high school athletes who fail to meet the eligibility requirements for participation in NCAA schools. Following is the definition of students who are considered "nonqualifiers" at NCAA institutions, as outlined in the *NCAA Manual*:

> A nonqualifier is a student who has not graduated from high school or who, at the time specified in the regulation (bylaw 14.3), presented neither the core curriculum grade point average or SAT/ACT score required for a qualifier.

Such students at Division I schools may not receive institutional financial aid and may not compete or practice during the first year of enrollment. Nonqualifiers at Division II schools are also restricted from practice and competition but may receive nonathletics institutional financial aid, provided the school's athletic director has documentation from the financial aid office or committee that such aid was granted to the student.

Partial qualifiers at Division I schools are defined in the Manual as follows:

> A partial qualifier is a student who does not meet the requirements for a qualifier [see information in this book regarding bylaw 14.3] but who, at the time of graduation from high school, presents a cumulative grade point average of at least 2.5 (based on a 4.0 scale).

Partial qualifiers at Division I schools may receive nonathletics institutional financial aid based only on financial need, but may not practice or compete during the first academic year in residence. The same is true of partial qualifiers at Division II schools.

The Junior College Opportunity

Junior Colleges provide financial aid and participation opportunites for both nonqualifiers and partial qualifiers. Young athletes in high school, therefore, who failed to apply themselves academically can redeem themselves in a junior college and still open the door to additional academic study and intercollegiate competition in an NCAA school. To be eligible to compete at a junior college, students must have graduated from high school, have received a high school equivalency diploma, or have passed a national test such as the General Educational Develoment Test (GED).

If young athletes have done none of these, they may still qualify by completing one term of college work, passing twelve credits with a grade point average of 1.75 or higher. These credits must have been completed after the student's class graduated from high school. The young athlete who failed to qualify for NCAA competition but is genuinely interested in getting a college education, therefore, can realize his or her goal by attending a junior college and meeting the following requirements. If the student athlete plans to transfer to an NCAA Division I school, he or she must

- graduate from a junior college
- complete satisfactorily a minimum of 48 semester or 72 quarter hours of transferable degree credit toward receiving the school's bachelor's degree
- have attended the two-year school as a full-time student for at least three semesters or four quarters (excluding summer terms)

If the student athlete plans to transfer to an NCAA Division II school, he or she must

- have attended a two-year school as a full-time student for at least 2 semesters or 3 quarters, *and*
- have graduated from the two-year college, *or*
- have presented a minimum of 24 semester or 36 quarter hours of transferable degree credit with a cumulative minimum grade point average of 2.0 on a 4.0 scale.

Student athletes who graduated from high school as qualifiers under the provisions of the NCAA's bylaw 14.3 but who attended junior colleges directly out of high school may also transfer to Division I or II schools. Such athletes are encouraged to read the *NCAA Manual* for the eligibility requirements that pertain to them. For additional information about junior colleges, write or call:

NJCAA
PO Box 7305
Colorado Springs, CO 80933
719-590-9788

THE NATIONAL SMALL COLLEGE
ATHLETIC ASSOCIATION (NSCAA)

The NSCAA was formed officially in 1966 when the original ten charter members from the Lake Erie Conference and the Eastern Shore Basketball League met with soon-to-be commissioner Del Noble to create the National Little College Athletic Association.

The original purpose of the Association was to provide small colleges the opportunity to participate in a national basketball tournament. The NSCAA has since grown large enough to sponsor national competitions for eight intercollegiate sports and has changed its name to the National *Small* College Athletic Association, having grown uncomfortable with the word little.

To qualify for membership, schools must have enrollments of under 1,000 full-time equivalent students. The students are not awarded athletic grants-in-aid but must meet NSCAA requirements to continue competition throughout their four years of eligibility. The NSCAA also awards both academic and athletic All-America honors and provides overseas trips for both men and women basketball players.

For more information about the NSCAA, students and parents are encouraged to write or call:

Gary Dallmann
Commissioner, NSCAA
1884 College Heights
New Ulm, MN 56073
507-359-9791

SPORTS GOVERNANCE: THE BIG PICTURE

That our "big picture" of college sports is influenced so profoundly by the media is unfortunate. The picture is not often what they paint. With true journalistic insight, many TV commentators, radio announcers, and newspaper columnists have found one of society's sore spots—our continuing disenchantment with anything bureaucratic—and have gnawed at it until the average person on the street is half inclined to lay waste the NCAA and any other regulatory organization that occasionally needs to flex its legislative muscles.

From Proposition 48 to the Clearinghouse, NCAA legislation is meeting increased media censure, much of it misinformed. Many in the media seem more interested in creating a story and less interested in the issues behind it. Evidently, intercollegiate and professional sports in this country are not the only parties guilty of vested interests. Newspapers are sold to the guy and gal on the street; they support society's media habit—and many of them seem willing to ingest almost anything to sustain the high.

Papers sell when columnists seek controversial if simplistic reasons for excusing people from their individual responsibilities and for blaming the nation's bureaucratic giants for getting in the way of young athletes. Fortunately, high school coaches, young athletes, and parents have access to volumes of information regarding NCAA, NAIA, and other regulations. Every reputable college and university in this country emphasizes the importance of a strong academic background for high school kids. Every high school counselor should know this and inform youngsters about college expectations and the requirements of the NCAA.

Expecting high school authorities to understand and act on the reasons behind such NCAA legislation is not unreasonable. Nor is it unreasonable for the newspaper columnists of this world to look at the issues to inform the public and to promote valuable educational experiences for young athletes. Most youngsters enroll in more than twenty full year courses in high school. Expecting that thirteen of them be academic, especially for youngsters wanting to play their sports in college, is not another form of social abuse. See Figure 2-8 for a related reproducible.

The issues involving the NCAA have little to do with bureaucratic impersonality. Although the NCAA, the NAIA, the NJCAA, and other regulatory organizations occasionally may have to plead guilty to such charges, they are not the bad guys in American sports. Expecting entering college freshmen to be well grounded in academics is not unreasonable, no matter what the newspaper columnists and unprincipled college coaches of the sporting world would have us believe.

I have indicated elsewhere in this book that vested interests in intercollegiate athletics are responsible for a wide range of abuses, from college graduates who are unable to read to under-the-table gifts that destroy the reasonable intent of amateur athletics. Even the NCAA has to be careful of vested interests. Because it is an organization governed by its membership, it must remain sensitive to its own self-interests to assure the protection of young athletes and university sports programs.

Consider, for example, that the NCAA operates with an annual budget of more than $180 million and that 75% of its total revenues are derived from a contract with CBS Sports to televise championship events, foremost of which is the NCAA Basketball Tournament. In fact, the NCAA Basketball Tournament accounts for a significant majority of the NCAA's total operational budget. That some officials, therefore, continue to talk about the possibility of an NCAA Football Playoff is not too surprising.

This section already has argued that the elimination of freshman eligibility will promote an early academic emphasis for student athletes new to college campuses. The opinion is shared by a variety of major college coaches, so it is likely to be discussed seriously by the NCAA for years to come. The vested interests of smaller schools to maintain athletic parity with the larger schools, however, will continue to be a stumbling block to immediate legislation in this area.

The NCAA, which includes each member institution, must continue to ask itself, therefore, if a football playoff or the continued eligibility of freshmen athletes is in the best interests of the athletes, the sports fans, or the schools themselves. Fortunately, the NCAA continues to ask itself these questions.

AN INTERVIEW WITH LORNA STRAUS, MEMBER OF THE NCAA ACADEMIC REQUIREMENTS COMMITTEE

Mike: "Lorna, thanks for answering some questions for me about the NCAA. Given your long-time association with them, you're a natural to come up with the answers I need."

Lorna: "It's my pleasure."

Mike: "Let's get right to the nitty-gritty. Is it safe to say that the significant numbers of schools out there that self-report inadvertent violations of NCAA regulations is proof that the NCAA has gotten everyone's attention?"

Lorna: "Absolutely, but it's hard to enforce all the legislation—not because there are so many cheaters out there but because the *NCAA Manual* is so detailed. You know, I entered this whole business with a great deal of good faith and have been pleased to learn that the vast majority of people I deal with have as much good faith as I do. Unfortunatetly, that's not 100%, and because that other small percentage is out there, we have to have this incredible number of rules in place."

Mike: "Yes, that sure makes compliance difficult sometimes."

Lorna: "It sure does and that's why one of the growth industries is compliance coordinators to help the universities with the interpretation of NCAA rules."

Mike: "Right, and that's why there are guys like me going into high schools to talk about bylaw 14.3 and the Clearinghouse, because most of the people in the high schools are having a tough time keeping up with all of it."

Lorna: "That's why I said at a recent meeting of the committee that our next issue was to get the word out, and the committee completely agreed with me. We wanted spots on the Final Four (in the NCAA Basketball Tournament), in NCAA football, and information to go out to all high schools. A lot of this has been done—for a long time—yet people are still saying, and I believe they're saying it in good faith, 'We didn't know.'"

Mike: "Right, it's amazing."

Lorna: "Yes, and I understand the frustration of the people in Kansas City (NCAA National Headquarters), because they annually send lots of information out to thousands of high schools across the country. Our concern is what happens to it at that point."

Mike: "Mine, too. My position during presentations at College Board conventions for the last several years has been that we have to get into the high schools."

Lorna: "That's right, some people are even saying the late elementary grades. And what people like you do—people in the writing and consulting sector—is raise the issues."

Mike: "Speaking of which, from your perspective, what one issue would you want to share with parents and young athletes about the NCAA and their university experiences?"

Lorna: "The purpose of all this is to get an education, so that the rest of one's life can be built upon the strong foundation that college provides. If the ticket to this education is going to be athletic ability, young athletes must never forget that underlying it is the reason they're going to college in the first place. Because professional sports careers are so unlikely, they must never forget the underlying purpose of going to college. The parents of youngsters who can run faster and jump higher than the rest of us share an important responsibility with coaches and counselors to assure that this happens."

LET'S WRAP IT UP

Finally, class distinctions are interwoven within the historical fabric of amateurism within this country. The NCAA and other regulatory organizations have not created these distinctions. Recent legislation, although well intentioned, is an affirmation of the integrity of a college education as well as the distinctions that separate segments of our society. This fact is unavoidable. To lessen the impact of such legislation and to accommodate at least some of the needs of disadvantaged students who want to play sports in college, the NCAA and other regulatory organizations would be well advised to reevaluate the relative advantages and disadvantages of freshman eligibility.

The elimination of freshman eligibility is but one solution, perhaps a single element in a comprehensive nationwide effort to resolve some of the abuses in college athletics without further depriving the culturally deprived. Without a genuinely sensitive aproach to the needs of colleges as well as to those of disadvantaged athletes, Caspar Whitney's desire in 1895 to have his sport "among the more refined elements" may be coming true.

Fortunately, the NCAA and other regulatory organizations are coordinated by men and women like Lorna Straus who are genuinely interested in the educational as well as the athletic well-being of the student athletes in our high schools and colleges. With their help and the ongoing involvement of folks like you and me, the many advantages of a college education will become available to larger segments of our society, certainly to the young men and women who devote so much of their time and effort to intercollegiate athletics.

Figure 2-1

ECONOMIC EARNING POWER OF EDUCATION

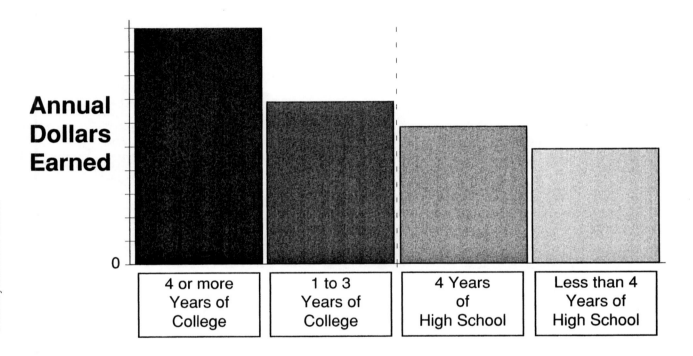

- 4+ YRS. OF COLLEGE earns 101% more than LESS THAN 4 H.S. YRS.

- 1–3 YRS. OF COLLEGE earns 39% more than LESS THAN 4 H.S. YRS.

- 4 YRS. OF H.S. earns 20% more than LESS THAN 4 H.S. YRS.

- 4+ YRS. OF COLLEGE earns 69% more than 4 YEARS OF H.S.

- 1–3 YRS. OF COLLEGE earns 17% more than 4 YEARS OF H.S.

SOURCE: *Occupational Outlook Quarterly*

33

Figure 2-1 (continued)

UNEMPLOYMENT RATES BY EDUCATION

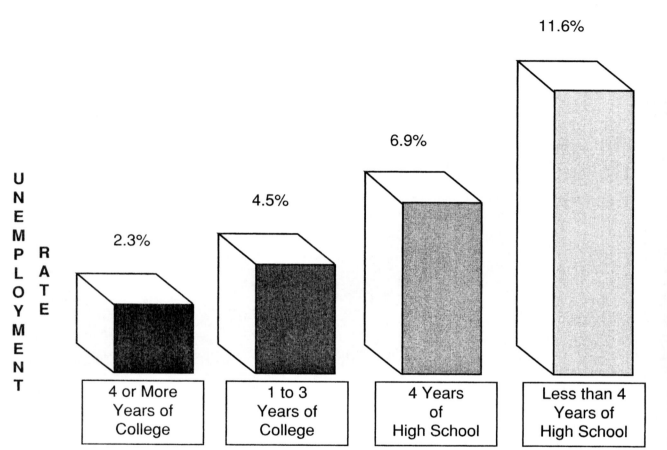

- LESS THAN 4 H.S. YRS. *5 × more likely to be unemployed* than 4+ YRS. of COLLEGE
- LESS THAN 4 H.S. YRS. *2 × more likely to be unemployed* than 4+ YRS. of H.S.
- 4 YRS. OF H.S. *3 × more likely to be unemployed* than 4+ YRS. of COLLEGE
- 4 YRS. OF H.S. *1.5 × more likely to be unemployed* than 1–3 YRS. of COLLEGE

SOURCE: *Occupational Outlook Quarterly*

Figure 2-2

ELIGIBILITY REQUIREMENTS FOR *INTERCOLLEGIATE* SPORTS

DIRECTIONS: The following discussion contains very important information. You *must* abide by it if you plan to play a sport in college. ***The Bad News:*** If you fall short in any area, you will not be eligible to receive a scholarship, practice, or play in an NCAA Division I or II school during your first year. For that matter, you may *Never* play a sport in college if you are declared academically ineligible. ***The Good News:*** The rules are not hard to follow. If you maintain a decent college-prep program in high school and study to the best of your ability, you will have no problem with the following requirements.

Be sure to write them down as we go along, and ask questions at any time. We're here to make sure you understand the rules.

The NCAA's Bylaw 14.3 (Proposition 48)

1. Graduate from high school.

2. Maintain a grade point average of _____ on a 4.0 scale and earn a composite score of _____ on the ACT or a _____ on the SAT *or* earn a lower grade point average but a higher ACT/SAT score. Ask your counselor or coach to see the NCAA "sliding scale." It shows the relationship between test scores and grade point average.

3. Maintain a program of at least _____ academic units (full-year courses), including the following:

   - English—4 years
   - Math—2 years
   - Social Studies—2 years
   - Science—2 years
   - Other:

NOTES:

NAIA REQUIREMENTS

The requirements of the National Association of Intercollegiate Athletics (NAIA) are similar to those of the NCAA. The NAIA also awards athletic scholarships and has its own set of eligibility requirements. Write them down as they are mentioned.

YOU MUST MEET ANY TWO OF THE FOLLOWING THREE REQUIREMENTS:

1. Graduate from the upper half of your high school class.

2. Earn a grade point average of _____ on a 4.0 scale.

3. Receive a composite score of _____ on the ACT or a score of _____ on the SAT.

For further explanations of some of the specifics of test scores and academic program, see your coach and counselor. You may have a unique situation that requires special consideration. Talk to your coach and counselor anyway, if only to make sure that you are meeting the requirements of either organization.

NOTES:

Figure 2-3

NCAA ELIGIBILITY
NCAA BYLAW 14.3

AFTER AUGUST 1, 1995 TO BE ELIGIBLE AT A DIVISION I SCHOOL:

1. *Graudate* from high school

2. Earn a grade point average of *2.5* on a *4.0* scale and obtain a *minimum combined score* of *700* on the *SAT* or a *minimum composite* of *17* on the *ACT,* or

   Earn a grade point average of *2.0* on a *4.0* scale and score a minimum combined score of *900* on the *SAT* or a *minimum composite* of *21* on the *ACT.*

3. The *NCAA* has developed a *sliding scale* to accommodate *variations* in *grade point average* and *SAT* and *ACT* scores. [See your coach or counselor for additional information.]

4. Complete a core curriculum of at least *13 academic units* (full year courses), including:
   - 3 in English
   - 2 in social studies
   - 2 in math
   - 2 in science (at least 1 lab course, if offered by your school)
   - 2 more in any of the above or in foreign language, computer science, philosophy, or nondoctrinal religion
   - As of 1995—2 more from among English, math, and natural or physical science

NOTE: NCAA Division II schools will require the same 13 academic units but will not use a sliding scale. They will still require a 2.0 grade point average on a 4.0 scale and a combined score of 700 on the SAT or a composite of 17 on the ACT. Contact your counselor or coach for additional information about NCAA Division III schools.

AFTER AUGUST 1, 1996 TO BE ELIGIBLE AT A DIVISION I SCHOOL:

1. *Graduate* from high school

2. Earn a grade point average of *2.5* on a *4.0* scale and obtain a *minimum combined score* of *820*on the *SAT* or a *minimum total score* of 68 on the subtests of the ACT or

   Earn a grade point average of *2.0* on a *4.0* scale and score a *minimum combined score* of *1010* on the *SAT* or a *minimum total* score of 86 on the subtests of the ACT.

3. The *NCAA* has developed a *sliding scale* to accommodate *variations* in *grade point average* and *SAT* and *ACT* scores. [See your coach or counselor for additional information.]

4. Complete a core curriculum of at least *13 academic* units (full year courses), including:
   - 4 in English
   - 2 in social studies
   - 2 in math, including algebra and geometry
   - 2 in science (at least 1 lab course, if offered by your school)
   - 2 or more in any of the above or in foreign language, computer science, philosophy, or nondoctrinal religion
   - 1 more from among English, math, and natural or physical science

Figure 2-4

AN NCAA UPDATE

The following information is provided to keep you informed of recent developments in the NCAA. As you know, we have a responsibility to assure that our athletes meet NCAA requirements in order to play a sport in college. We will be sharing this kind of information periodically so that you will be able to answer questions from students and parents and help our athletes with their educational planning. More detailed information is available in the Athletic Department. See me if you have any questions.

NEW NCAA LEGISLATION:

NEW DEVELOPMENTS:

LEGAL CONSIDERATIONS:

OTHER:

Figure 2-5

FORM 48-H AND THE CLEARINGHOUSE

HIGH SCHOOL PROCEDURE:

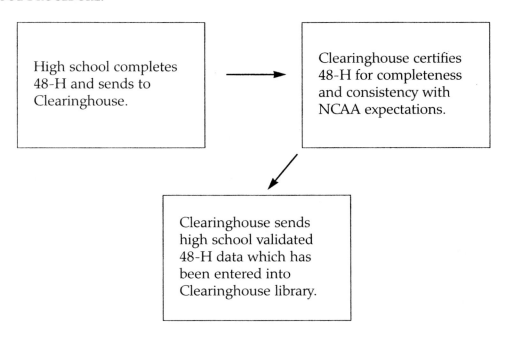

STUDENT ATHLETE PROCEDURE:

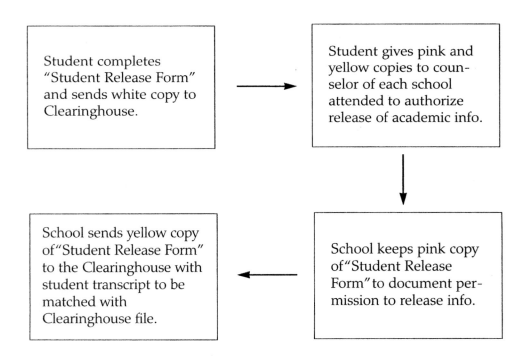

Figure 2-6

IC 3601.3

NCAA INITIAL-ELIGIBILITY CLEARINGHOUSE

Please print in black ink or type. Follow the instructions in the NCAA Clearinghouse brochure for high school students.

PART I: Student and High School Information

Section A: Student Information

Social Security Number ☐☐☐ - ☐☐ - ☐☐☐☐

Name _____ _____ ____
Last   First   MI

Address _____

City, State, ZIP Code _____

Country _____

Date of Birth ____ / ____ / ____   Phone (____) ____ - ____

Section B: High School You Currently Attend

H.S. Code ☐☐☐☐ - ☐☐☐   High School Graduation Date _____

H.S. Name _____

Street Address _____

City, State, ZIP Code _____

Country _____

Section C: Schools You Previously Attended (Grades 9, 10, 11, and 12)

H.S. Name _____

City, State (or City, Country) _____

H.S. Name _____

City, State (or City, Country) _____

(If more schools attended, attach extra pages.)

PART II: Authorization Signatures

I understand and agree to abide by the procedures in the NCAA Clearinghouse brochure for high school students. I authorize the high schools listed above to release to the NCAA Initial-Eligibility Clearinghouse my transcripts, including ACT and SAT scores, proof of graduation, and any other academic information or records, as requested by the Clearinghouse for determining my athletic eligibility. I further authorize the release of information or records obtained by the Clearinghouse to the NCAA and the institutions listed below. I understand and agree that the information provided to the Clearinghouse also may be used for research concerning athletic eligibility, the academic preparation and performance of student-athletes, and related issues. I also understand that the research may be published or distributed to third parties but that I will not be identified in any such published or distributed data.

_____   _____
Signature of Student   Date

_____   _____
Signature of Parent or Guardian (required if student is under 18 years of age)   Date

PART III: Permission to Release to Colleges/Universities

The Clearinghouse will respond to requests from NCAA member institutions for your eligibility information according to your instructions. *(Please note that the Clearinghouse sends eligibility information only when institutions request it.)* Check ONE of the following options:

☐ **Option 1.** I authorize the Clearinghouse to release my eligibility information to **any institutions** offering Division I or Division II sports upon request from such an institution.

☐ **Option 2.** I authorize the Clearinghouse to release my eligibility information **only to those institutions listed below.** I understand that if any institution not listed requests my information, the Clearinghouse must first contact me to obtain a release for that institution. (You may list up to five institutions below. For each institution that you list, please provide the code, institution name, city, and state. Codes are listed in the student brochure *Making Sure You Are Eligible to Participate in College Sports.* If you cannot find the institution on the list, leave the code blank but provide the name, city, and state.)

Code   Institution Name   City, State

☐☐☐☐ _____ _____

☐☐☐☐ _____ _____

☐☐☐☐ _____ _____

☐☐☐☐ _____ _____

☐☐☐☐ _____ _____

PART IV: Payment

The basic fee of $18.00 covers reports for all institutions that request information about you under Option 1, **OR** for up to five institutions listed under Option 2. This form will not be processed without correct payment or signed authorization from a school official for a fee waiver.

☐ Personal check, cashier's check, or money order in U.S. dollars drawn on a U.S. bank enclosed. Make checks payable to **NCAA Clearinghouse.**

☐ Credit Card: ☐ VISA   ☐ MasterCard

Card Number: ☐☐☐☐ ☐☐☐☐ ☐☐☐☐ ☐☐☐☐   Exp. Date: ____

Authorized Signature: _____

☐ **Fee Waiver (section must be completed by authorized high school official)**
Verification of Fee Waiver Eligibility: *I verify that the student named above has received a waiver of the* ☐ *ACT or* ☐ *SAT test fee (check appropriate box).*

_____   **School Seal**
Signature of Official   Title

_____
Printed Name of Official   H.S. Phone

PART V: Password

After _____ you will be able to access your file from a touch-tone phone to check on the status of your eligibility information. In order to use this option, you will need to provide a 4-digit personal identification number (PIN). Enter your PIN here: ☐☐☐☐

[White copy—Return completed copy to Clearinghouse at address below.]

NCAA Clearinghouse–Forms Processing, 2510 North Dodge, P.O. Box 4043, Iowa City, IA 52244-4043. Phone 319/337-1492. FAX 319/339-6988.

39

Figure 2-7

TO REMAIN ELIGIBLE IN COLLEGE

REMEMBER: To play a sport in college, you must meet high school eligibility requirements *and* you must maintain eligibility requirements while in college. Write down the following requirements as they are mentioned:

1. Be making normal progress toward a degree as defined by the institution you are attending.
2. Credit Hour Requirements:

	NCAA	NAIA	NJCAA
NO. OF HRS. BY YEAR:	_____	_____	_____
	_____	_____	_____
	_____	_____	_____
GRADE POINT AVERAGE REQUIREMENTS BY YEAR:	_____	_____	_____
	_____	_____	_____

Check with your advisor or coach in college to make sure you are maintaining your eligibility. These requirements may change during your college career.

HIT THE BOOKS AND EMPHASIZE ACADEMICS, YOU WON'T HAVE TO WORRY ABOUT THEM!

Figure 2-8

A GLANCE AT THE CORE CURRICULUM

What 13 Academic Units Look Like

Following is a sample high school program that contains 13 academic units. (They are underlined in each column.) It also contains room for additional academic courses. (They are listed in italics.) This program is required if you plan to play a sport in college. In fact, if you are serious about college, you'll take more academic courses than those mentioned in this sample. This is just a sample program; other variations are possible.

FRESHMAN

English 1, 2

Algebra 1,2

Physical Science 1, 2

Intro to Computers 1/Art 1

Physical Education

Social Studies Intro 1, 2

SOPHOMORE

English 3, 4

Geometry 1, 2

Biology 1, 2

Art 3, 4

PE/Health

Cons. Ec. 1/*Computer 2*

JUNIOR

English 5, 6

Algebra 3, 4

United States History 1, 2

Art 5, 6

Physical Education
  Business Course or (Language?)

SENIOR

English 7, 8

Chemistry 1, 2

Study and Work Program or (Language and Sci?)

Physical Education

Metal Shop 1, 2

THINK ABOUT:

- A foreign language; many colleges want it. (2 years)
- More academic courses (pay me now or pay me later!)

SEE YOUR COACH OR COUNSELOR IF YOU HAVE QUESTIONS!

THE REAL WORLD OF ATHLETIC SCHOLARSHIPS

First, a quick story. Several years ago, we had a quarterback who led us to a mythical national championship. He ran a 4.6 forty, threw the football sixty yards, maintained a B+ average, and attracted more recruiters than blitzing linebackers. They came from fifty schools and chased him relentlessly—at home, in school, and on the practice field. The real pros among the recruiters played within the rules; others did not.

Several disregarded simple rules of consideration by pestering his family with phone calls and unannounced visits. A couple tempted him by offering walk-on opportunities to his best friend, who was a good high school player but little more than a prep-team tackling dummy for Division I programs. One or two even made oblique promises of gifts for his parents. One, however, went well beyond implicit noncompliance, and in the process taught us a lasting lesson. He—the recruiter—also learned one.

He was a coach from a former powerhouse that was trying to muscle its way back to the front of the pack. Two or three prerace favorites were blocking his way, however, and the finish line was in sight, so he made a final desperate attempt to win the race: "How would you like to go out to your car tonight and find $5,000 in the glove compartment?"

His question was a first for our coaching staff (not a last) and was less tempting than insulting, so in a matter of minutes we hustled him from the chair in our office to the general proximity of his car in the parking lot. He was told never to call or visit our school again and advised not to contact friends and colleagues in the Chicago area.

He and his program were gone in four years. His school eventually was sanctioned by the NCAA and, worse, was shunned by many of the top high school programs in the country. The purpose of this story is not to proclaim our integrity but to affirm the power of high school coaches and other personnel. College coaches recruit blue chippers. High school coaches *make* blue-chippers—in all sports, male and female—and counselors work with them. The process results in skills for the athlete, influence for the counselor, and power for the coach, the kind of power that reaches beyond athletics to touch most of a young person's life.

RELATING POWER
TO ATHLETIC SCHOLARSHIPS

Because of this power, the high school coach must be the central figure in the coalition of persons who advise student athletes. Too many college recruiters are lured to the brink of abuse by quarterbacks who run 4.6 forties and throw a football sixty yards. They often jump off the brink if the athlete is a high school halfback who runs a 4.2 forty, a 290-pound tackle, or a 7'3" center.

The 6'5" female athlete who scores baskets at will may also be heavily recruited, but her sport in college is relatively unencumbered by the "dueling for dollars" mentality that motivates so many men's college programs. She will still, however, need the balance between academics and athletics that a knowledgeable high school coach can assure.

Others are also important. The high school counselor's power, almost as important as the coach's, is found in his or her knowledge of college and career planning and the relationship of both to the student athlete's ultimate selection of a school. This kind of power, especially when combined with the coach's influence on each of his or her athletes, constitutes a far greater force on student athletes than the charisma of most college coaches or the appeal of the scholarships they offer.

Scholarships have considerable appeal. To many high school athletes, a scholarship is more than an all-expenses-paid trip to academia; it is an affirmation of their athletic ability, a testimony to their lofty position in the school's pecking order, a confirmation of who they *are,* and, to some, another step toward the excitement, money, and fame of professional tennis, soccer, football, track, or basketball. As such, for all high school athletes, an athletic scholarship holds as much potential for harm as for good.

The parents of high school athletes are also powerful, often more powerful than anyone else. Parental power for good is maximized, however, when they know enough about scholarships and sports in college to look at both realistically. Many parents have too much invested in the accomplishments of their children. A child's accomplishment can be a parent's success, so they, too, can be overwhelmed by recruiters and their promises for self-esteem and future glory.

Coaches and counselors, therefore, must work closely with parents to influence their expectations and to secure their knowledgeable involvement in the process. Parents must be allies, not obstacles, when considering the scholarship process. Figure 3-1 provides a sample brochure that should be shared with parents and young athletes early in their high school careers, probably at an introductory meeting for freshmen. It has a football-basketball focus because I use it for our program, but it can be modified to reflect one or more different sports.

WHAT IS AN ATHLETIC SCHOLARSHIP?

Just what is this offer that rewards the hard work of so many talented young athletes and disappoints so many others? It is a form of financial aid from the college that includes tuition and fees, room and board, and books. Governed by the NCAA, the NAIA, and the NICAA, it can be guaranteed for only one year at a time and must be renewed each year, although many schools will promise (but not in writing) a scholarship each year for five years. In some schools, it amounts to as much as $20,000 a year or more; for most athletes, it is a college education, a fairly realistic assessment of athletic ability, and a sometimes misleading look at the future.

The "dollars" aspect of an athletic scholarship is quite obvious. The financial aid provided by a scholarship enables athletes to "play the price" of a college education. Exactly what they study in college is another question, a relatively detailed issue that suggests the "sense" of scholarships. Some parents need almost as much help as their children in working through these issues.

Many parents believe that colleges are all the same, that all offer fundamentally the same program of study and result in similar opportunities after graduation. Other parents are aware of the differences but allow themselves to be influenced by the athletic reputation of the school and the charm of the coach(es).

Still other parents are convinced that their child's selection to the all-conference team qualifies her as a future All-American at Nebraska. These parents are among the toughest to influence toward a realistic outlook regarding their child's college and career plans. Their narcissistic concern for their children's welfare often results in an unrealistic assessment of their athletic ability. That's why they are the logical early focus of informational activities provided by the high school. See Figure 3-2 for an excellent reproducible to share with parents.

WHO RECEIVES ATHLETIC SCHOLARSHIPS?

Every high school coach knows that many of his or her best athletes never receive even passing interest from college recruiters. The world of athletic scholarships is as competitive as the annual slugfest with the toughest cross-town rival, and perhaps moreso. The issues involving student athletes have been so prominent in the media that many parents believe that as soon as their child's season ends, the parade of recruiters begins. It's probably safe to say that most parents and student athletes alike are fundamentally unaware of the realities of intercollegiate athletics.

Our first job, therefore, is to share information with parents and young athletes, the kind of information that reorients perspectives by providing the realities of college scholarships. Fortunately, the information is not only revealing but interesting. It does, in fact, get their attention, if presented thoughtfully and completely. I always start with a couple of eye-openers.

The Facts of Athletic Scholarships

I like to share this story. I worked with a young tennis player one year who had decided to quit her high school tennis team to improve her national ranking. She then worked with a couple of different private coaches but, because of a recurring injury, couldn't sustain contact with any one of them for several months. Early in her senior year, her father met with me to discuss the "when" and "how" of tennis scholarships. I made several recommendations but, above all, advised him to ask one of her coaches to coordinate her scholarship search.

He agreed with the basis of my suggestion but felt that his many years' experience with the United States Tennis Association (USTA) had qualified him to "talk tennis" with college coaches. I was later informed by his daughter that very few college coaches wanted to talk to him. They responded as I had suggested they would. They would rather discuss a tennis player's potential with a marginally subjective coach than an obviously biased father.

To compound the girl's problem, many of the schools I eventually contacted for her had few scholarships available, some none. In most instances, the schools had only one or two scholarships to award and were offering them to players with higher national rankings. The girl, a potentially excellent player, ultimately was victimized by a recurring injury, a limited number of scholarships, and the wrong recruiting process. She eventually gave up competitive tennis.

I also provide *this* perspective on the availability of scholarships: I shared the rostrum at a College Board convention recently with the football recruiting coordinator from the University of Michigan. He provided some very interesting facts, one of which I still use. He indicated that his office annually mails about 8,000 questionnaires to high school football players who have somehow been brought to Michigan's attention.

He said that he receives players' names from commercial organizations, scouts hired by Michigan, high school coaches, players' parents, and even the players themselves. Once the player's name is entered into the program's computer, he will routinely receive mailings from the school and a questionnaire that requests specific information about him as an athlete and a student. Michigan's recruiting coordinator indicated that the questionnaire is only an initial request for information and, in some instances, nothing more than an act of courtesy to the person who made the referral.

Think about it. If major universities mail up to 8,000 questionnaires to high school athletes and ultimately award only a maximum of 25 scholarships, the odds against eventually receiving one are as high as 320 to 1. Even if the athlete is provided an all-expenses-paid visit to the campus (the NCAA allows Division I football programs to provide a total of seventy such visits to recruited athletes), the odds are still almost three to one against his receiving a scholarship.

Or look at it this way: There are over 100 major college football programs in this country, each of which provides a maximum of 25 scholarships to incoming freshmen annually. That's a total of 2,650 scholarships awarded each year, all of which eventuate from an initial mailing of almost a million questionnaires. The point is, high school athletes should be helped to put questionnaires in perspective. They, along with their parents, must develop a realistic understanding of the availability of scholarships.

Of the 265,000 seniors who play high school football each year, approximately 10,000 will receive all-conference honors. Less than a third of the 10,000 will receive an offer from a major football program. In fact, to illustrate even further, divide 265,000 seniors by 2,650 scholarships and discover that only one senior in every 100 will receive a scholarship.

Others will receive partial scholarships from NCAA Division I-AA, Division II, NAIA (National Association of Intercollegiate Athletics) schools, and junior colleges. The total number of scholarships available, however—most of which will be partials—will still be just under 10,000. Add to these statistics the fact that the NCAA has reduced the total number of scholarships universities may award athletes, and young athletes and their parents soon realize that a National Merit Scholarship is more likely than an athletic "free ride."

As an additional example, when I was working with the tennis player mentioned previously, both she and I discovered that there are only 279 Division I women's tennis programs. Each can award a *team* total of eight scholarships, with probably only one or two available for freshmen each year. The total number of tennis scholarships available nationally, therefore, is somewhere between four and five hundred, hardly enough to accommodate the expectations of thousands of young athletes who play tennis each year.

Considering Basketball Scholarships

Given the enormous negative publicity that college basketball programs have received recently, the average person is likely to believe that countless thousands of college athletes are suffering the slings and arrows of outrageous treatment. Consider the fact that there are just under 300 men's major college basketball programs in this country, and the NCAA is permitting them only 13 total scholarships per program.

The number of scholarshipped basketball players in major colleges, therefore, is just under 4,000. Now, add to that figure the fact that incoming freshmen players are competing for an average of only two or three scholarships per school, and it becomes clear that the total number of annual scholarships available to high school seniors is less than a thousand. Approximately 158,000 seniors play high school basketball each year.

The same numbers are true of women's basketball programs. There are just under 300 women's programs, each awarding a total of fifteen team scholarships. Although the women are allowed two more per team than the men, they still may award only three or four scholarships each year, bringing the total number available to high school athletes to just under a thousand.

Again, junior colleges, NAIA, and NCAA Division II schools award scholarships, mostly partials, so the total number of scholarships available to high school basketball players, men or women, is probably somewhere close to 2,000. Even at that, however, the real world dictates that only one in every one hundred high school basketball players will receive a scholarship, and most of those will be partials.

Looking at Other Sports

Recent decisions made by the NCAA, with input from groups like the Knight Commission, have resulted in the reduction of scholarships in all intercollegiate sports. If statistics regarding football, men's and women's basketball, and women's tennis open the eyes of high school athletes and their parents, consider the facts regarding the numbers of scholarships in other sports.

College men's tennis, for example, is allowed a total equivalency of 4.5 scholarships for the entire team. A coach with a very young team, therefore, may have no scholarships to offer during a given year. The same is true of sports like men's volleyball and golf, which also permit only 4.5 for the entire team. High school coaches and counselors, therefore, are encouraged to purchase a copy of the *NCAA Manual,* which lists maximum equivalency limits for all college sports, including women's sports and Division I-AA and Division II programs.

Coaches and counselors may want to know, for example, that there are approximately ninety-one NCAA Division I women's soccer programs in the country, each awarding a total of eleven team scholarships. With only two or three scholarships available for any given year, young soccer players are competing for a national total of only two to three hundred scholarships at the conclusion of their high school careers.

Your school may choose to provide such information to all counselors or to one specific person who is responsible for advising student athletes. However the school processes such information, it should be routinely shared with athletes and their parents to prepare them for the realities of athletic scholarships. See Figure 3-3 for a reproducible. They simply are not as available as most people believe, and the competition for them is intense.

A Word of Caution

The intercollegiate sports glass, however, is not half empty; it's half full. Junior colleges, the NAIA, and the NCAA's Division II programs offer athletic scholarships, and they provide a wide range of opportunities for young athletes to continue with a sport in college without a scholarship. We will discuss this in a later part of this section, when we look at "walking on" and discuss the advantages of junior colleges, the NAIA, and the NCAA's Division III programs.

The real world of college athletics may not involve as many scholarships as many young athletes believe, but the opportunities for sports competition are virtually unlimited. Although major college scholarships are relatively few in number, many partial scholarships are available, and many small college programs involve levels of competition that are among the finest in the world.

Every young athlete has a dream. Our jobs as parents, coaches, and counselors are not to destroy dreams but to promote them. A youngster's dream is his or her motivation, so each of us is advised to keep the dream alive by using these statistics cautiously. Dreams don't have to be destroyed by reality, just changed enough to make them more attainable.

SCHOLARSHIPS FROM THE WOMEN'S PERSPECTIVE

Given the past and continuing impact of Title IX, women's sports have grown considerably on most college campuses. Still a subject of debate, intercollegiate sports for women and the scholarships they provide often don't generate the revenue of men's sports and, as a result, suffer from budgetary restrictions. Such restrictions affect opportunities to conduct comprehensive mailings, to fly prospects to campuses for visits, and to transport recruiters around the country to watch student athletes and, ultimately, to meet them and their parents.

Because of these limitations, young women athletes are more dependent than men on their high school coaches for college contacts and for assistance with the entire recruiting process. Because recruiters for women's programs are unable to visit high schools as often as they would like, coaches must develop highlight tapes, resumes, and stat sheets for athletes with college potential and maintain routine communication with college personnel.

My earlier example of the young tennis player is illustrative. Her high school or private coach would have worked her through the process, and certainly would have made phone calls and developed highlight tapes to exhibit her skills in practice and competition. He or she also would have been able to arrange campus visits or meetings with coaches and would have had access to the kind of academic information the colleges require.

Another important consideration for women is the numbers of scholarships available to them in certain sports. Women's volleyball, for example, provides a maximum equivalency of 12.0 total scholarships; men's volleyball provides only 4.5. Women gymnasts, golfers, and tennis players also have more scholarships available to them than their male counterparts. This is another reason why the coaches of all women's sports should have a copy of the *NCAA Manual*. The coaches of some women's sports sometimes mistakenly assume that scholarship availability is comparable in men's and women's sports; it is not.

A representative of the NCAA's legislative services indicated recently that more scholarships are available to women than men in certain sports in an attempt to achieve total scholarship parity. Although coaches in men's volleyball are as dedicated to their sport as any other coaches, the NCAA considers it a minor sport; for women it is considered major. The same is true of gymnastics, tennis, golf, and swimming.

MAKING HIGHLIGHT TAPES

The development of highlight tapes, regardless of the sport, involves a few important considerations. It's usually a pretty good idea to provide two kinds of tapes for college coaches. The first is a video of the athlete performing in a contest, usually against formidable competition. It's generally a good idea to accompany such a tape with a stat sheet that identifies the player and describes the competition. A reproducible of such a sheet is provided in Figure 3-4.

The second kind of tape, especially important for sports like ice and field hockey, track, tennis, gymnastics—even basketball and football—is a skill tape. Skill tapes show the athlete executing the kinds of skills required of his or her sport: stick handling in ice and field hockey, beam routines in gymnastics, high jumping in track, or passing in football. Avoid lengthy tapes, whether they be performance or skill videos. Unless particularly interested in a prospect, many college coaches won't take the time to watch all of them.

If your school has a sophisticated audiovisual program, and you can edit and provide graphics for both kinds of tapes, so much the better. The quality of the tape won't find a scholarship for a mediocre athlete, but it will promote good athletes. As a close friend always reminded me—presentation is half the sell job. If such an AV program is not available to you, make the tapes anyway. They may provide the added boost the young athlete needs to make the jump from high school to college sports.

MAKING INITIAL CONTACTS WITH COLLEGE RECRUITERS

The same is true for your early contacts with college recruiters. Whereas men's major programs may span the nation in search of outstanding high school student athletes, the women's programs and the men's Division I-AA, II, and III programs are often restricted to local efforts. High school coaches, therefore, with assistance from counselors, must often make initial contacts.

Figure 3-5 provides a sample letter to use for such contacts. Notice that it provides relevant statistics about the student athlete's academic as well as athletic performance. It refers to her educational and career goals and provides information about such intangibles as leadership ability, personal values, and educational commitment. It also assures the coach that she will be with the college program for four years, a statement that college coaches appreciate. Even marginally talented players make substantial contributions to teams when they remain in school for four years.

RECOGNIZING THE UNLIKELIHOOD OF PROFESSIONAL SPORTS

A survey conducted by the Center for the Study of Sport in Society revealed recently that almost 50% of black inner-city youth expect to play a professional sport. Obviously, they see it as a way out of the inner city. My grandfather, Jim Thorpe, was fortunate enough to use professional sports as the road to a better life. Professional baseball with the New York Giants and, later, football with a variety of professional teams provided a route from the poverty of an Indian reservation to the relative security of middle-class America.

During his professional career, however, he was unable to integrate society's protocols with the sometimes brutal and often adolescent expectations of professional sport. His talent, therefore, filled every corner of his life while he was playing, but when his career ended, it left a void that he was unprepared to fill with anything else. The tragic cycle of his life was complete when the same road to professional sports and middle-class security led him back to near-poverty and premature death in a trailer park in California.

The tragedy of my grandfather's life is well known, but perhaps more tragic are the countless stories of young athletes, especially in inner cities, who seek a life of professional sports and never find it. They spend hours a day learning how to dribble and shoot a basketball, refining skills that are, at best, occupationally limiting. My grandfather, at least, had several years of money and glory. The vast majority of young athletes in our culture who seek professional careers never find them.

Again, look at the numbers. Approximately 158,000 seniors play high school basketball each year, and almost 70 rookies earn spots in the NBA. Of the high school seniors playing basketball, therefore, only four one-thousandths of one per cent will play professionally. The situation is similar in football. Almost 265,000 seniors play in high school each year and approximately 215 rookies make teams in the NFL. Only eight one-thousandths of one per cent of high school seniors can expect to play professionally.

These fractions are eye-openers to high school athletes and their parents. They are also critical for high school coaches and counselors because, when compared to the 50% of inner-city kids who expect to play a professional sport, they spotlight the dimensions of the tragedy that awaits a significant majority of young athletes.

Consider another sport. Professional tennis players are among the most visible in society. The U.S. Open and Wimbledon are viewed each year by millions of spectators around the world, and the top tennis players are seen almost daily on television commercials. The good ones can make a lot of money. During a recent conversation with an offical from the USTA, however, I learned that only a very few make big money and only the top one hundred in the pro ranks make the equivalent salaries of entry-level NBA or NFL players.

More than 30,000 senior girls play high school tennis each year; the number is approximately the same for senior boys. If only one hundred professional tennis players earn salaries which approximate the base salaries of NBA and NFL players, the expectations of high school tennis players for professional futures are similar to their counterparts in football and basketball.

And what if a youngster *does* make it in professional sports? In most sports, he or she can expect a career that lasts only three or four years. According to Roger Grooters, Director of Academic Advisement for athletes at Florida State University, "Fifty per cent of all the kids who play professional football end up flat broke when they're done, no matter how much money they made. Eighty-five per cent are divorced, and the average life expectancy of a pro football player is fifty-six years." He concludes his comment with the observation that pro football is not a good career choice.

The situation for professional tennis players may not be similar, but the lives of young tennis players are complicated by other issues. The Intercollegiate Tennis Association indicates that approximately 1000 to 1200 senior men play tennis in college. Interestingly, the USTA indicates that in a recent year only 15 of the top 100 professional tennis players in this country played in college, with only a couple of these actually graduating. Most professional tennis players, therefore, are beginning their careers well before college.

Such information must be shared with young athletes and their parents and used to steer kids in directions that lead to longer-lasting satisfaction and fulfillment. See Figure 3-6 for a reproducible. If professional sports make millionaires of only one in a million athletes, the odds are better that a youngster will be hit by lightning or, more appropriately, become a doctor or lawyer. High school coaches and counselors, then, must help student athletes find the academic as well as the athletic road to college. It may be less attractive and exciting, but it holds a great deal more promise for the future.

UNDERSTANDING RECRUITING

A knowledge of the recruiting process is essential if we are to help kids travel both roads. To gain such knowledge, we must understand recruiting from at least two different perspectives.

Recruiting from the College Perspective

College football coaches don't search the nation's high schools for civil engineers. College coaches invariably look for football players, good ones, tough kids who can help their programs. Intercollegiate sport showcases many of the world's finest athletes, in an arena that provides thrills for the spectators and pressure for the participants. A result is that some colleges spend more money recruiting three or four basketball players than they spend recruiting the remainder of the freshman class.

Certainly, they seek young people who are talented academically as well as athletically. College coaches who represent upstanding programs realize that good athletes who also are good students invariably make stronger contributions to the team than great athletes who are unable to learn their assignments or keep up their grades. Unfortunately, not all great athletes are good students. Within the past several years, therefore, at least 20% of the football and basketball players at major colleges have been "special admits."

More shocking, according to the report provided by the recent Knight Commission, half of all the football programs in the Division I colleges have been sanctioned by the NCAA. Most of these sanctions have been for relatively minor violations, but the fact remains: Intercollegiate programs sometimes don't play by the rules. Certainly not a startling revelation, such an observation still highlights the responsibilities of high school personnel when young athletes make the transition from high school to college.

According to the Knight Commission's report, in a typical Division I school only 33% of basketball players and 37% of football players graduate within five years. These statistics are consistent with a recent comment from an official for the NFL Players' Association, who indicated that two-thirds of the players in the NFL failed to graduate from college. Interestingly, he also indicated that players with college degrees last 50% longer in the NFL and receive salaries that are 20% higher than do nongraduates.

Surprising? Maybe not. Consider the comment from the Knight Commission that, throughout the 1980s, football and basketball players at Division I schools spent approximately thirty hours a week on their sports—more than they spent on their homework. Compare that statistic with one shared recently by the *Chicago Tribune*: "[In a recent year] 35.5 million spectators watched football games at 680 four-year colleges. According to a study by the College Football Association (CFA), $17.3 million was spent in one community solely from fans attending football games during the season."

That college coaches, therefore, are primarily interested in the "athlete" in student athlete should be surprising to no one. Consider the additional reality that major bowl games each year award almost $40 million to participating schools. College sports involve big bucks, and they require athletes who can help get them. The focus on the word "student" in student athlete, therefore, is the primary responsibility of the *high school* counselor and coach.

On the plus side, college athletes in other sports, particularly women, have graduation rates that are higher than those of nonathletes. In some instances, their rates of graduation are strikingly above the national average. Athletics and academics, therefore, *can* coexist at the university level, particularly when the Almighty Dollar is not lurking in every locker room.

Recruiting from the High School Perspective

For every "abused" college athlete, there are a high school coach and counselor who didn't do their jobs. It's that simple. Our job as high school coaches and counselors is only marginally to supply a product to colleges and universities. Contrary to the principles of marketplace economics, we are as concerned about our products after we sell them as before—or at least we should be. To the extent that we aren't, we increase the potential for abuse on the college level.

We also have the power to curb such abuses. If high school coaches instruct their players and the parents of their players to disregard the scholarship offers of unprincipled college coaches, such coaches inevitably will find themselves developing game plans to find new jobs. Similarly, the high school coaches themselves must reject the seduction that accompanies being on a first-name basis with high-profile college coaches. High-profile or not, underhanded coaches must be denied players.

If we don't give them the players, they don't win. And if they don't win—all the hype about academic emphasis notwithstanding—they lose their jobs. University presidents all over the country who glorify the classroom and de-emphasize the importance of athletics just as routinely fire coaches, upstanding and otherwise, who don't win enough games.

Our first task, therefore, is to promote the importance of academics. A sizeable number of our athletes will go to college; many will play a sport; some will receive athletic scholarships. In our entire coaching careers, we will be lucky to see one or two become professionals. The likelihood that women will play professional golf or tennis is as remote as that men will play professional football or basketball, so we are well advised to heed the words of one of the sporting world's staunchest and most articulate advocates of academics for athletes.

A few years before he died, Arthur Ashe said, "But I, and others, would like to see the riot act read to all beginning varsity athletes at the start of high school, informing them of what is expected, when and why, and what the consequences of noncompliance will be. It sounds simple, but it's not done."

"Noncompliance" *might* refer to local standards established by the school to determine eligibility; it *must* refer to the legislation required by the NCAA. And Ashe was correct. Generally, it is not done—to the extent that it is needed. Some high schools across the country—a few—have developed comprehensive programs to monitor the compliance of student athletes with the requirements of the NCAA's bylaw 14.3 (Prop 48); most have not. Much of the remainder of this section, therefore, is devoted to processes and materials for informing athletes and their parents about compliance requirements.

THE COUNSELOR'S ROLE
IN THE HIGH SCHOOL PERSPECTIVE

The counselor's role is every bit as important as the coach's. The counselor's knowledge of human development, career and college planning, and how each relates to the significant transition student athletes experience in and beyond high school is critical—at every stage of high school, but especially during the late junior and early senior years when college decisions must be made by the athlete and his or her parents. The checklist in Figure 3-7 identifies processes that must be followed by student athletes and their parents if the appropriate college is to be found.

Notice that it refers initially to the "Student Athlete Expression of Intent to Play College Sports." Use the form, which is provided in Figure 3-8, to announce a student athlete's interest in playing a sport in college. The form should be given to the counselor by the person who initiates it. Notice that it also requires information from the coach. The student or parent usually initiates the form, then gives it to the counselor, who in turn requests information from the coach, possibly in a meeting. In essence, the form alerts people that the process has started and requests relevant involvement for the most important people in the school—the counselor and the coach.

The other elements in the checklist in Figure 3-7 involve the obvious steps that must be taken when considering a college education. Some schools provide formal career and college searches. If your school has no such processes, you might consider developing them or simply eliminating reference to them in the checklist if you accommodate them in a different way. The important thing is that you use such a checklist to outline necessary steps for athletes and their parents. The more information you can provide in writing, the better the quality of your school's communication with athletes and their parents.

Counselors are important early in the student athlete's high school career. They must help athletes and their parents explore high school and college sports from a perspective other than that of the coach. Young athletes and their parents need a counselor's perspective to complement their understanding of

- the meaning of athletic success
- the definition of success as it relates equally to academics
- the advantages and potential disadvantages of participating in high school athletics
- the realities of competitive stress and the coping strategies needed to combat it
- the sometimes conflicting roles of parents as cheerleaders and family leaders
- the tendencies of young athletes to overidentify with their sports

Figure 3-9 provides a reproducible handout that should be shared routinely with the parents of freshman athletes, probably early in the year at a large-group meeting. It identifies the kinds of behaviors that parents should model for their children, and it encourages parents to maintain contact with the counseling office to secure the kind of assistance they might need as their children move through the school's athletic program.

Section 2 of this book has already discussed the NCAA, bylaw 14.3, and the needed processes and materials in schools to assure compliance. The counselor's role is to emphasize the realities of scholarships beyond mere compliance, to explore with parents and athletes the impact of athletic participation on adolescent development, to assist with the design of appropriate goals, and to assure student athletes that their athletic performance relates only incidentally to their value as people.

When the counselor complements the efforts of coaches and parents to help student athletes find a balance between athletics and academics, develop goals that seek a college experience for all the right reasons, understand the real value of athletic participation, and develop a sense of self-esteem that transcends athletic performance, young athletes can use sports to enhance rather than corrupt their development as adults.

RECOGNIZING IMPROPER RECRUITING TACTICS

Experienced high school counselors and coaches realize that the vast majority of college recruiters play by the rules. In fact, they generally represent their colleges and universities with pride and distinction. A few, however, like their self-centered counterparts in other segments of our society, have only their own best interests in mind. Unfortunately, they tend to be very good at what they do.

Inexperienced high school coaches and counselors may inadvertently allow themselves and their student athletes to fall prey to the tactics of such recruiters. Be alert, then, to some of the following strategies they may use:

- One of the most common tactics of a poor recruiter is to deprecate other programs. They forget that it's hard to work your way to the front of the pack when you're kicking everyone else in the seat of the pants. I learned a long time ago to be mistrustful of the recruiter who "bum raps" everyone else, and I want my kids to mistrust them, too, so I developed the material in Figure 3-10 to give to each of my athletes who might be interested in playing in college or who is being highly recruited. The handout also contains the remaining tactics in this section.

- On the other end of the continuum is the recruiter who claims the clear superiority of his or her program. No team consistently wins national championships any more. Besides, the student athlete's primary interest in the school *should* be its educational program. The recruiters who emphasize academics while discussing their sports program are generally the ones who represent the best programs.

- One of the most prevalent of improper recruiting tactics is the promise of a starting position to the recruit. The young athlete is indeed rare who can walk into a major college program and earn a starting position his or her first year. In most circumstances, the high school star has to achieve yet another level of performance before he or she can expect to even start in college, let alone become a star.

- Recruiters *can* promise a four- or five-year scholarship, but student athletes are advised to have them do it in the presence of parents and coach. As indicated already in this section, the NCAA allows only one-year scholarships, which are renewable each year, so recruiters are unable to put such promises in writing. If they make oral commitments, be sure they are made to a parent or coach, too. I always call the recruiting coordinator before any of my athletes visits a school to ask three questions: "What position do you have in mind for our athlete?" "How many years are you guaranteeing?" and "How good is your school's program in (the student's primary academic or career interest, if he or she has one)?" These three questions are essential early in the recruiting process.

- Beware of the recruiter who involves anyone from his or her booster organization. According to the *NCAA Guide for the College-Bound Student Athlete*: "No alumni or representatives of a college's athletic interests (boosters or representatives) can be involved in your recruiting. There can be no phone calls or letters from boosters."

This is one of the primary reasons that colleges receive sanctions from the NCAA. Often, the college's recruiters are unaware of the involvement of boosters in the process of trying to persuade an athlete to attend a particular school. High school personnel, therefore, must be watchful for phone calls or personal contacts from persons other than authorized personnel from the school's athletic program. Even if recruiters aren't responsible for such contacts, the program and the athlete can be penalized.

- Overzealous recruiters who visit the athlete at home more than three times are in violation of NCAA rules. The contact periods at school are similarly limited. High school personnel are encouraged to purchase multiple copies of the *NCAA Guide for the College-Bound Student Athlete* for distribution to coaches and counselors and to be available for recruited athletes and their parents.

- Promises of easy admission, unchallenging academic programs, or "friendly" professors are sure signs that recruiters care little about athletes beyond their ability to play a sport. Rarely will recruiters make such comments to coaches or counselors, but they will ease them into the conversation with young athletes. I had a middle linebacker one year who refused to talk again to a certain school because the recruiter made the mistake of saying: "Don't worry about admission; we'll take care of it." He may not have even intended anything improper. The comment, however, was enough to turn off 245 pounds of quality *student* athlete.

- Recruiters who promise return paid trips to their campuses are in violation of NCAA rules. High school student athletes are allowed only one paid visit to a maximum of five different schools. They can return to the campus often, but they must pay for each trip. Student athletes, therefore, must select their visits very carefully. The reproducible in Figure 3-11 provides some very helpful information for them when the recruiting process begins.

- The recruiter who swears up and down that the school's academic program in a particular field of study is the best in the nation may or may not be telling the truth. High school counselors must always investigate the quality of selected programs in schools. The information is more believable and helpful for the student athlete, and it can be used to assess the knowledge and truthfulness of recruiters.

- Finally, a typical recruitment ploy involves "walk-on" opportunities for a friend of the recruited student athlete. Several years ago, a recruiter from a major university discovered that a highly recruited tackle of ours wanted to attend the same university as his closest friend, an all-conference fullback on the same team. The fullback was a good player, maybe one of the best on the team that year, but he was not a Division I player. As enjoyable as the college experience might have been for the tackle, the walk-on fullback would have been beaten up on a daily basis as a prep-teamer. Such a tactic at first seems accommodating but ends up being nothing more than insensitive to the needs of the other young athlete.

This subsection has covered a wide range of recruiting tactics, some good, some bad. Coaches who sing the praises of their programs or schools may have much to brag about; they may also be "blowing in the wind." Our job is to help our student athletes tell the difference; they are well advised to be courteous, considerate, congenial, *and critical* of all recruiters. Even the best of them sometimes trip over their own enthusiasm.

LOOKING CAREFULLY AT WHAT IT MEANS TO WALK ON

"Walking on" is an opportunity for nonscholarshipped athletes to play a sport for a particular school. College coaches provide the opportunity for several reasons:

• Most obviously, the athlete may be quite talented, but not good enough to earn a scholarship. As indicated already in this section, some sports have few scholarships available during any given year, so coaches offer walk-on opportunities to players who have the potential to help their programs.

• Less often but probably as obvious, parents may be well connected with a particular university. A young athlete's mother or father may have played for the school; either or both of them may donate substantial money to the school each year. Whatever the connection, athletes with even marginal talent sometimes receive the chance to walk on for some schools. Although such an opportunity at first is a compliment to the youngster, when practice actually begins at the university, most of these athletes "walk on" the practice field but "hobble off." To many such young athletes, walking on is a disappointing and sometimes painful insight into the rigors of intercollegiate athletics.

• High school personnel must keep this reality in mind when they seek walk-on opportunities for their favorite athletes. Sometimes the bonds high school coaches develop with certain players and the respect they gain for them in the course of a season blind them to the players' limitations. The desire to help a player maintain his or her status in the eyes of a peer group or the inability to accept his or her limitations may help perpetuate unrealistic expectations. Coaches are advised, therefore, to secure a range of opinions from high school and college colleagues before recommending walking on for a particular player.

Other important considerations apply as well. Like most hunters, college recruiters tend to be territorial. Although they may at times search the entire nation, particularly if they represent major college programs, they usually maintain most of their contacts with high schools within their immediate regions—their own states, and four or five adjacent others.

They also establish loyalties with the coaches in the high schools they regularly recruit. This is an important consideration for potential walk-ons. They can expect better treatment and a more legitimate chance to play when the college coach is loyal to the player's former high school coach. College coaches are quick to provide fair treatment to players if they—the coaches—plan to return to the player's former school to secure help with future recruits.

Provide the information in Figure 3-12 to young athletes and their parents about walking on and keep the following points in mind if you plan to find a walk-on opportunity for one or more of your players:

- Be sure he or she has the talent to play at the level you are seeking. It's sometimes best to hurt some feelings now than perpetutate a set of expectations that can cause greater pain in the future.

- Make sure the student athlete plans to walk on at a school that has his or her academic program. The preliminary planning for all student athletes, whether scholarshipped or nonscholarshipped, must be similar.

- Contact the coach of each of the athlete's potential schools to determine his or her opportunity to play. I had a kicker one year who was willing to walk on but couldn't find a school in need of his skills. Ultimately, we found a good Division II program that met his educational and career needs. He matriculated, ended up earning a partial scholarship, and is now nearing graduation.

- Once the student athlete decides on a school, call the coach to get his or her name on the team roster. The athlete will then receive summer mailings and, in effect, become a full-fledged member of the team. In fact, by the time the team discovers the athlete's walk-on status, he or she will already be well accepted by them.

- Follow up with walk-on as well as scholarshipped players to informally assess the athletes' satisfaction with their treatment. If you have developed a relationship with the college coach, you can do much to assure a good experience for each walk-on. You also can provide valuable information for all your future athletes if you follow up with those who currently are in school. See Figure 3-13 for a sample letter to athletes. The reproducible is a form letter, so be sure to include a personal note at the bottom of each one you mail.

CONSIDERING DIVISION III PROGRAMS

Seriously consider the development of relationships with Division III coaches, too. Some of the finest colleges and universities in the nation have Division III programs. They may not provide scholarships for their athletes, but they offer the opportunity to continue a sport in college and to receive an excellent education.

Any presentation or discussion with student athletes and their parents, therefore, must emphasize both the good news and the bad news about intercollegiate athletics. See Figure 3-14 for a sample reproducible. Scholarships to play in college are not as available as most people believe or hope, but athletic ability can result in admission to highly selective schools that otherwise might not offer admission. Our football program, for example, has had players at every Ivy League school and a significant number of other prestigious schools across the country. Because most members of our community value high-quality education over athletic scholarships, I have used the talents of some of our best student athletes to get them into some of our nation's best schools.

All of these players, however, were excellent students as well as gifted athletes. Many of them did not quite have the academic credentials to qualify for admission without sports, but they all did well enough to be accepted, thanks to a social philosophy that at times rewards athletic ability as well as academic effort. They may have required the specific help of the college coaches to intervene with admissions officials, but they got into the schools.

That's the way it is. You and I may not agree with it, but colleges and universities, even the best in the country, need gifted athletes to win games, and that's what coaches are hired to do. Many of them will do what they can, therefore, to recruit qualified athletes, including working with university officials to offer admission to student athletes who otherwise might not qualify academically.

Keep the following process in mind, then, when you work with a young athlete who may fall short athletically of a major college sports program but has the athletic and intellectual qualifications to enter a highly selective school:

- Meet with the athlete and his or her parents to discuss the future in terms of the athlete's talent and an appropriate list of schools. This may not be as easy as it sounds. This early part of the process often involves very delicate discussions of the student athlete's ability to compete successfully at certain schools. I have often contacted college coaches, sometimes during one or more of the meetings, to have them share their opinions and intentions with the athlete and parents. Once the family has developed realistic expectations of the process, I proceed with the second step.

- Identify with the athlete and his or her parents the top schools on the list. Work closely with the counselor at this point to assure that the schools provide the educational program needed by the student. The counselor will also help the athlete and his or her parents identify the other characteristics in the selection process that warrant their attention, such as size of school, geographical location, ethnic and religious balance, and other such factors.

- If the resources are available to you, call the coaches at the top of the list and send letters to all the others. The sample letter in Figure 3-5 is appropriate. When you call, ask to speak to a recruiting coordinator or the coach responsible for recruiting your geographical area. Indicate that you have an athlete who has the potential to help them and who has the academic credentials his or her school requires. Describe the student athletically and academically and ask if you should send films or videotapes.

  College coaches rarely say no at this point, so send the tape(s) and tell the coach that you will call about a week and a half after you send the materials. Don't wait for the coach to contact you; you'll want to keep the process moving.

- Call the schools and discuss the coach's evaluation. If the coach is interested, give him or her the athlete's address and phone number. He or she will take care of the rest. Be sure, however, to meet periodically with the athlete to oversee progress. If the coach is not interested, inform the athlete and, as needed, identify additional schools to contact.

- As with scholarshipped and walk-on players, follow up with the student athlete to assess the quality of his her treatment.

The process requires ongoing discussion with the athlete and his or her parents and involves several contacts with college coaches, but it results in the mutual advantage of the school and the athlete and makes the high school coach look mighty good in the process.

KEEPING AN ATHLETIC SCHOLARSHIP

Coaches and counselors are advised to emphasize requirements for keeping an athletic scholarship in college as well as for getting one after high school. The NCAA requires good academic standing and satisfactory progress toward a degree for all college student athletes. They stipulate that such requirements are to be governed by "… the academic authorities who determine the meaning of such phrases for all students of the institution."

In addition, however, they mandate that third-, fourth-, and fifth-year student athletes satisfy a percentage of the degree requirements and the grade point average requirements of the institution for which they are playing. Coaches and counselors are encouraged to review the *NCAA Manual* for specific information. A knowledge of such information affirms their expert power and provides young student athletes with yet another reason to hit the books in high school.

Most high school students are unfamiliar with the graduation requirements of colleges and universities. Because most of them need only a D– average to graduate from high school, they assume the same of college. Most of them open their eyes a little wider when they realize that a C average in college puts them at the bottom of their graduating class. Use the reproducible in Figure 3-15 to share this information with your student athletes and any others who might benefit from it.

LET'S WRAP IT UP

The world of athletic scholarships is a good deal more complicated than most people realize. Just a glance at the 400+ pages of the *NCAA Manual* impresses most people with the complexities of NCAA legislation and the difficulty of assuring "fair play" in every aspect of intercollegiate athletics. The NCAA is doing what it can to keep the *student* in "student athlete" and to maintain the wholesome atmosphere that has characterized college sports.

High school personnel must complement their efforts. The assurance of "fair play" results as much from a knowledge of the rules as from their existence. No coach can create successful strategy without a knowledge of the rules of his or her sport. The NCAA has established the rules; high school coaches, counselors, parents and others who work with young student athletes must know them.

A knowledge of the rules will enable us to steer certain young athletes t appropriate alternatives. For some student athletes, a junior college may be their k only alternative if they want to continue with a sport in college. The NCAA's bylav was not designed to prevent kids from playing in college, just to provide an approj detour for those few who might require additional help; junior colleges can provide help. The reproducible in Figure 3-16 should be given to student athletes who can ven-efit from such information.

We must also know the rules written in the record of experience that many of us bring to our work with young athletes. Before a high school student athlete can make a decision about the right college, he or she must know something about several related issues:

- The college's graduation rates for athletes by sport, race, and gender.

- The average number of years it takes athletes to earn a degree.

- The availability of tutoring for athletes.

- The assurance that a fifth year, if needed, will be financed by the school.

- A knowledge of all the living arrangements.

- An understanding of the total time commitment during the season (meetings, tapings, weights, movies, etc.) and between seasons (conditioning, recruiting, etc.).

- The attitudes of professors toward athletes in his or her field of study.

- The likelihood of losing the scholarship if ineligible, injured, or not good enough.

- The kind of insurance coverage for injuries. For example, must it be supplemented by parents' insurance?

- The procedures for dealing with injuries. Can the family doctor be used? Are second opinions possible?

- Finally, how good is the program of study and what are the placement possibilities after graduation?

These and other questions must be asked by young student athletes every time they consider the merits of a college athletic program. College sports are available to a wide range of young athletes. Whether scholarshipped or not, they must never lose an academic and career focus. Remember the words of Amos Alonzo Stagg: "The day boys play football with one eye on the university and the other on professional futures, the sport will become a moral liability to the colleges." He made the comment in 1927. He also indicated, "Most of the evils that have beset [college sports] from time to time have been the direct result of student and alumni management, but the blame lies on the faculty doorstep."

We have made much progress since the days of Amos Alonzo Stagg, but much more needs to be done. High school coaches, counselors, and parents must work closely with young student athletes to assure appropriate college experiences for them. We will focus more on this issue in the next section. Fortunately, most college coaches play by the rules, but when abuses do occur in college sport, the blame no longer lies exclusively on the university doorstep.

A Word of Advice to Student Athletes

[YOUR SCHOOL'S LOGO HERE]

... and Their Parents

The Counselor and Coach Commitment

Your counselor and coach(es) are committed to providing the assistance you will need to realize your academic and athletic goals. As much as we would like to we can't guarantee you an athletic scholarship to college, but we can assure you and your parents that we will help you plan, work, and search for an appropriate college experience.

This brochure identifies for you and your parents the process and the people who will help you prepare for your goals.

Save it and refer to it each year to assure yourself that you are doing everything necessary to plan for your future college experience.

Sports may or may not be in that future. Ultimately, that is up to you. We are here to help.

So Stay in Contact with the 4 C's:

Coach
Counselor
Career Consultant
College Consultant

The World of College Sports

The world of college sports is as competitive as any activity in the United States. Players every year are getting bigger, smarter, and stronger. In football alone, the average lineman is 6'4" and bench presses over 400 pounds. Such athletes represent the finest in the world. High school athletes, therefore, are encouraged to remember the statistics mentioned in this brochure and to seek a college primarily as an *academic* experience.

What you do *now* in high school will determine in large measure what you will do in college, both on the court or the playing field and in the classroom. The success you realize in both areas will be the direct result of how hard you are willing to work now.

Sports requires an enormous amount of time. Now is the time to develop the right habits!

Hit the Books!

Figure 3-1 (continued)

Do You Need to Plan Carefully for High School and College Sports?

Consider these facts:

- Only 3% of high school football players receive a scholarship to play in college; most of those are partials.
- Only 1½% of high school basketball players receive scholarships to play in college—also mostly partials.
- Only 38% of Division I (major college) football players graduate at the end of five years. The percentage is lower for basketball.
- Tennis, swimming, and other kinds of scholarships are necessarily limited because of financial restrictions in many colleges.
- If you receive a questionnaire from a major college expressing interest in you as a football player, the odds are still as high a 320:1 that you'll ever receive a scholarship.
- If our school had started when our nation did, we would still have to wait a quarter of a century to have a graduate play professional basketball.

Academics Is The Answer!

How Do You Plan Carefully?

Your Freshman Year ...

- Sign an athletic code and get doctor's permission to participate. This must be done every year.
- Meet with your counselor to discuss your four-year plan as a roadmap to college. (Early December)
- Meet again with your counselor before registration for the sophomore year to discuss college entrance requirements and to assure compliance with the NCAA eligibility rules. (Early February)

Your Sophomore Year ...

- Take the PACT to practice for the ACT.
- Meet again with your counselor before registration for the junior year to assure compliance with the NCAA eligibility requirements.
- View the videotape the *ABC's of Eligiblity for the College-Bound Student Athlete*. It is available in the library and the Guidance Office.

Your Junior Year ...

- Take the PSAT in October to practice for the SAT.
- Meet with your counselor before registration for your senior year to be sure to meet

college admission requirements and to assure compliance with the NCAA eligibility rules.

- Secure a copy of the *NCAA Guide for the College-Bound Athlete* from your coach or the Athletic Director. Specifically read the section on athletic eligibility. Discuss it with your parents and coach.
- Sign up for a *Career Search* and a *College Search:*
- Meet with your counselor and the appropriate consultant to discuss the results.
- Take the SAT and ACT in the winter or spring of the year.
- Inform your coach of your interest in playing a sport in college.
- Visit potential colleges.

Your Senior Year ...

- Retake the ACT and/or the SAT as needed.
- Meet with your counselor early in the fall to review your transcript to assure compliance with the NCAA eligibility requirements.
- Meet with your coach to discuss your potential to play for certain colleges.
- Mail college applications.
- Review the *NCAA Guide for the College-Bound Athlete* and the videotape the *ABC's of Eligibility for the College-Bound Student Athlete.*

63

Figure 3-2

THE WORLD OF COLLEGE SPORTS

Athletics in College

College sports has changed considerably within the past five to ten years. Most significantly, Title IX has provided a wide range of opportunities for women to play competitive sports in high school and college. Women's facilities have improved; the range of sports has expanded; and the number of college scholarships has increased. Of equal significance, the competition for those scholarships has intensified, for both men and women.

Atypical just ten years ago, a 300-pound lineman in football and a 6'5" woman in basketball are commonplace today. Even more surprising is the fact that both are stronger and quicker than their smaller counterparts of ten years ago. Recently, the tallest player for a major university was the center on the *women's* basketball team. She was 6'10".

It is no longer uncommon for linemen in football to bench press 500 pounds or for backs to run 4.3 forties, nor is it surprising to find a variety of 7'0" men's basketball players or 6'3" women's volleyball players. College athletes in the United States are as gifted as any in the world, *and they are good students.*

Academics in College

The average graduation rate for college athletes is higher than the rate for nonathletes, especially for women. Whereas approximately half of all nonathletes graduate in five years, almost two-thirds of women athletes graduate. The average is lower for male athletes but still higher than for nonathletes. When college recruiters visit our school, therefore, one of the first questions they ask coaches about players is "What kind of student is she or he?" They have learned that poor students, no matter how good they are as athletes, don't stay in college long enough to help their teams.

The Challenge to You

If you want to play a sport in college, exercise your muscles and your brain *right now.* You'll benefit from both, even if you don't play a sport in college. Few athletes get to play a sport in college, so enjoy your high school participation. College is in your future; high school is now. Your coaches are here to help you with both. Let's work together to help you become the best *student athlete* you can be.

Figure 3-3

THE REAL WORLD
OF ATHLETIC SCHOLARSHIPS

The Numbers

According to recent NCAA legislation, the total number of athletic scholarships to be awarded in most college sports has been reduced. The major men's sports (NCAA Division I schools) have been most affected:

- Football has been reduced from a team total of 95 just a couple of years ago to 85. They still award a maximum of 25 to new students.
- Basketball has been reduced from a team total of 15 to 13.
- Baseball from 13 to 11.7.
- Tennis, volleyball, and water polo from 5 to 4.5.
- Cross-country and track from 14 to 12.6.
- All other sports have experienced similar reductions.

The NCAA Division II (smaller schools) scholarships, in both men's and women's sports, have been reduced in much the same way. Women's scholarships in Division I schools (the major sports programs) have remained as follows:

SPORT	TOTAL TEAM SCHOLARSHIPS
Cross-country and track	16
Basketball	15
Swimming	14
Volleyball	12
Field, soccer, softball, and lacrosse	11
Gymnastics	10
Tennis	8
Skiing	7
Golf	6
Fencing	5

Figure 3-3 (continued)

THE REAL WORLD
OF ATHLETIC SCHOLARSHIPS

What the Numbers Mean

There are just over 100 major college football programs in this country. Each can award a maximum of 25 scholarships to incoming freshmen. This is the largest number of scholarships awarded to incoming freshmen in any sport. That means that there are just over 2,500 total major college scholarships available to the 265,000 high school seniors (1 in every 106) who play high school football each year.

There are just under 300 major college (Division I) men's basketball programs in the country, each awarding only 2 to 3 scholarships to incoming freshmen each year. That means that of the 158,000 high school seniors who play basketball each year, only 900 (1 in every 175) will receive a scholarship to play for a major university. There are approximately 190 Division II basketball programs that also award scholarships—mostly partials. The situation is similar in women's basketball.

Other Sports

Because of the reduced numbers of scholarships available in other sports, they are less available each year. To their credit, the NCAA and other regulatory organizations are trying to put athletic competition in proper perspective on university campuses. Both men's and women's sports, therefore, may have only 3 or 4 scholarships available each year for incoming freshmen. Some schools have only 1 or 2 because of the total number of team scholarships already allocated to upperclassmen. Look at the numbers. If several colleges have awarded 6 scholarships in women's golf to athletes currently on their teams, they have none available to incoming freshmen.

What Does All This Mean?

Most important, it means that there may be a scholarship out there for you, if you work hard at your sport and in the classroom. Unfortunately, there are not as many as some of us think, but you may be one of the gifted few who receive them. Your coaches cannot guarantee a scholarship for you, but we will do whatever we can to help you, in your sport as well as in the classroom. The important thing is that you enjoy your participation in high school and do what you can to prepare for your future, whatever it may bring.

Keep in Mind

The numbers of scholarships per sport may change from year to year. It's a good idea to meet with your coach and counselor periodically to discuss scholarship availability, perhaps to check the *NCAA Manual* for exact numbers.

Figure 3-3 (continued)

THE TOTAL SPORTS PICTURE
WOMEN AND NCAA SPORTS

SPORT	DIVISION I	DIVISION II	DIVISION III
Volleyball	270	200	290
Soccer	90	60	200
Field Hockey	75	13	125
Softball	170	160	240
Swimming	160	50	180

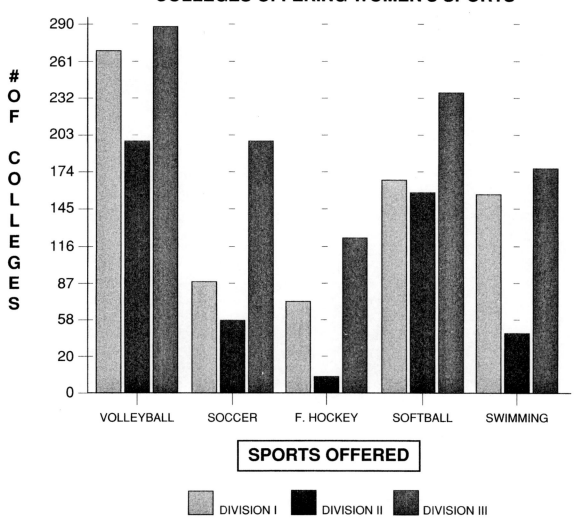

COLLEGES OFFERING WOMEN'S SPORTS

Figure 3-3 (continued)

THE TOTAL SPORTS PICTURE
DIVISION I SCHOLARSHIPS FOR WOMEN

SPORT	NCAA DIV I COLLEGES	H.S. SENIORS IN SPORT	FRESHMEN SCHOLARSHIPS AWARDED	TEAM SCHOLARSHIPS [TOTAL]	ODDS OF RECEIVING SCHOLARSHIP
Volleyball	270	85,000	3	10	1:105
Soccer	90	37,500	3-4	11	1:119
F. Hockey	75	13,000	3	11	1:58
Softball	170	56,250	3	11	1:110
Swimming	160	23,375	3-4	14	1:42

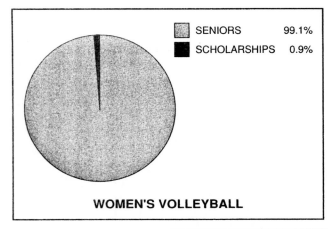

SENIORS 99.1%
SCHOLARSHIPS 0.9%

WOMEN'S VOLLEYBALL

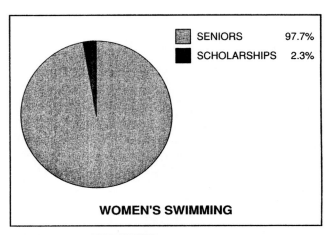

SENIORS 97.7%
SCHOLARSHIPS 2.3%

WOMEN'S SWIMMING

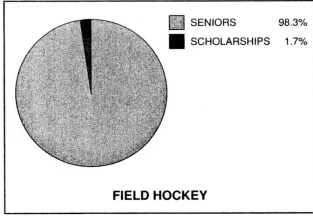

SENIORS 98.3%
SCHOLARSHIPS 1.7%

FIELD HOCKEY

Figure 3-3 (continued)

THE TOTAL SPORTS PICTURE
MEN AND NCAA SPORTS

SPORT	DIVISION I	DIVISION II	DIVISION III
Volleyball	60	—	—
Soccer	200	110	275
Baseball	270	155	260
Swimming	160	50	160

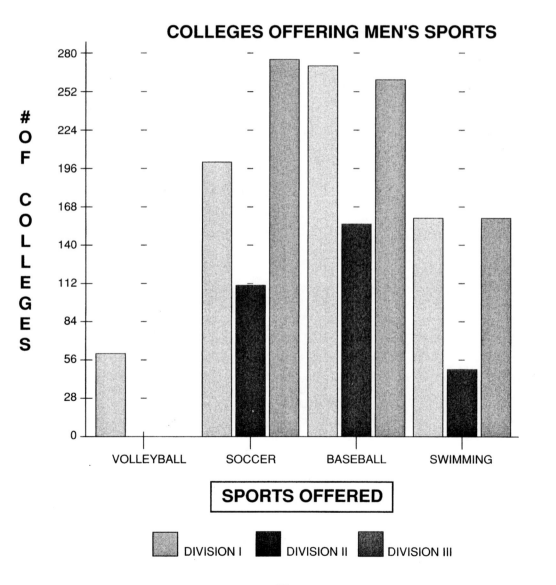

© 1996 by Michael D. Koehler

Figure 3-3 (continued)

THE TOTAL SPORTS PICTURE
DIVISION I SCHOLARSHIPS FOR MEN

SPORT	NCAA DIV I COLLEGES	H.S. SENIORS IN SPORT	FRESHMEN SCHOLARSHIPS AWARDED	TEAM SCHOLARSHIPS [TOTAL]	ODDS OF RECEIVING SCHOLARSHIP
Volleyball	60	5,000	1-2	6.3	1:55
Soccer	200	60,500	2-3	9.9	1:121
Baseball	270	107,000	3	11.7	1:132
Swimming	160	19,500	2-3	9.9	1:49

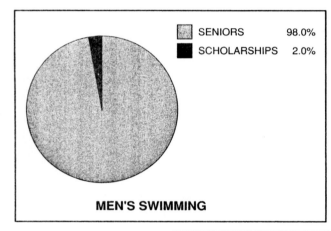

SENIORS 98.0%
SCHOLARSHIPS 2.0%

MEN'S SWIMMING

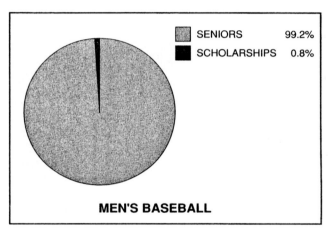

SENIORS 99.2%
SCHOLARSHIPS 0.8%

MEN'S BASEBALL

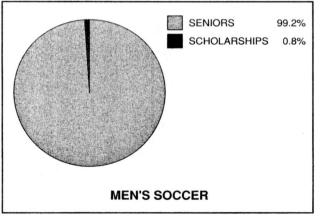

SENIORS 99.2%
SCHOLARSHIPS 0.8%

MEN'S SOCCER

Figure 3-4

PLAYER INFORMATION SHEET

The accompanying videotape illustrates the performance of:

Player Name: _____. The video is a:

highlight tape _____

tape of a game/contest _____ against (Opponent): _____.

RELEVANT INFORMATION: (AS APPROPRIATE)

Player's Position: _____

Player's Number: Offense: _____ Defense: _____

Color of jersey: _____

Player Size:

Height _____

Weight _____

RELEVANT GAME/CONTEST STATISTICS:

ACADEMIC/CAREER INFORMATION:

ACT score(s): _____

SAT score(s): _____

Class rank: No. _____ of _____ No. in class

Cumulative grade point average on a 4.0 scale: _____

Educational and career goals:

If you require additional information regarding this athlete, feel free to contact me at your convenience. When you have completed your review of the tape, please return it to:

(Coach's name, address, and phone number)

Thanks for your interest, and I look forward to talking to you.

(Signed)

Figure 3-5

SAMPLE LETTER TO COLLEGE COACH

Date

(Name
Address
City, State)

Dear (Coach):

Just a quick note to introduce you to Jessica Smith, one of the finest basketball players I have had the pleasure to coach within the past several years. Jessica was the center on this year's regional championship team, helped lead us to the second conference championship in her career, and distinguished herself and her teammates in the process. The team has the reputation of being one of the best in the school's history, and Jessica earned All-Conference, All-Area, and All-State honors.

Jessica is 6'2" and, although she has played with her back to the basket throughout much of her high school career, she has the ability to play any position other than point guard on the court. She has an excellent jump shot (averaging 22.3 points per game this season), can rebound as well as anyone in the area, and has the kind of court sense that results in assists and breakaway opportunites in every game she plays.

I have been coaching high school basketball for 25 years and am pleased to say that this is one of the best players I have ever coached. She will be a standout in college because of her basketball ability, leadership skills, and strong academic performance. Jessica will be with you for all four years and is likely to mature into an even better player than she is now. She already is an excellent student. She has earned a 3.4 GPA in a college prep program, a 25 composite on her ACT, and academic honors throughout her four years of high school.

I am certain that you will like Jessica. Call me at your convenience for additional information. I will be pleased to send videotapes for your evaluation. I look forward to hearing from you. Thanks for your time.

Coach

Figure 3-6

A PEEK AT THE PROS

Coaches and counselors often hear young athletes talk about futures in professional sports. A life as a professional athlete certainly is an exciting and profitable goal; it simply isn't as possible as most people think. Take a moment to consider the following observations:

Professional Football

Each year, approximately 265,000 seniors play high school football, and about 215 rookies earn a spot on a professional team. Simple mathematics tells us that .0008 of one percent (eight one-*thousandths* of one percent) of high school seniors ultimately will play professional football. Those are not very good odds. Then consider these statistics: A couple of years ago, a prominent university official indicated that about half of all professional football players end their careers with no money; 85% of them are divorced; and their life expectancy is about 56. Even if a young athlete does beat the odds to become a professional, he can expect these kinds of circumstances and a career that lasts only three to four years.

Professional Tennis

There are approximately 30,000 senior boys and 30,000 senior girls playing high school tennis each year. Only 100 professionals in men's and women's tennis earn as much as minimum-salary professionals in the NBA or NFL. The odds of making big money in professional tennis are three-thousandths of one percent for high school seniors.

Professional Basketball

The NCAA tells us that approximately 158,000 high school seniors play basketball each year and that almost 70 rookies make the pros. Again, consider the odds. Only .0004 of one percent (four one-*thousandths* of one percent) of high school basketball players can expect to play for a professional team. Look at it another way. If we have eight seniors per year on our high school basketball team, and if our school had started when our *nation* did, we would still have to wait *half a century* for our first professional basketball player.

Other Sports

Professional baseball, soccer, and track and field offer the same kinds of odds. Of the hundreds of thousands of young athletes who play these sports each year, only a handful ever play professionally. What does all this mean to you?

**Keep your goals but be realistic. Your chances are better to be a doctor
or a lawyer than to be a professional athlete. Your future will be
influenced much more by what you do in the classroom than
by your athletic ability. Play hard but**

HIT THE BOOKS!

73

Figure 3-7

CHECKLIST FOR STUDENT ATHLETES
AND THEIR PARENTS

The following checklist will assist you with the process of making the transition from high school to college sports. Because the transition involves academic as well as athletic issues, several people will be involved in your decision. Be sure to see them at the appropriate time.

DID YOU:

_____ Initiate the form, "Student Athlete Expression of Intent to Play College Sports?" Remember that your parents or coach can also initiate it.

_____ Meet routinely with your counselor to assure your compliance with the NCAA's Bylaw 14.3? If not, be sure to see him or her—at the *latest*—during your junior year.

_____ Watch the videotape the *ABCs of Eligibility for the College-Bound Student Athlete?*

_____ Do a Career Search?

_____ Do a College Search?

_____ Talk to your coach about your interest in college sports?

_____ Take the ACT and/or the SAT?

_____ Visit some of the schools you might want to attend?

_____ Schedule a meeting with your counselor and coach to discuss the college search and selection processes?

_____ Schedule a meeting with your parents and the college consultant?

_____ Review the *NCAA Guide for the College-Bound Student Athlete?*

_____ Mail your college applications?

REMEMBER: Contact your counselor or coach any time you have questions. Parents, feel free to call or make an appointment. My office phone number is:

Figure 3-8

STUDENT ATHLETE EXPRESSION OF INTENT TO PLAY COLLEGE SPORTS

Name of Athlete: _____ Student's counselor: _____

Sport: _____ Student's Coach: _____

This form is initiated by: _____ Date: _____

Once completed, please forward to student's counselor.

To Parents and Students: If you originate this form, please be sure to give it to your coach. The coach will complete the survey and forward it to your counselor. If you have hired a professional recruiter, please give his or her name and any suggested schools. If applicable, name of coach outside school:

_____

To the Coach: If you originate this form, please fill in the student's name, provide additional information as requested below or make arrangements to provide it, and forward the form to the student's counselor.

To the Counselor: The above-named student has expressed interest in playing an intercollegiate sport. (S)he is interested in satisfying the eligibility requirements of the NCAA or other regulatory organizations and in identifying schools that will satisfy his or her academic and athletic interests. Please use the "Information Sheet for Student Athletes" to work with this student.

From the Coach: Please provide the following information. If you would prefer to discuss the form with the counselor first, please feel free to do so:

NCAA Division (Your opinion) _____

1. Colleges of interest to student (to your knowledge): _____

    _____

    _____

    _____

2. Colleges expressing interest in the athlete: _____

    _____

    _____

    _____

3. Your suggestions of other colleges: _____

    _____

    _____

    _____

Please use the back of this form to provide additional information. Thanks.

Figure 3-9

FROM THE COUNSELING DEPARTMENT

A Complementary Perspective

Our school's coaches and counselors enjoy a shared responsibility with young athletes. We realize that the benefits of sports are maximized when young athletes develop the right attitude about their participation. We are concerned that our school's athletes guard against overidentifying with their sports and failing to realize the primary importance of academics. We recognize the realities of competitive stress and want to provide ways for young athletes and their parents to deal with it. We also acknowledge the challenges that parents face when assuming the sometimes conflicting roles of "cheerleader" and family leader. Counselors are available to meet with young athletes and their parents to complement the significant relationship that coaches have with them.

Academics and Athletics

Counselors are also available to oversee the academic progress that all students must make in order to realize the educational and career goals they will establish for themselves. Counselors are also familiar with the provisions of the NCAA's bylaw 14.3, which requires a specific academic program and grade point average of all high school student athletes who plan to play a sport in college. Periodic meetings with counselors are important to assure compliance with the NCAA.

This aspect of counselor involvement is particularly important because most young athletes and many parents are unfamiliar with the extraordinary competition for athletic scholarships. An athletic scholarship certainly is a worthwhile goal, but it is often unrealizable. Hard work in the classroom involves bigger, more realizable benefits. It must never take a back seat to sports.

Stay in contact, therefore, with your counselor *and* your coach. Both are committed to our young people as *student* athletes and are available to parents whenever they have questions or concerns. Let's be sure to work together during the next few years to guarantee your student a valuable sports experience.

Figure 3-10

WATCHING OUT FOR IMPROPER RECRUITING

High school athletes being recruited by one or more colleges must always be alert to improper tactics used by some recruiters. Most college coaches are honest men and women who are interested in you as a total person. Some few, however, are interested in you only if you can help their athletic programs. Such coaches are to be avoided. Fortunately, they are pretty easy to spot. If you are being contacted by one or more college coaches, keep these pointers in mind:

WATCH OUT FOR:

- The coach who "bum raps" other schools and coaches. Some coaches try to make their own light shine brighter by blowing out everyone else's. When they resort to this tactic, their own light isn't very bright in the first place. You want to know this.

- The coach who talks only about how great his or her program is. It may be a good one, but if that's the only thing he or she talks about, you are being recruited only to *keep* it good. College for you is much more than helping someone else maintain his or her reputation.

- The coach who promises you a starting position right away. Obviously, there are some entering freshmen who are good enough to be first string right away, but they are few and far between. Listen to the recruiter who is honest with you now, because only then will he or she be honest later.

- The coach who doesn't give an oral commitment to a four-or five-year scholarship. The NCAA allows only a one-year, renewable scholarship, but honest recruiters can promise more than one year. Make sure the recruiter makes such a verbal commitment to you, your parents, and your coach.

- The coach who puts you in contact with a "booster" from the college. The NCAA permits *no* contact with boosters. If you even talk to one, you jeopardize your future.

- The coach who promises easy admission, easy professors, or an easy schedule. He or she has no interest in you as a student.

- The coach who says that his or her school's academic program in your field of study is the best in the nation. Have your counselor check this out for you.

- The coach who promises to let your best friend "walk on" with the team. Rarely is such a coach concerned with the best interests of your friend. He or she is using your friend only to get to you.

There are other tactics to watch out for. Whenever you have a question or a concern, be sure to talk to your coach.

Figure 3-11

CONTACTS AND VISITS

High school athletes are as bound by NCAA rules and regulations as any college player. Your ignorance of these requirements could jeopardize your athletic future. Read the following NCAA rules carefully and share them with your parents. Be sure to talk with your counselor or coach if you have questions or need explanations.

CONTACTS WITH COLLEGE COACHES

- High school athletes can be contacted by a college coach only after the completion of their junior year. A contact is any face-to-face meeting involving even a simple "hello."
- High school athletes can receive letters from college coaches, faculty members, and students, but not until after September 1 of the junior year.
- Contacts are prohibited with university boosters at any time.
- College coaches may contact you at home or at school but as restricted by NCAA rules. Refer to the *NCAA Guide for the College-Bound Student Athlete* for specific information.
- During any contact, you may not receive T-shirts, college mementos, or financial inducements to sign with a particular university.

VISITS TO COLLEGE CAMPUSES

- The NCAA allows "prospective student athletes" one expenses-paid visit to five different universities. Select your visits very carefully; you are allowed only five of them. Remember, this restriction applies even if you are being recruited in more than one sport.
- You may not receive an official visit until you provide the college authorities with an official high school transcript and a score from the PSAT, PACT, plus SAT, or ACT taken on a national test date. See your counselor for information about the Clearinghouse and the Student Release Form.
- Each visit may not last more than 48 hours.
- You may visit any campus at any time beyond your five official visits if *you* pay all the expenses for each visit.

SEE YOUR COACH OR COUNSELOR FOR COPIES OF QUESTIONS TO ASK DURING AND AFTER YOUR CAMPUS VISITS. THEY ARE VERY HELPFUL.

Figure 3-12

SO YOU WANT TO WALK ON?

A high school athlete who has not received a scholarship but wants to play a sport in college may be given the opportunity to "walk on" at one or more schools. "Walking on" means that he or she becomes an unscholarshipped member of the team, is allowed to try to earn a position on the team, and is given the opportunity to earn a scholarship at some time in the future. "Walking on" can be an excellent opportunity for a good athlete who is serious about his or her sport, but it requires careful planning with your counselor and your coach. If you are interested in "walking on," follow this advice:

WITH YOUR COUNSELOR:

- Be sure you satisfy the eligibility requirements of the NCAA. "Walk-on" athletes are subject to the same rules and regulations as scholarshipped athletes.
- Do all the preliminary planning needed to identify a possible career. You may not settle on one, but look into it anyway. The experience is helpful.
- Find the colleges that provide programs in your career area. Develop a list of them. If you have found no career areas, identify the schools that provide a broad range of programs.
- Discuss the list. Be sure to bring your parents to this meeting.
- Select your top three or four schools from the list.

WITH YOUR COACH:

- Discuss your ability to participate on the college level. Be open-minded during this meeting. Remember, your coach has only your best interests in mind.
- Identify any additional schools at which you may have the chance to play. Be sure they, too, satisfy your career and educational goals.
- Contact the school(s) to secure the college coach's permission to "walk on."
- Mail applications, being sure to follow the admissions procedures specified by the college coach.

BE SURE THE SCHOOL(S) ARE RIGHT FOR YOU.
DON'T ATTEND A SCHOOL JUST TO PLAY A SPORT!

Figure 3-13

FOLLOW-UP LETTER TO FORMER PLAYERS

Date

(Player's Name
Address   Name of college: _____
City, State)

Dear (Player):

Just a quick note to see how things are going. As you probably know, I like to do a routine follow-up on former players. We are likely to have players this year or in years to come who are interested in attending your school. Your reactions to the school and the athletic program will be very helpful as they make their college decisions.

I'm interested in a few specifics:

- How would you describe the quality of the education you have received?
- Do you feel comfortable with the other students in the school? Are you associating with nonathletes?
- What is your current or planned major? _____
- How would you describe the coaches' treatment of you?
- Are you enjoying your experience there? Why or why not?
- If you had the decision to make all over again, would you choose the same school?
  —for athletic reasons?
  —for academic reasons?

Thanks for your help. And remember to stay in touch. Be sure to stop in when you get back into the area.

With warmest regards,

Coach

Figure 3-14

THOUGHTS ABOUT NAIA
AND NCAA DIVISION III SCHOOLS

High school student athletes who are interested in playing a sport in college need to know a little bit about the NCAA's Division III schools. These generally are the smaller schools that don't receive national coverage by the media but that have every bit as much tradition and history as the major colleges—sometimes more. They are not allowed to award athletic scholarships, but more young athletes play in Division III schools than any other, and they generally receive among the finest educations in the country. Think about these facts:

- Division III and NAIA colleges and universities constitute some of the best schools in the country. They are among the most prestigious and provide some of the best educational programs.

- Division III and NAIA schools provide some of the best placement opportunities in the nation after graduation—for both jobs and graduate schools.

- Most Division III and NAIA schools provide informal and personalized educations. Students usually get to know their professors quite well.

- Division III and NAIA schools provide increased contact with professors and fewer contacts with graduate assistants.

- Student athletes who are not being recruited by major college programs may still have the chance to play their sports in Division III or NAIA colleges.

- Division III and NAIA schools tend to be extremely competitive both academically and athletically. They have some of the finest athletes in the nation.

- Student athletes often receive preferential treatment regarding admission. *If you are competitive academically*—maybe not quite as competitive as other applicants—your involvement in sports will help you get into Division III and NAIA schools.

SEE YOUR COACH AND YOUR COUNSELOR
ABOUT THE POSSIBILITY OF A GOOD DIVISION III OR NAIA SCHOOL
IF YOU HAVE THE ACADEMIC CREDENTIALS.
THEY ARE EXCELLENT OPTIONS TO GOOD *STUDENT* ATHLETES.

Figure 3-15

STAYING IN COLLEGE

Getting into college is one thing; staying is another! Obviously, high school counselors give a lot of attention to college admissions requirements, SAT and ACT test results, recommendations, interviews, personal essays, and student resumes. We should also take a moment to mention what it takes to *stay* in college—not to shake you up or to apply any more pressure for your senior year but to make sure you don't get any surprises when you leave for college next year.

Good Academic Standing

Students in good academic standing generally maintain at least a C average (2.0 on a 4.0 scale) while in college. That means that for every D they might receive in one subject, they have to receive at least a B in another. Those students who fall below a cumulative C average after a semester or two are put on academic probation by the university. In essence, they are required to get their cumulative grade point back up to a C average, or they subject themselves to dismissal from the university for academic reasons.

Graduating from College

Think about it. If you maintain a C average throughout college, you will graduate at the bottom of your class. This isn't all bad; thousands of students do it every year. The point is, if you want to graduate in the middle or near the top of your class, you will have to maintain at least a B or a B+ average in college. And if you plan to keep a scholarship while in school, you will have to satisfy the academic requirements of the university to maintain "good academic standing."

The best way to earn the required grade point average in college to maintain good academic standing is to develop the necessary study habits in high school. If you develop the right study habits now, you won't have any problems in college. Talk to your teachers, counselor, or coach if you need some help in this area.

Figure 3-16

THOUGHTS ABOUT JUNIOR COLLEGES

A junior college may be your best bet for college next year! Junior colleges are schools that generally offer two kinds of programs for students who are interested in higher education. The first is called the transfer program. It enables you to enter the school as a college freshman, complete one or two years at the school, and transfer your credits to a four-year school. The second program is called a terminal program. It results in an associate's degree after two years and provides the qualifications for you to then find a job in your field of specialization. Certain junior colleges may award scholarships to recruited athletes. They provide excellent educations. Think about these facts:

- If you haven't done as well academically as you wanted, a junior college may provide an additional opportunity for you to improve your grade point average, then apply to a four-year school. Remember, you will be gaining college credits while you are improving your GPA!

- Junior colleges provide valuable educational and career experiences in their own right! They have some excellent programs that might meet your career interests.

- If you have failed to meet the provisions of the NCAA's Bylaw 14.3 (Prop 48), a junior college may provide the opportunity for you to continue to play your sport in college and ultimately to transfer to a four-year school. If you are in this situation, be sure to see your coach and counselor for additional information about attending a junior college to satisfy the NCAA's requirements.

- Junior colleges generally offer an open-door admissions policy. You probably don't have to worry about acceptance. You *do* have to plan on working hard in each of your classes!

- If you have been contacted by coaches at one or more four-year schools but must attend a junior college, be sure to meet with counseling personnel at the junior college to make sure you meet admissions requirements and to guarantee that the courses you take at the junior college will transfer to the four-year school(s).

- Junior colleges often provide academic help to students. You may benefit from such help. Check with your high school counselor to be sure that any junior colleges you apply to have the kind of help you may need.

SEE YOUR COUNSELOR OR COACH FOR MORE INFORMATION. A JUNIOR COLLEGE MAY BE JUST WHAT YOU NEED!

FOUR

THE HIGHLY RECRUITED STUDENT ATHLETE

First, a quick story. A ringing phone seems unusually insistent when you've been in bed for half an hour. Bordering between anger and apprehension, I groped for the speaker and found myself speaking to the mother of our star player:

"Mike, Sarah Thompson; I'm sorry to call you at this time of the night, but I can't stand it any more."

"No problem. Can't stand what?"

"These recruiters. They're driving us crazy, calling at all times of the night and setting up days to come by for a visit. I want this whole thing to end. We're about ready to throw all the names in a hat and pick one just to end this madness. I just got off the phone with one, and I had to call you."

"I'm glad you did. It's about time we did something about this. Call me at school tomorrow. Let's set up a meeting and figure out what we want to do."

"You've got a deal; I was hoping you'd say that. Sorry again for this call; I'll be on your doorstep one way or another tomorrow."

I had been coaching only six or seven years and was fortunate that year to have a fullback/middle linebacker who was being recruited by virtually every major football program in the country. Michigan wanted him to play defense; Notre Dame wanted him to play fullback. He was an unusually gifted youngster: smart, well bred, a gentleman in every sense of the word, and gut-level tough.

At that point in my career I could handle the athletes' in-season needs but was unaware of how to handle these kinds of post-season situations. Let's admit it. Not many of us are fortunate enough to run into this kind of an athlete very often. Such good luck can be a joy during the season, but it can be a pain in the neck afterward. And no matter where we are—inner-city Chicago or rural Wyoming, we may be blessed with such a player once in a while, so we had better know what to do with him or her.

DEFINING A "BLUE-CHIPPER"

A blue-chipper is a uniquely gifted young athlete in one or more sports who has displayed the skills and motivation to attract attention from a wide variety of university and college sports programs and, in the case of baseball, from the pros. Most obviously, blue-chippers are 6'11" forwards in basketball, high school halfbacks who run 4.3 forties, or field hockey players who score at will. Less obviously, they are athletes who usually are blessed with a kinesthetic sense that "slows down time," that enables them to "see" everything during the actual performance of their skills, whether such skills involve triple somersaults in the pike position, back walkovers on the balance beam, or quick openers up the middle.

They are so gifted and have grown so accustomed to the undeniability of their physical talents that they have learned to trust their bodies. The softball or baseball player trusts his or her built-in instrumentation when pitching; so does the basketball player when shooting. The wrestler "senses" moves; the football or soccer player "feels" opponents approaching from the side; the diver or gymnast "knows" when to come out of a turn for a landing or entry into the water.

To many of us, the performance of such skills involves little more than a confusing blur of motion, a disjointed moment in time, ended before it begins. It involves an uncoachable skill. The native ability of many blue-chippers to perform increases their value in the sports market and makes them the focus of recruiting activity as well as media attention. Once this happens—once they realize they are somehow "special"— blue-chippers can experience a world of contradictions—admiring but potentially abusive, fantastic but tragically real, and exciting but surprisingly short-lived.

This "special" athletic genius can take control of their lives. It can assume an existence of its own. From Van Gogh in painting and Mozart in music to Einstein in math and science, genius is so undeniable that it demands expression. Music echoed through Mozart's mind; he simply wrote it down. Completed paintings appeared in Van Gogh's mind; he simply put them on canvas. Einstein's mind worked until entire blackboards were filled with equations. And Michael Jordan found himself in "the zone," making a succession of 3-point shots that even he couldn't understand.

The point is—and this may be the focus of our concern as coaches, counselors, and parents—the undeniability of such genius can sublimate everything else in one's life. Athletics are no different. The youngster who dribbles her way through a maze of defenders and "double-pumps" a lay-up and the young halfback who litters the field with would-be tacklers create moments that mystify themselves as well as everyone in the stands.

It's no mystery that they like it; they enjoy the crowd's reaction. Even more, they sense fulfillment and personal satisfaction each time they express their genius. Such expression can become addictive and ultimately leave room for little else in their lives. A result is that classwork can suffer; relationships at home can change; social behavior can be transformed. Talent in one area can retard development in others. Athletic genius, then, can promote not only media and community attention but emotional immaturity.

It's no wonder that so many gifted young athletes make so many poor decisions—in so many different areas of their lives. Many in the media would have us believe that sports provides a way out of poverty; such an influence is too obvious to deny. Sports also provides an improved self-concept, an elevated social position in the school or community and, most important, the opportunity to express a natural talent that is undeniable—at times tyrannical in its demands.

That's where we come in. Athletically gifted youngsters need help in combating the insistence of their own bodies. They need help in developing other areas of their lives that may not guarantee such immediate satisfaction or suggest such obvious future advantage. A way out of the ghetto and the yellow brick road to fame and fortune are two of the more obvious temptations confronting young athletes. Less obvious but equally powerful is the imposition of their own talent.

Fortunately, with our help, they can translate these talents into a powerful sense of self, expanded opportunities for personal and educational growth, and satisfying and meaningful lives. They need our help to realize these benefits. Without the sense of direction provided by a respected adult, many of these youngsters travel a road that leads thousands of gifted athletes to a destructive preoccupation with one dimension of their lives.

On Being a Blue-chipper

Blue-chippers live in a contradictory world. That they can be confused at times and that highly visible sports personalities can deny their media-created images as role models is not surprising. An admiring world tempts them with drugs and sex on one hand and expects exemplary behavior on the other. Their talents provoke a disregard for the development of the very personality characteristics that are most important for them when they try to live up to the expectations that the rest of us impose on them.

If coaches and others really believe that athletic participation develops character, then we may not be asking too much when we expect athletes to display it whenever they find themselves in the spotlight. *Expecting* them to display it and *helping* them to develop it, however, may be two different things. Coaches, counselors, and parents, therefore, share a responsibility with young athletes; we are expected to do everything in our power to make their involvement in sports as character building as possible.

The difference between some blue-chippers and the average young athlete is not simply a matter of talent. You've probably heard the old saying, "Adversity doesn't develop character; it reveals it." Well, so does athletic competition. It can pose a higher degree of adversity to the young athlete with average talent. He or she has to work harder to make the team or to achieve any kind of recognition—especially something as competitive as an athletic scholarship.

Every coach knows that such young athletes constitute the core of his or her team. Not everyone can be a blue-chipper, even though most youngsters want to be. With the insight that comes with experience and the help of a knowledgeable coach, such "average" young athletes learn the lessons of courage, hard work, and commitment. Relieved of the demands of athletic "gifts," they learn the value of hard work. This is the essence of the "character-building" nature of athletic participation.

The point is, it is more available to the average athlete. Gifted athletes often fail to realize the benefits of such hard work. Their talents are so obvious and their skills so natural, participation comes easily to them. The recognition they receive, then, from friends, acquaintances, teammates and opponents, and the media is inconsistent with the effort they have exerted. And whenever reward overshadows hard work, problems result.

At that point, the young athlete *expects* recognition and the immediate gratification that results from the expression of his or her talents. Such expectations can spill over into schoolwork ("Pass me to keep me eligible; I'm scoring 25 points a game"), chores at home ("I don't have time"), and social relationships ("Give me anything I want; everyone else does"). Such expectations don't characterize every talented young athlete, but they reflect the behaviors of a surprisingly large number of them. These are the youngsters who genuinely need our help.

Without such help, many of these gifted young athletes seek immature, underdeveloped goals in life. Like children, they disregard long-term satisfactions in favor of immediate pleasures. They focus on scholarships to college to play a sport, only incidentally to further themselves personally and professionally. They expect professional sports futures and the immediate attention of friends and acquaintances. At the extreme, they can become so spoiled that they disregard social protocols, rules, and even laws to satisfy their own needs.

These are, of course, extreme characterizations. The media, given their attention to atypical behavior, however, have established such characterizations as almost normal. Talk shows and television tabloids devote so much attention to the social anomalies and extremists among us that they may, in fact, be redefining normal behavior. The impact of such media coverage serves to influence impressionable youngsters, many of whom are young athletes—if not to sanction—at least to legitimize such behaviors.

This is all the more reason that coaches, counselors, and parents must work closely with youngsters to compensate for such media and other external influences. We must impress upon young gifted athletes the value of hard work in all areas. Think of the NCAA's Prop 48 as just such an opportunity. If not adversity, it may pose challenges to gifted young athletes to learn the value of hard work in the classroom and at home, in areas where their natural gifts are unable to make life easy for them. Parents must be among the first to offer and to *seek* help in this regard.

On Being the Parent of a Blue-chipper

Few parents are prepared to handle the responsibility of discovering a blue-chipper in the house. How could they? Most parents are so busy guiding their kids through the developmental jungle of adolescence that they often avoid rather than resolve such related issues. No one can blame them. Let's admit it—the problem is further complicated by the tendency of many parents to identify with their children's accomplishments, to accept a young athlete's successes as their own.

This, too, is understandable. The bond between parent and child is so strong and the desire for parents to assure the success of their kids so pronounced that they can't help but take pleasure in their young athlete's accomplishments, but they must be careful in this regard. Parents walk a fine line between encouraging the personal growth of their children and expecting it, between perceiving athletic success as the growth of the child and perceiving it as the affirmation of the parent.

When parents work closely with school coaches, counselors, and athletic directors, however, they broaden their understanding of the needs of their gifted youngsters and tend to promote athletic participation for all the right reasons. They identify allies in the struggle to raise successful and responsible young adults. The coach may be the first person to contact. Figure 4-1 will help parents initiate needed dialogue with coaches.

The Blue-chipper and the High School Coach

This book has emphasized repeatedly that the high school coach's responsibilities go well beyond game or contest strategy and player motivation. If coaches go into education to promote the wholesome and purposeful development of young people, then their responsibilities include much more than developing highly recruited sprinters or All-State goalies. We assume the pleasurable task of working with parents and helping youngsters develop educationally and socially as well.

We help do that on the court or field every time we emphasize teamwork and fair play, and we do it in the school building when we demand considerate behavior and attention to responsibilities at home and in the classroom. Such expectations are particularly appropriate for uniquely gifted young athletes. We need to provide a counterbalance for the demands their talents make on them. Our demands must be every bit as intense if they are to work.

We perform that responsibility by doing the following:

- *Maintaining contact with the home.* Coaches can establish relationships with parents during pre-season and post-season meetings, occasional phone calls whenever dialogue is needed, and periodic mailings. Each of these contacts opens the door to further communication and a mutual understanding of the need to work together to promote the best interests of young athletes.

  See Figures 4-2 and 4-3 for sample mailings. The first extends an invitation for a meeting to discuss poor academic performance or misbehavior. The second offers help to discuss planning activities, especially for the talented athlete who can expect to be highly recruited. Both contacts promote not only important communication but the value of your program and your involvement with kids. These are excellent selling points for parents and school administrators.

- *Meeting occasionally with young athletes.* Coaches are encouraged to advertise an open-door policy with other teachers in the building to be informed of the academic and behavioral progress of their athletes. Everyone in the building knows that coaches have a big influence on the work habits of the school's athletes. Coaches often are asked to use their influence with certain students to promote improved classwork or behavior. To the extent that they exercise this influence by working with teachers, they identify themselves as resource persons in the building and establish supportive relationships with teachers and others.

Figure 4-4 provides a reproducible to initiate such meetings with young athletes. It is easy to use and provides space for a written record of the conversation. It also serves to document each incident for future reference in the event additional interventions with parents and school authorities are necessary.

- *Promoting study habits.* I visited an inner-city school not long ago that assigned young athletes to an "Early Bird" study hall whenever their grades slipped below C level. The students were expected to arrive at school approximately 45 minutes prior to the start of the regular school day and meet with tutors from the National Honor Society to get help with the completion of assignments and preparation for tests and quizzes.

  Once their grades improved, they were released from the program. I was impressed by the school and community support the program received. I also was intrigued by the coach's statistics indicating that larger numbers of his athletes were remaining eligible and eventually graduating from school. He was improving the success of his program while performing a valuable service for the community.

- *Emphasizing a team or family concept during practice and contests.* The singularity of their talents draws enough attention to gifted athletes. Coaches need not single out their performances at team meetings or even post-season banquets. Leave that to the media and everyone else in the school and community. Coaches *can* provide specific praise to them individually after a game or during one-on-one meetings. Gifted athletes must realize that they are members of a team and that their performance, though at times individually outstanding, would be impossible without help from their teammates.

- *Being the "God figure" young athletes make of them.* This sounds contrived, but no one should be surprised at the fact that junior high and senior high school athletes look at most high school coaches as "God figures." An acquaintance, a professor at the University of Virginia, developed such a hypothesis when, a few years ago, he studied the academic achievement of junior high and senior high school students. He concluded statistically that educational performance improved significantly when high school coaches—his only intervening variable—helped young athletes plan their educational programs and apply themselves academically.

  Such intervention has its drawbacks; some persons in the school may resent the intrusion, and many coaches may not want the additional responsibility without some kind of compensation. Schools that overcame these obstacles, however, discovered significant improvement in the educational performance of young athletes, suggesting the need for schools to use athletic motivation as an inducement to improved classroom achievement.

That coaches are important in the lives of young athletes is no startling revelation. Their involvement in nonathletic settings can promote the same kind of commitment and dedication that young athletes evidence on the playing field or court. In addition, their involvement as resource persons can help others in the building with their relationships with young athletes.

WHAT IS THE COUNSELOR'S ROLE?

Counselors provide a complementary relationship with parents and coaches. They may not be "God figures," but they represent a caring, relatively nonjudgmental force in the lives of most students. Counselors have access to important information about young athletes: test scores, transcripts, teacher comments, grades, academic progress reports, and behavioral referrals. Such information enables them to develop a "big picture" of the student's immediate needs and possible futures.

This picture is important at registration time, when the athlete and his or her parents are planning an educational program. It is important when college and career decisions are made. It is critical whenever personal or social problems begin to interfere with the young athlete's classwork or emotional and psychological development. And it is extremely helpful when youngsters begin to feel the extraordinary pressures that competition can impose on them.

The counselor's role must be seen as complementary, not just peripheral. Teamwork is important for athletic programs; it is at least as important to parents, coaches, and counselors whenever they help young athletes. Certainly, parents must assume primary responsibility for the young athlete's future. Coaches, however, can influence youngsters to reach for such futures, and counselors can use their knowledge of adolescent development to extend that reach.

Working together, these people create a more powerful influence on the young athlete's life than when they work separately. Parents are often unaware of eligibility and recruiting tactics, let alone the several opportunities available to accomplished young student athletes. Coaches are limited in their knowledge of college academic programs and admission requirements. And, in spite of the young athlete's local reputation and media attention, counselors usually are unfamiliar with his or her ability to play a sport in college.

Collectively, however, all of them can find answers to their questions and provide the kind of help young athletes need to make reasonable decisions about their academic and athletic futures. The first step, then, for parents, coaches, and counselors is to combine their efforts, as emphasized in Section 3 of this book, and initiate the process that results in such decisions.

Important Steps to Take

Figure 3-1 in Section 3 outlines some of the steps to take to guarantee the academic emphasis of the college selection process. Let's take a closer look at some of those steps, particularly as they relate to the highly recruited athlete. The academic emphasis is often more difficult for them, given the attention they are receiving for their athletic ability.

- *Find the right academic program.* A challenge for any student, matching aptitude and interest with the appropriate college program is especially difficult for the highly recruited athlete. Students and their parents can devote hours to aptitude tests, interest inventories, and discussions of possible careers without making any decisions regarding the "right" program of study in college. That the process may be frustrating, however, is no reason to avoid it.

Some students *do* discover insights into themselves that lead to college programs and eventual careers. Even those who experience only frustration learn more about college majors and their relationship to the significant number of careers are available. Even if the process results in indecision, it provides information and promotes a better understanding of the reasons underlying a selection decision. It also helps create an academic orientation in the mind of the young athlete—a predisposition that will accompany him or her to college.

- *Find the* Best *Schools.* The *best* schools may be those with highly ranked academic programs that match the young athlete's educational and career interests, or—for the undecided—they may be those with the academic breadth that allows for a range of educational and career decisions. Best schools also will satisfy other requirements the student may have identified in his or her search process, such as class sizes, geographical location, relative difficulty, size of campus and student body, makeup of student body, and a range of other issues, all of which are identified later in this section.

  The point is, student athletes should have a college or colleges that interest them irrespective of their athletic futures. I was fortunate to be able to enjoy a playing career in college that lasted into my senior year. Two weeks into fall practice, however, and hoping for a future chance at professional football, I incurred a cerebral hemorrhage. Within seconds, my future changed. Fortunately, I was able to find satisfying alternatives. All young athletes must have similar alternatives in the event unexpected injury changes their lives.

- *Visit Several Schools.* Parents are well advised to promote college visitations as early as possible in a student's high school career. There's something about a college campus that can be motivating to high school students. Ultimately, the experience can serve as a goal for the student; and, for student athletes making selection decisions, a visit can result in that indescribable sense that enhances the desirability of certain schools.

  Visits for young athletes actually anticipating an upcoming decision should be started during the spring of the junior year. That provides enough time to think about the other factors that affect the decision. Additional visits will be made later when scholarship offers begin coming in, but all initial decisions should be made as if the young athlete were not going to play a sport in college.

- *Mail applications early in the senior year.* Consistent with the notion that athletics should not influence initial college decisions, young athletes should be encouraged by their parents, coaches, and counselors to mail applications to *best* colleges early in the senior year. Such a process assures an appropriate college in the event of injury, and it eliminates much of the confusion that can result later when young athletes and their parents become overwhelmed by the sudden attention they receive.

An additional consideration: If the college is highly selective and admission is questionable, be sure to apply to one or two other schools to which admission is guaranteed. Then contact the college coach to determine the degree of his or her involvement in the admissions process at the highly selective school. He or she may want to approach the admissions office on behalf of the athlete. Parents may want to contact the high school coach to have him or her make the call, at least to determine the best process for mailing the application. The process may vary among colleges.

This initial process of selecting appropriate schools is very important. Share the reproducible in Figure 4-5 with student athletes who are likely to be highly recruited and forward a copy to their parents sometime in the junior year to get them thinking about the process.

DEALING WITH COLLEGE RECRUITERS

The phone call to the college coach suggests a whole range of related considerations. Blue-chippers receive enough mail to decimate a small forest, and they are contacted by recruiters as soon as the NCAA gives colleges the green light. At first exciting and complimentary, the process can become exhausting. Like all salespersons, recruiters sell their programs; they can be pleasant, persistent, and persuasive.

They are a necessary part of the process. To assure that recruiters are held in check, however, highly recruited athletes and their parents require the help of a knowledgeable high school coach as well as others in the school building. A meeting early in the school year is perhaps the best way to coordinate the recruitment process. As emphasized elsewhere in this book, the meeting should involve the young athlete, the coach, the counselor, and maybe the athletic director and the school's college consultant, if it has one. Figure 4-3 provides a sample letter to mail to parents.

The purpose of this initial meeting is to focus on the schools in which the young athlete and his or her parents are interested and to determine a procedure for handling recruiters. Such a procedure can consist of several different components:

- If the number of early contacts has been relatively small, each of them can be called or sent a letter that outlines the parameters of the experience for everyone. A sample letter is provided in Figure 4-6. Notice that it avoids dictating terms; it simply makes reasonable requests regarding the timing of phone calls and visits. Our purpose is not to discourage recruiters, just to promote a little consideration.

- Again, if the number of early contacts has been small, this is the time to review the student athlete's original list of schools and determine which of them need to be contacted regarding possible recruiting. Some young athletes are highly recruited in one geographical area and don't hear from colleges in other parts of the country. It's possible that none of the schools in a certain geographical area will have the appropriate program of studies. Once such a determination is made, other schools have to be contacted. The coach is the best person to do this.

- If the student athlete is highly recruited by a significant number of schools, the coach generally should offer his or her services to "run interference" for the family. Figure 4-7 provides a reproducible letter that informs college coaches of such a decision. Because high school coaches speak the language of most recruiters, they are the logical people to provide this service to families. It can be helpful to the families and a miracle of public relations value!

- If decisions are possible at this point, young athletes and their parents can avoid the recruiting process entirely. This is yet another advantage of having young athletes engage in the college search process before recruiting begins. The information gained during such a search can be used to make quick decisions when recruiting begins, at least to narrow down the alternatives from which the young athlete and his or her parents will choose.

If decisions are possible at this point, or whenever they are finally made, coaches should use the reproducible in Figure 4-8 to inform the other recruiters that the athlete has made a decision or has narrowed his or her list of schools. At that point recruiters must be helped to understand that no further contact is warranted. Most will not seek such contact because of their need to intensify the recruiting process with other athletes on their list. Some few, however, will want a final shot; they should be discouraged from taking it.

The high school coach is the focal person in this early meeting and the one who has the most work to do when the meeting is over. He or she, therefore, must be relieved of other responsibilities that can double the work load. Additional letters of recommendation, the processing of applications, and additional meetings that do not really require his or her presence should be handled by someone else in the coalition.

Easy reference to the right materials can save a lot of meeting time and unnecessary discussion. Among the most important and time-saving materials in this section are the lists of questions that highly recruited athletes must ask of recruiters and others during and after campus visits. Before those visits are made, however, the high school coach must call each school to get the answers to three important questions:

- "What position do want him or her to play?" Basketball players may want to play guard rather than small forward. Sprinters may want to focus on the 100 and 200 meter sprints instead of intermediate distances. Wrestlers may not want to drop one or two weight classes. Football players may want offense as opposed to defense. Softball players may want to play shortstop rather than first base. Obviously, each of these preferences is dependent on previous discussion with the high school coach and acknowledges the inevitability of compromise. Asking it of the college coach, however, provides information that may be helpful when future decisions are made.

- "Are you guaranteeing financing for five years?" Although the NCAA permits only one-year scholarships, most upstanding programs will commit to four or five years. They are unable to make such commitments in writing but will make them orally. The high school coach is the best person to elicit such statements.

- "How good is the recruited athlete's program of study?" This suggests that the athlete is a student first and that the high school coach is interested primarily in the student's education. The answer also exposes the recruiter's knowledge of the school's academic programs. The relative degree of that knowledge reveals the recruiter's interest in potential players as *student athlete*s.

ASKING THE RIGHT QUESTIONS
DURING THE COLLEGE VISIT

If the young athlete's decision is dependent upon one or more campus visits, he or she will need the answers to several additional questions. The following issues are particularly important and warrant discussion before each visit. Answers to these questions are especially helpful to parents who are certain to discuss each school before a decision is made at home. Refer to Figure 4-9 for a complete listing of questions and a reproducible to distribute to student athletes. The following information provides further insights into several of the questions:

Ask Recruiters

- "Will I be red-shirted?" Red-shirting adds time to the total college experience but sometimes provides the opportunity for graduate study. In addition, some few athletes want to play right away. In such instances, this question should be asked immediately in the recruiting process. (See Figure 6-2, "Important Terms.")

- "What happens to my scholarship if I'm injured or ineligible—or just not good enough?" Again, for the highly recruited athlete, most upstanding programs commit to multiyear scholarships or, at least, answer this question honestly, especially as it relates to eligibility. Everyone in the coalition except the counselor—coach, parents, and student—should ask the same question at an appropriate time.

- "If injured, may I use my family doctor? Who determines my fitness to resume competition after an injury? Will such injuries be covered by a team insurance policy?" A friend's daughter received a basketball scholarship in college and tore ligaments in her ankle during her sophomore year. The family's insurance had to pay for the initial treatment. In addition, the girl returned to the team before her physical therapy was complete. She never completely recovered from the injury.

Ask Players at the School

- "About how much time do you devote to your sport?" Answers to this question relate to available study time, time spent in meetings, practice, travel, the training room, and other sports-related activities. Recent research indicates that athletes are spending at least as much time with their sports as they are with their studies. It's important that young athletes enter college with their eyes wide open in this regard.

- "How do you like the living arrangements?" Some schools put all their athletes in one dorm. Some athletes like this; others do not because it restricts their contact with other students and necessarily limits the quality of the college experience. Often, athletes are housed in a single dorm more for the convenience of the coaches than for that of the players. Young athletes and their parents want to know this.

- "Can I get academic help?" Are coaches the first contacts regarding needed tutoring, or does the school have a comprehensive program of academic advisement?

Academic advisement is a growing reality on most college campuses. The quality of the program is an important consideration, especially for the parents of student athletes.

Ask the School's Nonathletes

- "If you had it all over to do again, would you choose this school to attend? Why or why not?" Nonathletes will provide honest answers to this question, and many will be able to provide good reasons for their answers. Recruited student athletes should also be sure to ask this question of students in their intended field of study, if they have selected one.

Ask School Officials and Admissions Officers

- "What are the graduation rates for athletes? For athletes in my sport?" This is a critical question. Some sports programs have reputations of not having graduated African-American athletes in several years. This is a startling statistic, one that must be revealed during the recruiting process. Admissions officers must share this information with you.

- "What is my eligibility for additional financial aid?" The answer to this question involves the processing of additional forms. Families are advised to take the time to do this, given the fact that Pell Grants are available to supplement athletic scholarships.

QUESTIONS TO ASK
AFTER THE CAMPUS VISIT

Figure 4-10 provides a reproducible that should be shared with student athletes and their parents early in the recruiting process so that they can incorporate important questions into their planning activities. Most of the questions are self-explanatory, but the following few may require brief discussion:

- "Did any of the recruiters have bad things to say about the other schools that are recruiting me?" Integrity is revealed in a variety of ways. Perhaps the most obvious is the inclination to "take the high road" regarding observations of opposing programs. Recruiters who criticize or berate other programs are revealing more of themselves than of the other programs.

- "Would I attend this school if I had no intention of playing my sport?" This may be one of the important questions a young athlete can ask of himself or herself before making a decision about particular schools. The glamour of sports competition and the media attention received by certain programs and their coaches can color a young athlete's decision to attend that school. Parents must be sure to discuss this question at length with their young athletes before making a final decision about which school to attend.

Figure 4-11 provides a suggested format for parents and young athletes to help them focus on the right issues when making a decision. The top-priority items are crucial when making a final decision, so they are given the highest point values. Some of the items can be shifted around to reflect the values of the young athlete and his or her family, but the top items should remain the most important. They constitute the fundamental reasons for going to college in the first place.

- "What is the nature of the relationships among coaches, players, and nonathletes?" This question embraces several in Figure 4-10 and reveals insights into how the young athlete will feel on the campus. This may not seem to be an important issue early in the recruiting process, but it grows in importance as the final decision approaches.

- "Does the school satisfy all the requirements that I identified earlier with my parents and counselor?" This is, perhaps, the single most important question to be answered during the process of making a final decision. It contains all the reasons the student decided to go to college in the first place, and it places athletic competition in its proper perspective. For that reason, it is the first question asked on the form provided in Figure 4-11.

A FINAL WORD ABOUT BOOSTERS

I was pleased a couple of years ago to be honored by the University of Nebraska's Masters Program as one of their distinguished alumni. I was particularly pleased because as a student at Nebraska I developed such profound respect for the quality of the education they provided me, especially in their English department. I had a most enjoyable visit with them.

During my stay, I was thumbing through a copy of the *Nebraska Alumnus*, reading an article about the school's history when I bumped into the following quote: "… a Cornhusker football team might be good for the local economy." A passer-by couldn't help but notice the smile on my face and asked if I was enjoying the article. I said "Yes" and acknowledged that I just read what probably was one of the classic understatements in the university's history.

I don't know specifically about Lincoln, Nebraska, but I do know that several communities across the country realize up to $17 million during the local university's home football games every fall. That comes down to 2 million to 3 million dollars on each of six or seven weekends for local restaurants, hotels, souvenir shops, bars, and assorted businesses. It may be true that university athletic programs are losing money, but *someone* in the area is cashing in on the thrill of competition.

Recognizing a well-worn chronology of booster abuses, the NCAA has restricted the involvement of boosters in the recruiting process; boosters may have *no* involvement in the process. Because the NCAA imposes several other restrictions regarding recruiting and because it is representative of all the regulatory organizations, be sure to distribute Figure 3-11, "Contacts and Visits" to student athletes and their parents early in the recruiting process.

LET'S WRAP IT UP

Much of the information and many of the materials in this section are also appropriate for the student athlete who may not be heavily recruited. The primary focus of the section, however, involves the importance of distinguishing between the gifted and the not-so-gifted athlete. As a coach with thirty-one years' experience, I am eternally grateful to the young athletes of average ability who worked hard for everything they earned.

Certainly, I appreciated the young kinesthetic genius who worked his magic on game days; without him, our football program would have realized less success. I learned early in my career, however, that such players may be the arms and legs of great teams, but that the average player is the team's heart and soul. They are the athletes who go on to enjoy some of life's greatest accomplishments.

When we're fortunate enough to work with gifted young athletes who extend themselves beyond significant ability levels, we enjoy an experience that few coaches realize. When effort meets ability, it can create experiences we never forget. These athletes also go on to achieve significantly in life; it's just that they often require a different approach to promote such effort.

Coaches, parents, and counselors are challenged to devise ways to overcome the demands of what must be described in some cases as genius. The imposition of such ability often leaves room for little else in one's life. Our job is to help such young athletes develop the kind of perspective that enables them to capitalize on such ability to realize the benefits of a richer and fuller life. The materials in this section will help.

Figure 4-1

SAMPLE LETTER
FROM PARENT(S) TO COACH

Date

(Coach's Name
Address
City, State Zip)

Dear (Coach's Name):

First of all, let us indicate how pleased we are that Shelly has had such success in gymnastics this year. It really is pleasurable to see her, as just a sophomore, win the state's balance beam title and do so well in the All-Round competition. We are especially pleased because we know how hard she has worked these past several years.

We also are pleased to acknowledge the contribution you have made to her success. Without your instruction and support, she certainly would have had a much more difficult time. We write this letter to seek some additional support. The parents of one of last year's top gymnasts have told us that the next two years may become a bit frantic around here if Shelly continues to realize such success. Between the media and college recruiters calling, we might need some advice.

You are the logical person to provide it. For that reason, we would like to meet with you sometime within the next couple of weeks to discuss Shelly, the student athlete, and everything her future is likely to involve. Would you check your calendar, please, and give us a call to discuss the particulars of such a meeting? Thanks for your help, and we look forward to hearing from you.

Sincerely,

(Parents)

Figure 4-2

LETTER REGARDING
ACADEMIC PERFORMANCE OR MISBEHAVIOR

Date

(Parents' Names
Address
City, State Zip)

Dear Mr. and Mrs. (Parents' Names):

I write this letter to seek and to offer some help. I have just been notified that Tommy has received three notices of unsatisfactory progress: English, geometry, and Western Civilization 1. He also has received two behavioral referrals, one from his English teacher, the other from the math teacher. I have spoken to him at practice, and he assured me earlier that he would get to work to improve his academic performance, but apparently he is still having problems.

I think the time has come for the four of us to meet, maybe even in the counselor's office. We can talk about Tommy's program and his reaction to it. We want to determine why he is experiencing such difficulty and causing occasional misbehavior problems.

As you must know, I really like Tommy. He has worked hard in practice and has never caused us one problem on the team. Maybe such a meeting can steer some of his motivation for sports into the classroom. He certainly has a great deal more ability than these referrals would indicate.

Please give me a call to discuss the particulars of such a meeting. If you feel the counselor's attendance would be helpful, I will contact her to schedule the appointment, then get back to you with the actual time and place. Thanks for your help, and I look forward to hearing from you.

Sincerely,

(Coach)

Figure 4-3

LETTER TO PARENTS REGARDING
TALENTED ATHLETE

Date

(Parents' Names
Address
City, State Zip)

Dear Mr. and Mrs. (Parents' Names):

Well, Tom did it! He made the contribution to this team that everyone expected from him and, in the process, distinguished himself as one of the best baseball players in the state. I can't guarantee anything, but I expect that he will be pretty highly recruited by several colleges across the country. His home run production was the best in the school's history, and his batting average of .482 has already earned him All-State and All-America honors.

You and I have much to discuss. The recruiting process can get pretty complicated, but it can result in a great college experience—if we plan well now. We will need to discuss Tom's educational and career plans if he has any, and we'll have to talk about the colleges he may already have identified with his counselor. In fact, a lot has to be done before the actual recruiting process begins if Tom and you are to ask the right kinds of questions of college coaches.

I will be involved as well. I would like to discuss that with you also. Please do me a favor, therefore, and check your calendar for an appropriate time for us to get together, then give me a call to arrange for a meeting. My number is 999-9999.

I know Tom has given you a great deal of pleasure already; he's a great kid. I, too, have enjoyed his contribution and would like to help him realize more success on the college level. Give me a call at your convenience.

Sincerely,

(Coach)

Figure 4-4

COACH'S INTERVENTION
WITH STUDENT ATHLETE

TO COACHES: Use this form whenever a teacher contacts you about one of your student athletes. The athletic department does not care to see the form. It is provided only for your convenience, if you should choose to use it.

STUDENT ATHLETE'S NAME: _____

DESCRIPTION OF INCIDENT (Be specific. If the teacher's concern is with academic progress, secure from him or her relevant grades and the names of incomplete assignments.):

MY INTERVENTION (Provide a detailed description. You might want to refer to this form at some time in the future.):

DATE OF INTERVENTION: _____

Figure 4-5

IS COLLEGE IN YOUR FUTURE?

To Student Athletes and Their Parents:

Many high school athletes look forward to a continuation of their sports in college. In many instances, these expectations can be very realistic; in others, they are not. When the time comes, be sure to talk to your coach about college sports. He or she will be able to give you all the help you need to make that important transition in your life. In the meantime, if a college sport is what you want, keep the following pointers in mind:

1. *Search out the right academic program.* Talk to your counselor about interest inventories, career searches, and the college exploration process. You may not end up with a definite career focus, but the process will introduce you to several very important considerations about your future. It will also provide the academic orientation you need when you go to college to hit the books and to realize success in your studies.

2. *Find the best schools for you.* When you have completed the process, you probably will have developed a list of colleges that meet your academic, career, and personal requirements. You'll be surprised at some of the things your counselor tells you about the college selection process. It's an eye-opening experience!

3. *Visit several schools.* After you have developed a list of schools that are just right for you, visit several of them. Everything else being equal, a visit to a college campus is the best way to determine if that school is what you want. If it doesn't result in a decision, at least it will give you the information you need to eventually make that decision.

4. *Apply to two or three schools early in your senior year.* We don't want to jinx you with this memo, but sports in college is not a sure thing for you. You may get injured between now and then, or you may discover a sudden disinterest from college recruiters next year. Even if you are highly recruited, the work you do to select the right college program will make the recruiting process a whole lot easier next year.

SEE YOUR COUNSELOR AND YOUR COACH
FOR ADDITIONAL INFORMATION
ABOUT THIS BIG STEP YOU ARE PLANNING!

103

Figure 4-6

SAMPLE LETTER TO COLLEGE COACHES
REGARDING RECRUITING

Date

(Coach's Name
Address
City, State Zip)

Dear (Coach's Name):

Well, the recruiting season is about to get under way, and it's great to know that you are interested once again in a couple of our kids. I know that you're wrapping up your season now, so I won't take much of your time. I just wanted to let you know that I have spoken with our athletes about the process and am planning to meet with their parents soon. If this year is anything like past years, we probably will have a lot of contact with each other.

Let's start off by doing you a favor. I'll give you a call in a few weeks to discuss my kids and your degree of interest in each one. That way I don't have to pester you trying to sell one or more of them. I can get some tapes out right away so you have time to evaluate them before we talk. I have one or two that I have strong feelings about. They are players and have the potential to really help your program.

Once you let me know the names of the players you want to recruit, we can talk about a meeting schedule and the best times to make phone calls. That kind of preliminary planning has always helped in the past.

I'll give you a call in a few weeks. If you want to talk before then, give me a call at your convenience. I hope the remainder of your season goes well. I look forward to talking to you.

Sincerely,

(Coach)

Figure 4-7

LETTER TO COLLEGE COACHES

Date

(College Coach's Name
Address
City, State Zip)

Dear (Coach's Name):

First of all, on behalf of Pete Zankowicz and his parents, I'd like to thank you and your school for your interest in him as a prospective football player. You and I have talked often about Pete's football and academic abilities, and both join that crowd of recruiters who believe that Pete will realize every bit as much success in college as he has enjoyed in high school.

In fact, "recruiting" is the reason I write this letter. Pete and his parents have met with me often to discuss his athletic and academic plans and to identify those schools that seem to have the right kind of program for him. Yours is one such program. Because there are others, however, and because all of them want to talk to Pete and his parents about their programs, I have been asked to "run a little interference" for them.

Pete has done so much for me over the years that I want to help him and his family, so, if you would be so kind, I'd appreciate your contacting me each time you would like to get a hold of the family or Pete. We can talk a little bit, and I can forward the information to the family or have them call you to discuss the issue further.

I'm sure you understand the reasons for this request and will do what you can to give me a call whenever you want to talk to Pete or the family. I would appreciate any phone calls at school. My number is 999-999-9999. I can be reached here any day. If unavailable at the time of your call, I promise to get right back to you. I would prefer no calls at home, but if a call is necessary, I can be reached at 777-777-7777.

Thanks for your understanding, and I look forward to hearing from you.

Sincerely,

(Coach)

Figure 4-8

SAMPLE LETTER TO REJECTED SCHOOLS

Date

(College Coach's Name
Address
City, State Zip)

Dear (Coach's Name):

First of all, let me thank you for your interest in Sally Marcos. I have enjoyed working with you through-out the recruiting process. You and your program are a pleasure to work with.

The bad news is that Sally has decided on another school, one that comes closer to meeting her educa-tional and career needs. Sally, her parents, and I discussed the issue at considerable length, and their decision is final. They weighed a lot of factors in the decisional process and came up with a school that seems best for her.

Obviously, your school was among those they seriously considered, primarily because of the merits of the academic program and your ability to sell them on your athletic program. It's too bad about Sally as far as you folks are concerned, but I know we will do business again in the future! In fact, I have a cou-ple of kids you might be interested in for next year. Give me a call so we can talk and maybe you can keep an eye on them.

Good luck with your program, and I hope to talk to you again soon.

Sincerely,

(Coach)

Figure 4-9

QUESTIONS TO ASK *DURING* YOUR VISIT

Before you decide to make your first visit, it's a good idea to think carefully about
tion you are going to need to eventually make a decision. Once you do, you'll be ab
kinds of questions. Following are some good ones to get you started.

ASK THE RECRUITER:

1. What position (event) do you want me to play (perform), and how many others are you recruiting for the same position?
2. What is your philosophy of offense? Defense? Are you considering any changes?
3. Will I be red-shirted?
4. If I need a fifth year, will you finance it?
5. What happens to my scholarship if I'm injured or ineligible?
6. Whom do I see if I have academic problems?
7. Has drug use been an issue at your school? Athletic program?
8. Are all injuries handled by a team insurance policy?
9. If injured, may I use my family doctor? Who determines my fitness to compete after an injury?
10. What is expected of players during the off-season?

ASK OF THE PLAYERS AT THE SCHOOL:

1. What does your typical daily schedule look like? In-season? Off-season?
2. Approximately how many hours a night do you study?
3. What generally are the attitudes of professors in different fields of study? In my field of study? Toward athletes?
4. How do you like the living arrangements?
5. Do you have an academic advisor? Is he/she any good?
6. Are the coaches available to help if you have academic problems?

ASK OF NONATHLETES AT THE SCHOOL:

1. What do you think of the quality of the education you are receiving at this school?
2. If you had to do it all over again, would you choose this school to attend? Why or why not?
3. What is the general opinion of athletes on this campus?

ASK OF SCHOOL OFFICIALS/ADMISSIONS OFFICERS:

1. What are the different graduation rates for athletes? In my sport?
2. About how long does it take someone in my sport to earn a degree from this school?
3. What is the placement rate and the average starting salary for graduates in (your field of study)?
4. What is my eligibility for additional financial aid?

LET'S TALK! BRING YOUR PARENTS IN!

Figure 4-10

QUESTIONS TO ASK *AFTER* THE VISIT

You will have to ask yourself several important questions *after* you have visited your schools in order to decide ultimately on the right school. These questions will provide a good start. Take the time to think about your answers, and be sure to talk to me, your counselor, and your parents about answers that may be difficult for you. Remember, you want the right athletic *and* academic experience, so *all* these questions are important.

1. Did any of the recruiters have bad things to say about the other schools that are recruiting me?

2. Did any of the recruiters promise that I'd compete right away, even be a starter? (If they did, they may have been less than honest.)

3. Would I attend this school if I had no intention of competing in my sport?

4. Do the coaches and players seem to care genuinely about each other?

5. Will I be successful academically in this school? Athletically? How do I measure up to everyone else?

6. Were the coaches and players I met honest, available to me and others, friendly, genuinely interested, or did they seem phony?

7. Were the coaches interested in academics? Did they ask me about my educational and career interests? Were they knowledgeable about my intended program of study? If not, did they introduce me to someone who might answer my questions?

8. Will I fit in with the rest of the student body at this particular school? Will I be comfortable associating with them for four or more years?

9. How will I feel if one or more of the coaches leaves? Will I still be happy with the school? My sports participation?

10. Does the school satisfy all the requirements that I identified earlier with my parents and counselor? *This probably is the most important question.* Give it a lot of thought, and be sure to talk it over with me, your counselor, and your parents.

TALK TO ME *ANYTIME*—ABOUT *ANY* OF THESE QUESTIONS.

Figure 4-11

SELECTING YOUR ONE, *BEST* COLLEGE

Now that you've taken the time to study a range of colleges for the academic program a[ ]
right for you, the time has come to make a decision. Because there are so many excelle[ ].
there, you and your family probably will need help making such a decision. This form should help. It
asks that you respond to a series of questions involving different aspects of your decision with the name
of the college that is the single best answer. Obviously, academic considerations are the most important,
so they receive the highest numerical value. Be honest as you complete this form, and be sure to discuss
areas of disagreement with your parents, explaining your reasons with as much objective information as
you can find.

1. (Worth 10 pts.) Which college meets all the program requirements I developed earlier with my counselor and parents? College: _____

2. (Worth 9 pts.) Which school meets all the other characteristics I desire in a school, such as geographical location, size, etc.? College: _____

3. (Worth 8 pts.) Which school would I attend if I had no intention of playing a sport? College: _____

4. (Worth 7 pts.) Which school had the best graduation rate and job placement possibilities after graduation? College: _____

5. (Worth 6 pts.) Which school satisfies my playing needs best: offensive philosophy, position, likelihood of playing, etc.? College: _____

6. (Worth 5 pts.) Will my schedule of sports activities provide enough time to do well in my academic program? College: _____

7. (Worth 4 pts.) Which school offers the best financial package? College: _____

8. (Worth 3 pts.) Are the professors accepting of athletes, and are relationships among teammates and coaches positive? College: _____

9. (Worth 2 pts.) Are the living arrangements to my liking? Will they promote study? College: _____

10. (Worth 1 pt.) Are injuries handled appropriately, insurance costs met? College: _____

Now add up the numerical value for each college.
The one with the highest number *may be* your one, best school.
At any rate, this process has given you something to think about
and discuss at home. Contact your coach and counselor
if you need more help.

GOOD LUCK!

Section

Section
FIVE

STUDENT ATHLETES AND THE HIGH SCHOOL COACH

First, a quick story. I attended a social gathering recently at the home of the strength coach of a prominent professional team. He had worked with pro basketball and football players, and had coached football in college and, several years earlier, in high school. We strolled through his home and found ourselves standing with him in his office, studying a display of team portraits and the autographed pictures of former players—one of them a picture of his first high school team.

Though several of the photographs were of Hall of Fame athletes, he talked mostly about his high school team, even sharing detailed stories about some of the players in the picture. One player in particular stood out in his mind. Finally, he spoke of him:

"You know, Mike, the relationship with high school athletes is really special."

"Yeah, it sure is. Their love of sports is as pure as it gets."

"This kid's the perfect example," he said, as he pointed to a boy in the middle of the picture. "I'll never forget him. We had just played our last game. I think we were about .500, maybe 4 and 4. We won the game, and Mike was a senior. I had just finished talking to the kids; always a really emotional thing that last game of the season."

"Yeah," I said, "sometimes it can leave a big hole in your gut."

"That's the truth. But I got done with my talk, and I walked around the locker room talking to the kids, telling them what a great season it had been."

Here his voice began to quiver: "And I saw Mike standing by his locker, still wearing his game uniform."

111

Now his eyes moistened: "So I walked up to him and said, 'Great season, Mike. Come on, buddy, let's get that stuff off and get showered.'"

Then, as a tear rolled down his cheek, he said, "And you know, that kid just stood there crying. He told me, 'I just don't want to take it off, coach; this is the last time I'll ever wear these pads.'"

I smiled in acknowledgment.

"Twenty-five years ago," he said, "and it still chokes me up."

I guess high school coaches don't enjoy a corner on that kind of emotional market. Many teachers can share similar stories, so can college and professional coaches. Certainly parents can. In the world of sport, however, in spite of the media's claims that money is king, such stories happen everywhere—especially in high school, where player and coach share mutual respect and a simple, unencumbered love of sports. My friend is one of many such coaches who have the sensitivity to realize it.

THE JOB OF THE HIGH SCHOOL COACH

That the responsibilities of high school coaches reach well into the lives of their players, therefore, goes without saying. That they understand the full scope of such responsibilities is the focus of this section. Most high school coaches expect more of themselves than of their players. They devote long hours during the season to practice and preparation for contests, and afterward, they meet with seniors and their parents to discuss college, write letters, make phone calls, and meet with recruiters.

Some few, however, restrict themselves to responsibilities involving only practice and games. They forgo the added responsibilities that accumulate when the season ends. They do this for several reasons:

- Some feel that meager coaching stipends fail to promote involvement with youngsters beyond the season.
- Some are unfamiliar with the protocols and processes for contacting college coaches.
- Some work in litigious communities and fear legal reprisals from dissatisfied parents, so they avoid the process entirely.
- Others bump into obstacles such as inaccessible phones, secretaries, or office equipment.
- Still others move into other sports and have no time for spill-over from the previous season.
- And, let's admit it, some just can't find the time for the extra work.

These latter coaches generally get involved in sports for the wrong reasons. They ask what playing or coaching can do for them, not what they can do for kids. They may even have good win-loss records and prominent reputations, but their motives are suspect. Such coaches, in spite of their apparent success, contribute little more to sports than an already pronounced preoccupation with winning.

Unfortunately, we can't do much about them, but we can help the well-intentioned coaches who care about kids and would provide more help if they knew how. Certainly, I can't pay them more (I wish I could!), but I can share a few ideas that will get them started in the right direction.

IN UNITY, THERE IS STRENGTH

The idea most worth sharing acknowledges the significant power of high school coaches. I remember my first year teaching English in a large, Chicago-area high school. One of my supervisory responsibilities involved a study hall of some 600 kids during the last period of the day, the worst time to ride herd on a group of frenetic 16-year-olds awaiting the final bell. I was wringing wet by the end of most days, but the experience generally went quite well.

I often wondered at the time, however, what would happen if 600 kids suddenly decided to talk or throw paper airplanes or run relay races up and down the aisles of the auditorium. What could I do? That one thought represented one of my earliest acknowledgments of the raw power of kids, especially kids in large groups. It was a significant learning experience and one reason why I always enjoyed mutually respectful relationships with teenagers.

High school coaches have that kind of power, and some college coaches—generally the most successful—realize it. They know that if large groups of high school coaches were to deny them any recruits, their college programs would fold. Like the students in my study hall, high school coaches usually fail to realize the dimensions of their collective power—which is unfortunate for today's high school coach.

It also is unfortunate for intercollegiate athletics, which is being diminished by the contradictory interests of coaches and players on the one hand and the intentions of the NCAA and university presidents on the other. Still attracting the attention of millions of people, intercollegiate athletics is being weakened by the vested interests of coaches, boosters, and even the players themselves.

High school coaches have the power to revive it. In combination with counselors and parents, they can control the flow of athletes to every university in this country, large or small. I was approached by the executive vice president of one of this country's largest and most influential service organizations a couple of years ago and asked if I thought we could organize something comparable to the Knight Commission for high schools.

I was intrigued by the idea, but after some discussion concluded that high schools are denied the kind of regulatory clout available to universities through the NCAA. Both he and I agreed, however, that high school personnel, parents, and young athletes could combine their knowledge and strength to create local coalitions that would work with the kinds of schools that help themselves as well as the young athletes they recruit.

Figure 5-1 illustrates the concept and provides a reproducible that high school coaches and counselors can use to share with parents during informational meetings. It suggests that the knowledge of the coach and counselor, the influence of the parent and coach, and the talent of the athlete generate power. Such coalitions can give or deny that power to recruiters, who have little power—unless high school personnel and parents give it to them. Already emphasized in the conclusion to Section 1, this position is so important that it will be repeated periodically throughout this book. Before we go on to a different issue regarding high school coaches, let's consider power from just one more perspective.

WHO HAS THE *REAL* POWER?

Having taught educational supervision on the university level for more than twenty years, I know that power has been the subject of considerable study. I know, for example, that theorists have identified different kinds of power. Consider just three: charismatic power, coercive power, and expert power. Charismatic power generally results from the force of one's personality. It is often complemented by position. Head coaches of major university programs often have charismatic power.

Coercive power results from the ability to *force* someone to do something. It may involve control of resources, the ability to withhold, or the ability to reward. It usually avoids physical force, although the media often provide ample evidence of that as well. Coercive power isn't necessarily bad. We have all experienced it—every time our parents made us do something we didn't want to do but that was in our best interests.

Expert power results from the ability to control others by the force of intellect or knowledge. Usually others grant such power willingly because of the benefits they receive from the shared knowledge. We can find expert power—to varying degrees—in every enterprise, from schools to businesses. The most successful seek and nourish it; the less successful often disregard it. Some schools, for example, are run by administrators who depend more on coercive power or hierarchical authority than expert power.

To the extent that schools fail to promote expert power and the wisdom that results from it, they run the risk of failing to meet the needs of their students and parents. This section, then, emphasizes the need for all of us to develop and coalesce the expert power of coaches and counselors with the coercive power of parents and coaches. The charismatic power of college coaches has grown disproportionately strong over the years. The time has come for high school personnel and parents to do something about it.

The High School Coach and the Pre–High School Athlete

The high school coach's expert power is most evident and, probably, most impressive to young athletes and their parents when the coach visits feeder schools (junior high schools and K through 8 programs) to make presentations. High school coaches can be powerful influences on the academic and behavioral motivations of athlete and nonathlete alike. Fortunately, no one expects them to be sophisticated speakers—just honest, sincere, and perhaps moderately entertaining representatives of their high schools.

If they display confidence and a solid value system, families will listen to them, and parents will be inclined to encourage their children to participate in the sports programs they represent. High school coaches, therefore, are encouraged to volunteer their services to work with feeder school personnel to develop informative and entertaining programs for sixth, seventh, and eighth graders and their families. Such programs can cover a wide range of important topics:

- The "Real World of Athletic Scholarships." Such a presentation may be especially appropriate for youngsters *before* they enter high school. It may help promote a strong academic orientation before they walk through the front door in the fall.

- Drug Prevention. The high school coach who shares startling statistics and anecdotes about the dangers of drugs does much to discourage kids from using them.

- The Importance of Academics. Coaches can discuss such a topic with or without an accompanying discussion of athletics.

- Getting Involved in the High School. Statistics indicate that involvement in extracurricular activities in high school correlates positively with success in later life. Coaches can talk about the range of programs available to youngsters.

- Success Stories. Coaches who share success stories of their former athletes with the community use their expert power to good purpose. Such programs are well received by community organizations for luncheon meetings and invariably do much to promote the high school within the community. Most important, such presentations, whether in feeder schools or community organizations, help establish the kinds of relationships that are so important among youngsters, coaches, and parents.

THE RELATIONSHIP BETWEEN COACH AND PLAYER

This relationship warrants special mention. Sports competition touches a great many people: coach, player, parent, athletic director, counselors, school administrators, fans—anyone who organizes or attends athletic contests. Because the word "competition" sparks such divergent reactions among them, the coach must be the first to define it appropriately for his or her players. On the one hand, the philosophy of "win at all costs" influences the behaviors of thousands of coaches, regardless of the sport. On the other, it has become a phrase that receives the severest condemnation from critics of sports abuses.

At the one extreme, some coaches focus on winning to the exclusion of integrity, fair play, and the best interests of their players. At the other, schools renounce coaches for not promoting "fun," for not playing every athlete equally, for seeking to win games or contests at the expense of player involvement. If each of these positions represents opposite ends of the continuum, the more realistic purpose of sports competition must be somewhere in the middle.

Coaches must find that purpose and behave in ways that are consistent with it. I suggest that the purpose is embodied in the words of Vince Lombardi, who said, "Winning isn't everything. The *will* to win is everything." Many coaches will recognize immediately that a misinterpretation of Lombardi's quote has caused a lot of confusion among coaches and players. Some people believe that Lombardi said, "Winning isn't everything; it's the only thing."

Such a misinterpretation of Lombardi's philosophy has done an injustice to the memory of the man, and it has provoked a world of abuses in American sports. Coaches must do what they can to reorient the thinking of players, parents, and fans alike by introducing young athletes to a philosophy that puts competition in the right perspective. Like Lombardi, we must emphasize with young athletes that the work they put into a contest, the desire that marks their effort, and their commitment to be everything they can be are much more important than winning a game or an event.

The *willingness* to practice hard and to commit to a winning *effort* are the real victories in sports competition, even if the contest itself is lost. Now don't get me wrong; I'm not giving kids an easy way out. I'll push them as hard as I can in practice and expect nothing but their best in a game, but once they've given everything, I will ask for no more, and I will congratulate them after the contest—win or lose.

I recognize, as does every other coach, that winning is the purpose of any game, whether it be field hockey, checkers, or tic-tac-toe—and a winning effort generally involves sacrifices. It involves hard work from everyone, increased pressure on game days for the talented players, and, yes, sitting on the bench for the less talented. If winning is one of the primary purposes of the contest, the talented players must take the field or the court during the contest, and the less talented must make their contributions in practice and in support of their teammates during contests.

Such a position is consistent with Lombardi's philosophy. The *will to win* or *to play* in the contests is more important than the contests themselves. When children are young, eight or nine or ten, they must have every opportunity to discover the extent of their talents. Equal participation at this time in their lives may have merit. Having discovered the extent of those talents, however, they must be helped to accept them, not to entertain unrealistic expectations of themselves and their coaches. The limited athlete must be rewarded by acknowledging his or her commitment to team values and hard work, not by playing at a level of competition he or she simply can't handle.

When parents or others push for equal playing time in sports competition that requires sophisticated skills and pronounced athletic ability, they subject the less-talented youngsters to potential embarrassment and deny them the opportunity to learn one of sport's most fundamental lessons. Simply stated, the lesson teaches anyone, young or old, that we are never failures when we work at something. Most of these youngsters find *practice* the best time to work on their skills—not the actual competition.

Parents don't experience the drills and individual attention the less-talented athletes receive during practice. Any youngster with potential will work long and hard on his or her skills during practice and, once they are actualized, will experience more actual competition. Expecting youngsters to learn the game or develop their athletic skills during competition is like expecting them to drive a car before they learn how to operate one. It simply won't happen.

As Coach Lombardi might have said, whenever we commit ourselves to a goal and work hard to achieve it, even if we don't reach it, we are not failures. Whether the goal involves winning the game or playing in the game, if we work hard to achieve it, we are not failures. Failures give up; they don't try. They accept falling short of their goals, so they avoid making an effort.

This is the purpose of sports competition, not just to win but, more fundamentally, to make the effort to win. Youngsters who learn this lesson early in life will be successful, whether they made All-State or rode the bench as seniors—whether they started for their junior high basketball teams or were members of the supporting cast. They will set goals for themselves and work hard to accomplish them. By so doing, they will never fail.

They will find satisfaction in their lives; hard work really is its own reward. People who accept it and find pleasure in it accomplish significant things in life. They may not become All-Conference players in high school or get into very many games in junior high school, but the values they learn stay with them for the rest of their lives. All coaches must teach this lesson; it constitutes the core of the relationship between player and coach.

To that end, coaches must pledge themselves to the positive development of their athletes. Figure 5-2 outlines the coach's pledge. (It is borrowed from my earlier book, *Building the Total Athlete.*) It can be read by parents to establish reasonable expectations of the people who work with their children. It can be read by the children to understand the responsibilities of this significant person who is about to enter their lives. And it can be shared by coaches at meetings with parents and young athletes to promote their understanding of the importance of a coach's responsibilities.

The coaches who read this book are encouraged to agree with the statements contained in the pledge—even the statements that require their post-season involvement with parents and athletes. Theorists everywhere are promoting consensus-building activities within all organizations. This pledge will help create consensus, the kind of mutual understanding that every relationship deserves—especially one as important as the one that exists between player and coach.

THE ATHLETE AND PARENT PLEDGE

Consensus building is a two-way street. The coach should pledge his or her responsibilities; the athlete and parent must pledge theirs. Also borrowed from my book, *Building the Total Athlete,* Figure 5-3 lists the responsibilities of athletes and asks them and their parent(s) to commit to them by signing the form. By agreeing to such statements before practice or competition, young athletes and their parents understand the expectations of the program and are more inclined to abide by them as the season progresses.

Such a procedure also meets the provisions of substantive due process and avoids legal problems if the school should have to discipline a young athlete for violation of behavioral or training rules. Each of the expectations also makes for excellent discussion during meetings early in the school year or before the season starts. All adults and most kids have learned that we can achieve consensus a lot easier before, rather than after, a problem occurs.

THE COACH'S RESPONSIBILITIES

The Coach's and Athlete's pledges involve specifics that warrant periodic reminders. To achieve the larger functions of each pledge, therefore, coaches, parents, and athletes must perform certain tasks. The following checklists are provided to coaches to remind them of these tasks. Later sections of this book provide similar checklists for parents, counselors, and athletes.

The Coach's Pre-season Responsibilities

Figure 5-4 provides a reproducible that can be taped over the coach's desk or left somewhere in the office to remind him or her of a few of the tasks that must be performed in order to provide the kind of help young athletes require if college is to be a realistic experience for them. Parents are also encouraged to notice that coaches have significant responsibilities prior to the start of the season.

Because they have so much influence over their athletes, they should instruct them—even the most talented—to conduct a college search as if they had no intentions of playing a sport in college. Nothing is more heartbreaking to a young athlete during his or her last year of high school than to incur a career-ending injury or to discover widespread disinterest from college recruiters and to have no alternatives available.

High school coaches, perhaps more than anyone else, have the power to get young athletes to regard college as an expanse of opportunities extending well beyond the field or court. Young athletes should be considering those opportunities well before competition during their senior years. The senior year is too late. They should be exploring college for its academic and career opportunities—at the latest—during the spring of the junior year. Just one word from the coach can provide the impetus parents need to get young athletes moving in this direction.

Coaches also have the task of notifying college recruiters of promising young athletes. Such a responsibility involves any player who can make a contribution to any college program, including Division III, NAIA, or junior colleges. Many coaches focus only on the very talented athletes because they attract the greatest number of recruiters. Such a tendency is understandable. What high school coach doesn't want to meet the head coach of North Carolina and eventually watch one of her players on TV vying for a National Championship?

I certainly enjoyed receiving a Certificate of Appreciation from Notre Dame and watching one of my fullbacks start thirty-three games for them, eventually becoming a captain during his senior year. But I also found comparable satisfaction in watching many of my players head for the Ivy League or a top-notch Division III school, play a sport they loved in college, and become extraordinarily successful when they left school to work and raise their families.

Consider the sample letter in Figure 5-5, therefore, as a way to introduce young athletes to selected colleges and universities during their junior year in high school. Such a letter alerts colleges to promising young athletes and encourages them to maintain contact with them over the summer and early in the senior year. At the very least, it gets the young athlete's name in the athletic program's computer and makes future contacts that much easier.

The Coach's In-season Responsibilities

The primary in-season responsibility of coaches is to promote academics. Yes, yes, I know, how can a coach with thirty-one years' experience forget that the number-one in-season responsibility is to win? Well, there's always that, too, but good coaches can do both. They can behave in ways that are consistent with their philosophies. They can deal with strategic and motivational issues in planning sessions, work the team during practice, and still assure that each athlete is satisfying his or her academic responsibilities.

Several high school athletic programs across the country have developed study halls for student athletes who fall below expected standards of achievement, usually a grade of C. These high schools also have developed referral forms like the one in Figure 5-6 that encourage teachers to comment about not only the academic but the behavioral progress of students. Needless to say, the procedure has improved the classroom performance of thousands of young athletes, and it has been appreciated by teachers who find the high school coach to be a very effective ally.

Generally, athletic study halls share the following characteristics:

- Reasons for the athlete's involvement are distributed to parents and athletes early in the school year. Usually, the eligibility requirements as established by the state and the school are used as baseline standards. The practice of sharing this information early in the year accomplishes at least three things: (1) It informs parents that they have help as they seek an academic orientation for their children; (2) it satisfies the legal need to inform parents and athletes of eligibility requirements; (3) it gets the attention of young athletes, who suddenly realize that sports involves significant academic as well as athletic responsibilities.

- Teachers are asked each week to submit forms that identify students who need the program. Generally, such early intervention prevents ineligibility and provides the resources that keep small problems from becoming big ones.

- Athletic study halls usually function on an "early-bird" basis. That is, they usually start approximately 45 minutes before the beginning of the regular school day. As such, they don't interfere with practice after school, but they do bite into early-morning sack time—just enough inconvenience to get the attention of every athlete in the school.

- Athletic study halls often involve tutors from the National Honor Society or other programs in the school that provide services. Many of these tutors are excellent role models for some of the younger athletes, particularly those tutors who are also athletes.

- Athletic study halls usually are supervised by one or more coaches who are relieved of their regular supervisory assignment during the day. Most administrators are willing to make such accommodations because of the significant PR value of such programs. Parents really like them!

- At the end of the study hall each day, the supervising coach fills out the form in Figure 5-7 to inform head coaches of the attendance and work habits of each athlete in the study hall. Athletes who miss the study hall or don't use the time profitably usually receive some extra "attention" from their coaches—the kind that motivates even the most intransigent student athlete.

- Students remain in the athletic study hall until the coach receives notification from the referring teacher that the student's achievement has improved.

This is not a big time-consumer for coaches, and it gets the job done. Those schools across the country that routinely lose young athletes to ineligibility are well advised to organize such study halls. They are also encouraged to establish liaisons with classroom teachers, who appreciate their help and who can do much to promote their programs.

Coaches must also maintain statistics during the in-season and assure press coverage and recognition for deserving athletes. In-season and post-season honors and press coverage do much to sell young athletes to recruiters. In order to handle such statistics effectively, coaches should contact the local media early each year to identify the local, state, and national records held by high school athletes in their respective sports. Such comparisons can be important to provide a sense of perspective for college recruiters.

They also are important for athletes and their parents. I know of a young basketball player who led her county in scoring for two consecutive years and enjoyed the passing attention of the local media but didn't realize that she held the county's all-time record for scoring until it was broken three years after her graduation. Her coach simply hadn't taken the time to find out or to use the information to promote her for All-State honors.

These kinds of oversights are unforgivable. Athletes deserve recognition for their efforts and can use it to find satisfying college experiences. The coach's job is to help make sure it happens.

The Coach's Post-season Responsibilities

Now is the time for the coach to share this consolidated information with colleges as well as the media. Generally, letters like the one in Figure 3-5 should be mailed to college coaches, and resumes of the athlete's individual statistics should be included. The same resume can be shared with coaches' groups and sportswriters to secure post-season honors for deserving players. Following the mailing to selected colleges, the coach should make a follow-up phone call to determine the college's interest and to discuss additional information such as highlight or skill tapes.

A sample phone conversation is provided later in this section and outlines the important topics to be covered during the discussion. This phone call may be the single most important step for the high school coach in the recruiting process, because it

- initiates a dialogue with the college
- promotes a positive relationship with the coach
- identifies the degree of his or her interest in the athlete
- provides the chance to supplement written recommendations
- clarifies the college's process for making a decision about the athlete, including time lines
- provides opportunities for future contacts that may benefit other athletes

Post-season is also the time for the coach to meet with the athlete and his or her parents to promote some sensitive but candid dialogue about the athlete's ability to play a sport in college. Figure 5-8 provides a sample letter for inviting the parents to such a meeting. This can be a very difficult meeting, not just for the athlete and his or her parents, but for the coach. During the course of a season, coaches grow so close to many of their athletes that they sometimes assess their skills unrealistically. "Thinking with your heart instead of your head" may have a place in coaching, but not when assessing the athlete's ability to play in college, and especially not when sharing such information with the parents. Our desire to want only the best for our kids sometimes results in our nudging them in the wrong direction. If Mary wants to play basketball for the University of Tennessee or Tom wants to play hockey for Notre Dame, we want them to have it. Unfortunately, this push for happiness can sometimes result in embarrassment or danger for our young athletes.

Consider this story. When a friend of mine was playing football at a major midwestern university, he bumped into one of the freshmen coaches in the library, a graduate assistant. (We played back when universities actually had freshmen teams!) After some initial small talk, the conversation went something like this:

"I hope the varsity practices are going better than ours with those freshmen."

"We're doing OK. Why? You guys having a problem?"

"Well, how about this? We have a quarterback, kind of a little kid. If I stood him in the middle of this room and told him to throw a football in any direction, he couldn't hit a wall!"

"Come on," said my friend. "No one can be that bad."

"This guy is. Word is his dad promised $100,000 to the athletic department if football gave him a scholarship."

My friend went on to tell me that the young man quit football about halfway through the season. Think about it. When all was said and done, if the son had known about the father's "good intentions," would he have been grateful? Certainly, this is an extreme story. Back then, however, it happened more often than we might expect. The point is, even the most well-meaning parents can watch their good intentions ultimately hurt their children.

Coaches, therefore, must be among the first to look at an athlete's abilities realistically, and they must help parents do the same. This meeting also is the time to discuss the following:

- The ins and outs of the recruiting process.
- Forms of financial aid beyond a possible scholarship.
- The continuing appropriateness of the student athlete's earlier list of colleges.
- The continuing appropriateness of the criteria that resulted in that list.
- The graduation rates of schools on the list and any others that are expressing interest in the student athlete.
- The possible need to include the counselor and the athletic director in future meetings.
- The responsibilities of each person in the meeting. Generally, the coach is the point person. As such, he or she can expect to be notified each time the family receives a phone call or another letter from a particular school, certainly when a decision is made. In the case of highly recruited athletes, the coach may help the family narrow the list of schools, then call each one requesting that he or she be contacted instead of the family.

In addition, one of the primary responsibilities of the family is to be cordial but noncommittal during discussions with recruiters, unless, of course, they have made a decision, in which case everyone should meet once more to discuss the decision, then conclude the process. My advice to young athletes has always been, "Don't burn any bridges behind you." I have seen too many young athletes say no to a school early in the process, only to discover later that it was their best offer.

A CLOSER LOOK AT THE FIRST MEETING

Assessing a youngster's athletic ability with the player and his or her parents involves a great deal of care. Insensitive comments at this point can compromise future relationships between the coach and the athlete and his or her family. Such insensitivity can even echo through the community and stifle any interest in sports programs. Coaches must, therefore, keep the following suggestions in mind during this first meeting:

Usually, it's a good idea to ask the athlete early in the meeting for his or her self-assessment. Earlier conversations during practice or competition have already influenced this self-assessment, so it is likely to be consistent with the coach's. In addition, young athletes tend to be surprisingly realistic about their abilities, sometimes to the point of being self-deprecating. The coach's job, therefore, is to help young athlete's and their families find a realistic balance between fantasy and self-deprecation.

Each time a young athlete's fantasy must give way to reality, however, coaches must use their opinions as prods, not bludgeons. Even when youngsters hold little athletic promise for the future, coaches must share their opinions sensitively. Whether it be leadership, hard work, or self-discipline, every youngster has evidenced *some* strength that can become a positive focus at those times when he or she must be discouraged from playing a sport in college.

Sometimes the coach should focus on a different level of competition. The exceptional student who falls short of a Division I offer can enjoy the attention of Division II or III schools and a variety of Ivy League colleges. For example, while the student and his parents were in my office, I have called one or more Division I schools that expressed moderate interest in a player to determine their exact recruiting intentions. I recall one coach telling me that they were interested in a particular young man but that he was quite far down their list of recruits.

I even handed the phone to the athlete, so he could hear the assessment directly from the coach. When he hung up, I called a couple of Ivy League schools, all of which were extremely interested in him. He eventually attended one of them, started for four years, benefited from the best education in his field, and landed a job after graduation that wouldn't have been possible had he attended the Division I school that interested him earlier.

This experience suggests the related consideration that coaches sustain a focus on the student athlete's academic program throughout the discussion with parents. Coaches from some of the least reputable academic schools in the country are among the sports world's most charismatic recruiters. They have to be. They have little else to offer young athletes but a recurring litany of compliments and sports-related promises.

Young athletes who want to play immediately in college and parents who are caught up in the intrigue of the recruiting process sometimes fall prey to their tactics. All high school athletes, highly recruited or unrecruited, are influenced more by dreams of playing in college than visions of success in the classroom. Parents sometimes allow such dreams to influence their involvement in the process.

High school coaches must not let this happen. This first meeting is the place to assure a focus on academics, which allows a more realistic look at the youngster's athletic abilities. Be sure, therefore, to mention academics early in the meeting, even to ask the athlete's parents if they share your concern that the youngster's most important decision should involve the college's educational program and available career opportunities. Such a question will set the tone and make mutual assessments of athletic ability that much easier.

Finally, at the conclusion of the meeting, be sure to document the decisions that resulted from the discussion. Take notes during the meeting and share them in substance with the family in a follow-up letter. Be sure also to list the follow-up responsibilities of each person. The athlete, for example, may have some letters to write; the coach may have some phone calls to make; the parents may want to visit the counselor to seek recommendations.

Last, the follow-up letter should identify next steps. Such specifics as college visitations, shared correspondence to and from college coaches, and future meetings should be listed, including times and dates. Recreate the meeting and document areas of agreement and disagreement. Then file the letter. Follow the same format for future meetings—with parents, the student athlete, and college coaches. Keep this principle in mind: "If you didn't write it down, it didn't happen." Lengthy disagreements about "who was going to do what" or "who said what" are avoided with proper documentation.

Looking at Such Meetings from the Parents' Perspective

The parents of student athletes must also have a well-prepared agenda when attending or requesting such meetings, especially when dealing with a high school coach who may be unfamiliar with, or resistant to, the college search process. High school coaches who are unfamiliar with the recruiting and college selection processes may react defensively to parental expectations for help, especially when such help can be so time-consuming. Parents are encouraged, therefore, to keep the following suggestions in mind when seeking such meetings with high school coaches:

Always do your homework before the meeting. If possible, bring a list of schools that satisfy the academic and career interests of the student athlete. Indicate to the coach that you already have met with the student's counselor to discuss these schools. Mention the counselor's perceptions of admissibility. If the athlete is highly recruited, solicit the coach's help to match the list with the schools that have expressed interest in him or her.

If the athlete is unrecruited, seek the coach's help to stimulate the interest of coaches from the schools listed. If the coach agrees that the youngster has the ability to play a sport in college, and if the student has good academic credentials, seek a cooperative effort to gain admission to a reputable college that will satisfy his or her athletic and academic goals.

Enter the meeting with a willingness to solicit and value the coach's opinions about the student's athletic ability. You may not agree with the opinions, but you must use them as the starting point for meaningful discussion. Whether or not high school coaches are blessed with years of accumulated knowledge, they must be treated as experts if they are to feel useful during the college selection process.

Share the student athlete's goals with the coach, then seek his or her help with ways to realize them. Student athletes are helped best when parents, coaches, and other school personnel perceive themselves as colleagues combining their skills to establish a well-organized college selection process. This "coalition" of forces can do a whole lot more for kids than individuals working separately.

KEEPING RECORDS

Good coalitions require organization. Parents, coaches, counselors, and the student athletes should keep records of meetings, phone calls, letters, and other materials related to the process. Such files should be brought to each meeting of the coalition to share relevant materials and to integrate them into discussions and future activities. Figure 5-9 provides a reproducible "Record of Contacts" that coaches and parents can use to document phone calls to and from college recruiters.

The form even provides a place to indicate the coach's *perceived* interest in the athlete. Certainly, this is only an opinion, but it can provide the substance for important discussions with others in the coalition at a future time. The section regarding the substance of the discussion is also important, especially as it relates to what others have been told by recruiters!

ALERTING COLLEGE RECRUITERS
TO THE UNDERPUBLICIZED ATHLETE

Many outstanding athletes playing for schools in remote areas of the country receive local recognition but rarely experience the kind of recruiting attention they deserve. They may be excellent athletes, but, for a variety of reasons, colleges know little about them. High school coaches may not share information routinely, or the player may be a late bloomer, only recently having developed into a college-level player. Many of them are too far removed from the mainstream of sports activity to attract attention from awards committees and recruiters.

Whatever the reasons for their lack of recognition, these athletes require help from coaches, counselors, parents, or others who feel they are qualified and deserving of consideration from university programs. Coaches are the most obvious persons to provide that help in the following ways:

- They can send letters introducing players to university programs after the junior year to encourage college coaches to watch them in the senior year.

- Sometime during the student athlete's senior year, generally in the middle of the season, they can send letters that share recent statistics, honors such as Player of the Week, continued academic excellence, leadership contributions to the team, size, strength, and speed. In the case of baseball, softball, track, and other spring sports, coaches will have to send such information before the season starts in order to initiate the recruiting process before the school year ends.

- At the conclusion of the season, they can send another letter that shares final individual and team statistics, improvements in size and speed, recommendations from opposing coaches, and an educational profile, including current GPA, test scores, and academic and career interests. Refer to Figure 5-10 for a reproducible that lists the kinds of statistics that should be shared with colleges. This particular form was shared by Libertyville High School, a midwestern school that does an excellent job with its student athletes.

- At the conclusion of the season, they can also call various university programs—such calls to be made after high school coaches meet with the athlete, his or her parents, and counselors. We will discuss the nature of this phone conversation later in this section.

- This also is the time to send videotapes of games or individual events. Generally, game videos should reveal the athlete's performance against the toughest opponents on the schedule. If the athlete has unique skills such as kicking in soccer or football, spiking in volleyball, high jumping, long jumping, or pitching, skill tapes can be sent to college coaches. Such tapes should focus on the successful performance of the skill, showing the height or length jumped, the speed of the pitch (If possible), and the distance of the kick. Skill tapes also are important for other athletes. Field hockey players use them to show the player's ability to keep the stick on the ball. Football players use them to highlight pass-receiving skills or throwing motions, basketball players for defensive agility and shooting, and so forth. Game tapes and highlight tapes can provide the important "peek at performance" that so many college coaches require to make recruiting decisions.

- Tell the college coach that you will be calling two or three weeks after the tapes have been received to discuss his or her evaluation of the player's college potential. If the athlete is obviously outstanding, the college will call, probably often! If the athlete is marginal but suggests good growth and skill potential or has a level of commitment that will guarantee success, the high school coach should call to maintain or further the college's interest. Players sometimes possess intangibles, such as unusual toughness or dedication, that must be shared with college coaches and that require more than one phone call.

- Send additional letters both from you and opposing coaches throughout the process. Also include reference to any additional honors the athlete may have received in the interim.

WHEN SOMEONE OTHER THAN THE COACH IS NEEDED

Let's face it, sometimes high school coaches fall down on the job. We have discussed this circumstance already, so we will avoid further reference now. The point is, when this happens, *someone* has to fill the void. Often, it's a parent or another school official. Unfortunately, college coaches prefer not to talk to the parents of athletes because of an obvious bias. When this becomes necessary, therefore, consider the following suggestions:

- Seek out opposing coaches who might be willing to send letters and make phone calls. They won't want to devote long hours to helping a player from another school with the recruiting process, but you'll be surprised at their willingness to provide a helping hand.

- Develop skill tapes and secure game tapes from the school to forward to college coaches. One look at superior performance on a tape can dispel suspected bias.

- Refer to Figure 5-10 for the kinds of statistics that should be shared with colleges. They can be secured from newspapers or from your school's athletic department. In the case of distances, heights, and times for individual events, be sure they are certified. Again, opposing coaches can be very helpful in this regard.

- Be sure to have your son or daughter write a letter to college coaches expressing his or her interest in playing in college. This letter can also include reference to honors and statistics.

- Make sure the letter from the student athlete includes his or her resume, which should mention height and weight, speed, strength (if appropriate), GPA, class rank, SAT and ACT test scores, educational and career goals, athletic and academic honors received, names of high school coach and guidance counselor, social security number, graduation date, and address and phone number. Sample resumes will be provided in a future section.

- The letter should also include a personal statement explaining why the student athlete wants to compete on the college level, and it should reveal as much as possible about the character and uniqueness of the athlete. The ideal letter enables college coaches to feel that they actually know the youngster and want to meet him or her.

- If necessary, contact one or more commercial organizations that help student athletes find scholarships to college. Some of these organizations are reputable and have excellent computer bases for finding schools, if you cannot rely solely on coaches and videotapes to sell young athletes to university programs.

MEETING THE NEEDS
OF FEMALE ATHLETES

Many female athletes often find themselves in circumstances similar to those of under-publicized male athletes. Their problems are further complicated by issues such as the following:

- Restricted budgets at the university level. The coaches of women's sports in college simply don't have the same opportunities to travel that many men's football and basketball coaches enjoy. A result is that they are more dependent on high school coaches for statistics and videotapes.

- These budgetary restrictions reinforce the tendency for women's college programs to recruit regionally. Although many men's programs do the same thing, the largest programs have the financial ability to travel cross-country to find and recruit promising athletes.

  This is not usually a big problem for women, unless the student athlete is interested in an educational program that is regional or plays a sport like field hockey that is generally restricted to one geographical area. If such is the case, the athlete's parents may have to finance trips to schools beyond the immediate region to facilitate the recruiting process.

- Women's programs at both the high school and the college levels tend to attract some of the least-experienced coaches. They may not be bad coaches; they simply lack the experience of other coaches in major men's sports. This inexperience affects the quality of coaching in high school and the ability of coaches to engage purposefully in the recruiting process.

- High schools also are experiencing problems finding women to coach girls' sports. A recent report in one midwestern state indicates that fewer than 50% of all girls' sports are coached by women. This is not to say that men are unqualified; they just don't provide the same kinds of role models that women provide in their respective sports.

- In spite of recurring media attention to issues like gender equity, women's sports programs still attract fewer spectators than men's sports. Some major women's sports like basketball, volleyball, track and field, gymnastics, and swimming may enjoy large crowds—particularly at championship events—but by and large, most of them don't enjoy the revenue-producing potential of major men's sports.

Women's programs struggle for a larger share of the financial pie—even for their very survival on many university campuses. This is not to say that women athletes are less talented than men. Many of them are performing at levels that were considered impossible only a few years ago. Formerly restricted to the grandstand and considered by men and women alike to be enthusiastic but comically uninformed, many women are now abandoning the sidelines for the personal satisfaction and the thrill of "getting in on the action," and they are doing it with amazing talent and style.

Helping Young Women with the Recruiting Process

All of us who are interested in the world of sports must continue to assure equality of opportunity for women who seek the same kinds of satisfactions and benefits from sports participation that their male counterparts enjoy. Coaches and parents alike can help by following recruiting procedures that are similar to those suggested for the underpublicized male athlete:

- Parents of talented young women are encouraged to videotape games and events to be shared with college recruiters at some future time. The coaches of many girls' programs in high school often fail to tape contests or individual events. Because tapes are so important for college coaches with restricted travel budgets, parents will have to supply them if their youngsters are to be recruited.

- Share newspaper clippings and other media information with college coaches, particularly if such information includes statistics and descriptions of superior performance. Such information can be very impressive.

- Maintain comprehensive statistics and certify them when possible. Parents, for example, are well advised to learn how to record athletic performance. Most high school programs have student volunteers record statistics like rebounds in basketball, spikes in volleyball, strikeouts in softball, and blocked shots in field hockey. Often, they fail to record assists in basketball and unassisted double plays in softball.

  Parents are encouraged, therefore, to learn how to take such statistics, then to volunteer their time to help during high school contests. They will feel more comfortable with the validity and the breadth of the statistics, and they will have a better chance to certify them before sharing them with college recruiters.

- Finally, coaches and parents are encouraged to help young women develop comprehensive resumes and revealing cover letters to be sent to college recruiters and to secure recommendations from opposing coaches, or officials.

Increasing numbers of women are taking to the courts, the diamonds, and the fields to experience directly the pain and pleasure of sports competition and to demonstrate not only their exceptional athletic ability but their knowledge of competitive strategy. They not only have entered the arena, therefore, they have commanded the respect of all spectators for their enthusiasm, dedication, and skill. Parents, high school personnel, and college officials must do all they can to assure continued progress in this area.

DIALOGUING WITH COLLEGE COACHES

Before we conclude this section, let's take a final look at the phone conversation between the high school and the college coach. Because this conversation is so critical within the recruiting process, high school coaches must be careful with the kinds of questions they ask and the nature of the information they provide. Figure 5-11 provides a "conversation" checklist to use each time a call is made to a college coach.

High school coaches must remember that such conversations are mutually beneficial. The young athlete will receive some kind of concession, a scholarship or admission to a top-notch school, and the coach will sign on a youngster who has the ability to help him or her win games. Because these phone calls have different purposes, let's look at two examples. The second relates to the unrecruited athlete and the first to those that are highly recruited:

"Coach Brown, Mike Koehler from Plainfield High School."

"Mike, how are you doing? It's good hearing from you."

"Nice talking to you, too. I just wanted to take a minute of your time to talk about Brian Phillips. I know you guys are interested in him and that you're talking about a visit. I had a couple of questions to toss out beforehand."

"You bet; what's on your mind?"

"Well, first of all, I'm sure you're still offering five years to the kids you bring in."

"Yeah, we are. That's policy. You know that we can't put it in writing, but we tell the kids we bring on board that they have a five-year scholarship."

"And that's what you'll be offering Brian?"

"Absolutely, I don't know if we've mentioned that already, but we certainly will."

"Well, I'll mention it to him, too, now that I've verified it with you. I also wanted to check on the quality of your petroleum engineering program. You know that Brian is interested in that field?"

"It's one of the best in the area. I'll have the engineering school send out some information to Brian."

"Good, I was going to ask that you do that. Also, what about your intentions for him? Offense? Defense?"

"Mike, he's our number-one recruited fullback. I've talked to him, and I know that's what he wants to play in college. Fortunately, that exactly what we need next year. We think we've got a match!"

"Well, that's good news. I'll pass that on to Brian, too. He has four more visits he's planning on and, as far as I know, hasn't made a decision yet, but you can bet we'll be in touch throughout the process. I know I can expect the same from your end."

"You can count on it! You know how badly we want Brian. He can do wonders for us, and I know that our school is just what he wants."

"Well, thanks, Coach. I appreciate your help and your honesty. I'm sure we'll be talking soon."

Most such conversations last a lot longer than this one. The answers from college coaches may be less predictable and generally give rise to additional conversation. This example does illustrate the need for the high school coach to determine the specifics of the scholarship offer, the quality of the academic program the athlete wants, and the college's indication of where they want to use him.

Answers other than those provided in this example provoke additional conversation and may terminate the relationship with that particular school. Most important, the college coach has provided this information to the high school coach, not just to the athlete. The more people who have answers to these questions, the more likely the college is to honor them.

Clearly, these two coaches will have more conversations. What is important for high school coaches to remember, however, is that the high schools are *helping* the colleges. The role of the high school coach is not dictated by the college coach, but is formed by the needs of the athletes, the families, and the other young athletes they represent. That role is no different when they are discussing an unrecruited player with a college coach:

"Coach Brown, Mike Koehler from Plainfield High School."

"Hi, Mike, it's good talking to you. How've you been?"

"Hangin' in there. I just wanted to take a minute of your time to let you know that I have one for you. This kid's a player and a student, just what you guys have been looking for."

"What's his name? What does he play?"

"Well, his name is Bill Morris, and he's been our starting fullback for the past two years. He's about five foot ten and weighs 205 pounds; not real fast, maybe a 4.8 forty, but a tough runner and one of the best blockers I've ever had. Are you guys in the market for a good fullback?"

"Well, it just so happens we are. Our two top fullbacks graduate at the end of this year. Does it look like this guy's going to grow any more?"

"Yeah, it sure does. His dad is only about 6 feet, but he weighs about 230 and is in pretty good shape."

"What does he look like academically? Can we get him in?"

"Without a doubt. He has a 29 composite on the ACT, a 1300 on the SAT, and is in the top ten percent of his class."

"Bill Morris, huh? You know, I think I have heard something about him. Do me a favor; can you send out tapes?"

"I'll get 'em out within the week. Coach, you're going to like this kid. Tell you what. I'll get the tapes out right away, give you time to evaluate Bill, and then give you a call to talk about your evaluation. I want to help him as much as possible. He's a top-notch student and is very interested in your school. I'll give you a call in a few weeks. How's that sound?"

"Sounds about right. That'll give us time to make our evaluation. Hey, Mike, thanks for the call; we'll talk again."

Certainly, such a conversation will be preceded and followed by letters, probably from the athlete as well as you. It also will involve sending the athlete's resume and probably forwarding a copy of the application for admission to the coach. The important thing is, this kind of conversation opens the door for good young athletes to play their sports in the kinds of colleges that satisfy their academic and career goals, maybe even schools to which they might not be admissible without sports.

Such phone conversations are critical within the recruiting process and, fortunately, are relatively easy to make. High school athletic directors must help by having phones available to coaches and budgeting the expenses for making such calls. Fortunately, the costs are more than outweighed by the public relations value the school receives when parents enjoy such a beneficial partnership with coaches.

FOLLOWING UP WHEN THE ATHLETE GOES TO COLLEGE

The relationship doesn't end when the student leaves for college. As indicated in Section 3 of this book, high school coaches can maintain valuable information about the quality of college programs by following up with former players at those schools. Figure 3-13 provides a sample letter that high school coaches can send to former athletes to secure their current perceptions of the school athletically and academically. Such information is useful for future players who may be recruited by the same school.

Figure 5-12 provides a letter requesting similar information from the college coach. I am borrowing this figure from my *Football Coach's Survival Guide* because of its relevance to the material in this section. Such a letter lets the college coach know that you maintain an interest in each of your athletes, and it encourages him or her to work closely with each of them to be able to continue recruiting your school for future prospects.

LET'S WRAP IT UP

The length of this section is the surest clue to the importance of the high school coach's involvement in the college selection process for young athletes and their families. Without the coaches, the process may realize only marginal success. Even with them, it requires careful planning and coordinated effort. Most important, the efforts of high school coaches that extend beyond the season to work closely with student athletes and their families should be appreciated.

Such involvement is time-consuming but extremely satisfying. It enables coaches not only to influence the youngster's immediate performance on the playing field or court, but to touch their lives well beyond high school, to make that "real difference" that is so important to many of us. In that regard, coaches and parents have much in common.

If they do their jobs well, both stand in the shadows while others claim the prize. Both enter the competition each day, however, with renewed enthusiasm and the stubborn desire to keep trying. We both claim our titles having no special talent, just a willingness to work hard and to assume the presumptuous responsibility of "creating others in our own image," but the rewards are great.

To illustrate, let's close this section as we started it, with a story from my friend, the professional coach. We met recently to discuss an upcoming move he was planning. We found ourselves discussing the challenges of starting a new program and of dealing with the unique problems associated with professional athletes. Predictably, he mentioned how much easier and more enjoyable it was to work with high school students. And then he said: "Most of my career has been in the pros—five world championships—and I've coached in college. But, you know, if I hadn't had those seven years in high school, I think I'd be somehow unfulfilled. You can't ever go back, so I know I probably won't coach in high school again, but I'm sure glad I had those seven years. My career wouldn't have been the same without them."

Mine wouldn't either.

Figure 5-1

LOCAL COALITIONS

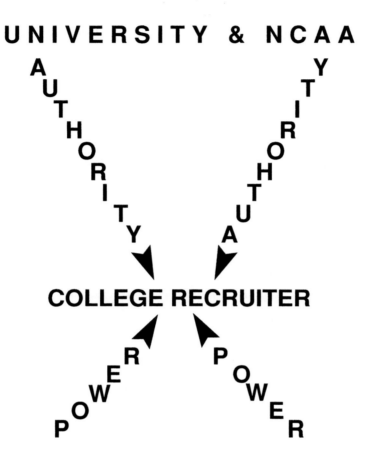

PARENTS, STUDENTS, COACHES, COUNSELORS
LOCAL COALITIONS

Figure 5-2

THE COACH'S PLEDGE

The *Coach's Pledge* extends beyond a knowledge of athletics and reaches into the life of each of his or her players. It is one of the most important responsibilities in the school and involves at least the same level of commitment that coaches expect of their players. Mutual respect and team membership are to be expected equally of player and coach and, for the coach, involve the following promises:

AS A COACH IN MY SCHOOL, I PROMISE:

1. To be a model of appropriate language and behavior.

2. To respect and dignify each of my athletes as an individual.

3. To promote the safety of each athlete and to ask no more in practice or competition than each is capable of delivering, but …

4. To promote the conditions and circumstances that encourage each athlete to realize his or her full potential.

5. To impose time demands that acknowledge the primary importance of each athlete's academic and family responsibilities.

6. To promote among all athletes and coaches a solid sense of team membership.

7. To reflect in my coaching the best and most recent thinking-strategy in my sport.

8. To assist, whenever appropriate and mutually convenient, with the post–high school planning of my players as it relates to athletics.

9. To be available to parents at times that are mutually convenient.

10. To work, whenever appropriate, with other school personnel to guarantee the best interests of each of my student athletes.

Figure 5-3

THE ATHLETE'S PLEDGE

Individual and team success in sports results from commitment. The extent to which young athletes are able to make such commitments reflects their maturity as well as their dedication to family, friends, school, and team. Your coach already has made a similar kind of commitment. You will receive a copy of it. For these reasons, we ask you to read and agree to the following *Pledge*:

AS AN ATHLETE IN MY SCHOOL, I PROMISE:

1. To be a worthy representative of my teammates and coaches, abiding by school and community expectations of my behavior and reflecting my team's values of commitment and hard work.
2. To maintain my health and fitness levels by following the training rules as prescribed by the Athletic Department.
3. To reflect the knowledge that a commitment to victory is nothing without the commitment to hard work in practice.
4. To attend every practice unless excused by my coach.
5. To understand that my future as a responsible adult relates more to my academic than my athletic activities.
6. To find the time to satisfy my family relationships and responsibilities.
7. To accept the responsibilites of team membership: cooperation, support of my teammates, shared responsibilities, positive interaction, and mutual respect.
8. To reflect good breeding by expressing my feelings and ideas intelligently and appropriately.
9. To reflect my belief that true strength involves gentleness and that even the toughest athlete is sensitive to others.
10. To behave in a way that is consistent with the philosophy that winners don't brag and losers don't make excuses.

I have read the above statements and promise to live up to them:

(Signature) _____

Date: _____

I, too, have read these statements and promise to do what I can to help my child live up to them.

(Parent Signature)_____

Date: _____

Figure 5-4

THE COACH'S RESPONSIBILITIES TO STUDENT ATHLETES

Use the following checklist to determine through the year if you have met the needs of your student athletes.

Pre-Season

DID I:

_____ Maintain updated athletic and academic statistics of college-bound student athletes?

_____ Notify appropriate colleges of student athletes who are likely to compete at their level?

_____ Tell student athletes to conduct a college search as if they had no interest in playing a sport in college? (Athletes may get injured or discover that no one is interested in them.)

In-Season

DID I:

_____ Continually update statistics of student athletes?

_____ Motivate student athletes to perform well in the classroom *and* on the field or court?

_____ Assure appropriate press coverage and other forms of recognition for deserving athletes?

Post-Season

DID I:

_____ Consolidate all statistics and forward to appropriate colleges?

_____ Meet with athlete and parents to identify schools that are consistent with athletic and academic abilities?

_____ Seek post-season honors and recognition for deserving athletes?

_____ Review with athlete and parents the NCAA bylaws regarding recruiting and financial aid?

_____ Determine graduation rates at schools on student athlete's list?

_____ Maintain contact with parents, athlete, and counselor as appropriate?

(This form is reprinted from Mike Koehler's *Football Coach's Survival Guide,* published by Prentice Hall. It also was used in the videotape, the *ABCs of Eligibility for the College-Bound Student Athlete,* marketed by the College Board.)

Figure 5-5

SAMPLE LETTER FOR ATHLETE
IN JUNIOR YEAR

Date

(Coach's Name
School
Address
City, State zip)

Dear (Coach):

Just a quick note to introduce to you Marcy Thomas, probably one of the best volleyball players in the school's history, certainly one of the best I have ever coached. Marcy is 6'0" and has a vertical jump of 32". She also has good growth potential. At the end of this year, her junior year, Marcy will be just 16 years old. She is an excellent spiker, currently holding the school record for career spikes, and, I'm pleased to say, she has another year to go!

Marcy is also an excellent student. Currently, she ranks 12 in a class of 410 with a grade point average of 3.92 on a 4.0 scale. Marcy hasn't taken her ACT or SAT tests yet but did receive a score of 68 on the verbal section of the PSAT and a 72 on the math section. In addition, her Selection Index score of 208 qualified her as a Semifinalist in the National Merit competition.

I realize that you are unable to recruit Marcy at this point; I simply wanted to introduce her to you with this letter and to offer my services to provide additional information within the next several months.

Feel free to contact me with any questions. I'll be in touch again as Marcy's career progresses. Thanks for your time.

Sincerely yours,

(Coach)

Figure 5-6

REFERRAL FORM
Athletic Study Hall

TO: *Classroom Teachers*

Please use this form to refer student athletes for remedial work to the Athletic Study Hall. Once assigned, the student will receive tutorial help to gain a better understanding of the subject matter and assistance with the completion of incomplete work. Please fill out the form completely. Someone will be in touch with you shortly after you deliver the form to discuss the specifics of the student's needs.

Thanks for your help.

Student's Name: _____

Date of Referral:_____

Please list incomplete work, including tests, quizzes, and homework:

In one or two sentences, please describe the student's classroom behavior:

Grade to date: _____ (Please deliver the form to the *Athletic Dept.*)

FOR ATHLETIC STUDY HALL USE:

     Date student assigned to study hall: _____

     Date student released from study hall: _____

     Comments:

Figure 5-7

ATHLETIC STUDY HALL
Daily Attendance and Behavior Report

Date: _____

This form is designed to provide attendance and behavioral information about the student athlete(s) who have been assigned to the Athletic Study Hall in order to improve their academic achievement. Please refer to the list for the names of any athletes in your sport, notice their attendance and behavior, and discuss either with them as appropriate.

Thanks for your help. The success of this study hall is dependent on the quality of assistance we receive from head coaches.

NAMES OF STUDENTS: **ATTENDANCE**   **BEHAVIOR**

(X = present)

Figure 5-8

SAMPLE LETTER
Invitation to Parents for Meeting

Date

(Parents' Names
Address
City, State Zip)

Dear Mr. and Mrs. _____:

The time has come for us to sit down to discuss (student's name)'s plans for college. Hopefully, (student's name) already has explored some careers and has met with (his or her) counselor to discuss colleges and identify a list that satisfies (his or her) educational and career needs. If your family has such a list, please bring it when we meet to discuss appropriate colleges. If such a list has not been developed, please have (student's name) make an appointment with (his or her) counselor to discuss this issue before we meet. The list need not be definitive, but my experience has indicated that it always provides a good starting point.

We will meet in my office at a time that is mutually convenient, probably after school because such meetings can become rather lengthy. If we require more meetings or if we need to include the counselor or anyone else, we can always meet again at a time decided at this first meeting.

Please check your calendar at home and give me a call at your convenience to arrange this meeting. Thanks for your help, and I look forward to seeing you soon.

Sincerely yours,

(Coach)
Phone: _____

Figure 5-9

RECORD OF CONTACTS

DIRECTIONS: Use this form to document phone calls to and from college recruiters. Be sure to include all relevant information and to recreate all conversations as well as possible. This documentation will be very important for future discussions with recruiters as well as during meetings with all the parties who are helping to find the appropriate college experience for the student athlete.

1. DATE OF PHONE CALL: _____

2. INITIATED BY WHOM? _____

3. NAME OF RECRUITER AND COLLEGE REPRESENTED: _____

   _____

   _____

4. SUBSTANCE OF CONVERSATION: _____

   _____

   _____

   _____

   _____

   _____

5. AS APPROPRIATE, YOUR *PERCEPTION* OF THE DEGREE OF HIS OR HER INTEREST IN THE ATHLETE: (Place a check mark on the continuum)

   Low _____ High
        1   2   3   4   5

141

Figure 5-10

ATHLETIC STATISTICS FOR COLLEGE-BOUND ATHLETES*

BASKETBALL (BOYS & GIRLS)

1. Assists (per game)
2. Rebounds
3. Free Throw Percentage
4. Field Goal Percentage (both 2 and 3 point)

BASEBALL & SOFTBALL:

1. Batting Average
2. Fielding Average
3. ERA (pitchers)
4. Won-Loss Record (Pitchers)
5. Runs Batted In (RBI)
6. Extra Base Hits
7. Stolen Bases

FOOTBALL:

1. Tackles (defensive player)
2. Assists (defensive player)
3. Sacks (defensive player)
4. Interceptions (defensive back/linebacker)
5. Fumbles Recovered
6. Yards Rushing (running back)
7. Receptions—yards, average, touchdowns (running back & ends)
8. Attempts, Completions, Total Yards, Passing/Rushing (quarterback)
9. Kickoffs—attempts, longest, average (kickers)
10. Punts—attempts, longest, average (punters)
11. Kickoff Returns—attempts, longest, average
12. Punt Returns—attempts, longest, average
13. Points Scored—touchdowns, extra points
14. Field Goals—attempts, longest, average, total points scored

SOCCER:

1. Goals
2. Assists
3. Blocked Shots

*SOURCE: Libertyville High School

142

Figure 5-10 (continued)

ATHLETIC STATISTICS FOR COLLEGE-BOUND ATHLETES*

CROSS-COUNTRY, TRACK & FIELD

1. Times and Distance
2. Distance in Field Event (shot put, discus, long jump, triple jump)
3. Height in Field Events (high jump & pole vault)
4. Major Conference, Invitational or State Places

GYMNASTICS:

1. Event & Scores
2. Major Conference, Invitational or State Places

SWIMMING:

1. Event & Times
2. Dives, Difficulty, Scores
3. Major Conference, Invitational or State Places

VOLLEYBALL:

1. Blocks
2. Assists
3. Kills
4. Aces

WRESTLING:

1. Individual Record and at What Weights
2. Season Takedowns
3. Season Reversals
4. Season Escapes
5. Season 2 point & 3 point near fall points
6. Falls
7. Major Conference, Invitational or State Places

TENNIS:

1. Record & Position
2. Major Conference, Invitational or State Places

GOLF:

1. Scores
2. Major Conference, Invitational or State Places

*SOURCE: Libertyville High School

Figure 5-11

COACH'S CHECKLIST
Phone Conversations re: Student Athletes

COACHES: Be sure to use the following checklist to guarantee that you cover all the essential topics about your student athletes during initial phone conversations with college coaches or recruiters. Then, use the "Record of Contacts" to document the substance of this and every subsequent conversation. Maintain a file. It will be very helpful when you summarize conversations for parents or before each conversation with recruiters.

ABOUT THE ATHLETE:

_____ 1. Academic motivation, including class rank and GPA *as appropriate.*

_____ 2. Size and speed, including reference to growth potential.

_____ 3. Relevant statistics regarding athletic performance.

_____ 4. Educational and career goals.

_____ 5. Special strengths, including leadership potential and commitment.

_____ 6. Special skills and/or ability to play more than one position.

ASK THE COACH ABOUT:

_____ 1. Guarantee for five-year scholarship.

_____ 2. Projected college playing position for athlete.

_____ 3. Quality of academic program of study in which athlete is interested.

_____ 4. Degree of interest in athlete.

_____ 5. His or her interest in videotapes and any follow-up procedures.

Figure 5-12

COACH'S FOLLOW-UP LETTER

Dear Coach _____,

Just a quick note to see how things are going. We're hanging in there on this end and still graduating some pretty good football players. Because one of those players is in your program, I wanted to drop you this note to see how he's doing. I remember how excited he was when you and he came to an agreement; he's been excited ever since.

Have somebody drop me a short note to let me know how he's fitting into your plans and how his schoolwork is coming. If he's falling short of the mark anywhere, I can still exert a little influence on this end!

I hope all is going well for you and your program, and if I can help you in any way, please don't hesitate to give me a call.

I look forward to hearing from you.

> With warmest regards,
>
>
> Head Football Coach

SIX

STUDENT ATHLETES AND THE HIGH SCHOOL'S SUPPORT SERVICES

First, a quick story. Several years ago, an acquaintance of mine, a high school counselor with almost thirty years' experience, found himself facing litigation. A counselee of his was one of the top soccer players in the school's history, a young man who was being courted by major universities everywhere in the country. Unfortunately, he also was a student who enjoyed pounding opposing goalies more than hitting the books.

As a result, my friend found himself constantly reminding the young man to study at night and to get the help he needed in each of his classes to improve his grade point average and class rank. He also reminded him about the NCAA's eligibility requirements, which, at that time, involved a 2.0 grade point average in a core of eleven academic units.

Like many of his colleagues, my friend met often with student athletes, generally after grades and progress reports were distributed, to count their academic credits and to provide whatever pep talk they needed to improve or, at least to maintain acceptable grade point averages. Whatever he said or did with this particular student worked, because the young man had a 2.1 grade point average when graduation time rolled around.

They ran into a problem in the spring of the student's senior year. The counselor had assumed that a consumer economics course satisfied the high school's interpretation of the NCAA's core curriculum. It did not. What followed was the family's realization that their child was academically ineligible, a series of meetings with the parents and the school's administration to resolve the situation, the sudden disinterest of college recruiters, and the parents' decision to sue the counselor and the school.

WHAT IS THE COUNSELOR'S ROLE REGARDING STUDENT ATHLETES?

The parents didn't win the law suit, but the situation provoked lengthy discussion throughout the school, particularly in guidance department meetings, where counselors heard each other resurrecting claims of not being all things to all people and questioning the scope of their responsibilities with student athletes. This is not the first group of counselors to ask such questions. The relatively recent introduction of new NCAA eligibility requirements and the growing predictability of their change has provoked parents, students, and coaches to ask the same questions.

Finding answers to such questions is not easy. Parents and students must ultimately be responsible for abiding by the eligibility and recruiting requirements of the NCAA. Certainly, coaches must be aware of them when asked to assist student athletes and their families with the college selection process. But counselors, more than anyone else in the school, are expected to be the resident experts regarding high school course selection and its relationship to life after high school. How do counselors satisfy such an expectation when NCAA regulations are subject to annual change? They can answer this question in several ways, but two responses in particular have been tried in many schools.

Finding a Solution

One solution is to have individual counselors maintain files of NCAA information, try to familiarize themselves with it, and refer to it as needed when meeting with a student athlete who wants to play in college. This solution has several advantages. It characterizes the counselor as a generalist who has broad knowledge of college requirements, and it underscores his or her indispensability to all students. It also spreads the responsibility of advising young athletes to all counselors and provokes a sharing of information and ideas within the department. Finally, it enables the department chair to conduct in-service activities regarding intercollegiate athletics that are relevant to every member of the department.

The obvious disadvantage of such a process is that it adds yet another area of responsibility to a group of professionals who find their jobs expanding each time changes are made in state and federal, let alone NCAA, legislation. The task of keeping up with NCAA bylaws is significant, especially considering, when all is said and done, that it affects such a small percentage of students in the counselor's caseload.

An alternative that has found favor in some schools is the identification of one counselor, usually also a coach, to handle referrals involving student athletes who actually plan to play a sport in college. The counselor usually is given a reduced load to handle such referrals and, in effect, becomes the school's resident expert on the NCAA, other regulatory organizations, and the realities of college athletics.

Although apparently feasible, this solution is usually ineffective. Most schools don't enjoy the financial luxury of assigning all student athletes to one counselor. Normally it involves a reduction in the caseloads of all the other counselors, a practice that curls the toes of budget-minded administrators. It also involves logistical problems. Most youngsters and their parents don't realize that college athletics is a viable option until they become juniors or seniors in high school.

By then, the academic die is cast. All the important decisions involving NCAA legislation have been made, and the student athlete has all but finalized his or her transcript. Counselor involvement is most important during the student's freshman and sophomore years when academic decisions are being made and when coursework is being completed. Because many schools involve up to 60% of their students in interscholastic athletics, they can't expect one, two, or even three counselors to be responsible for all of them.

A more realistic alternative is to have one counselor responsible for gathering and distributing information to other counselors, organizing informational meetings for young athletes and their parents, and being available to answer very general questions about intercollegiate athletics. The school's administration might accommodate this additional responsibility by paying the counselor an extracurricular stipend or freeing him or her from one or more supervisory responsibilities.

Such an alternative maintains the involvement of every counselor in the school with every young athlete. Even the noncollege-bound athletes experience the pressures of competition and an occasional overemphasis on winning, and they may be the *most* unrealistic about future sports participation. Working with young athletes, then, as suggested in Section 3, involves much more than assisting the college-bound or the marginally talented youngster. It involves every young athlete who commits himself or herself to sports competition.

The remainder of this section, therefore, considers counselors as generalists and assumes that all counselors will work with the student athletes in their caseloads. Such a task may be burdensome, but the involvement of all counselors guarantees an important sharing of information and identifies all counselors as valuable resources to their students. To provide such a service, counselors are dependent on the school's athletic department, specifically the athletic director.

STUDENT ATHLETES AND THE SCHOOL'S ATHLETIC DIRECTOR

Athletic directors play a vital role in the high school's interscholastic program. Too often perceived as keepers of the financial flame and schedule makers, athletic directors often find themselves painted into an organizational corner, trying desperately to expand their responsibilities beyond their offices and the equipment room. They realize, as department heads, that they are as responsible for student learning as anyone in the academic wing and that their programs influence the lives of a significant majority of kids in their schools.

College-bound student athletes constitute a much smaller percentage in schools but involve a disproportionate amount of the AD's time. Much of that time should be devoted to sharing information about the eligibility and recruiting requirements of the NCAA and other regulatory organizations, and it should involve occasional meetings with the guidance department to coordinate the efforts of the two programs.

Consider, for example, a sports-minded youngster's reaction to being cut from a team. Such rejection can be devastating to the social and personal adjustment of many adolescents. Athletic directors, therefore, should send the names of students who have been cut from athletic teams to the guidance department for distribution to the counselors of the children. Figure 6-1 provides a reproducible. Follow-up meetings between the counselor and the student can help put athletic involvement in the proper perspective and provide the support the student needs to either reaffirm his or her willingness to try again or find an alternative activity.

NCAA updates, as provided in Figure 2-4, maintain the information counselors, coaches, parents, and others need to help young athletes plan for future sports competition. Such information, provided concisely and conveniently, is easily filed by counselors and coaches and provides quick reference to important information each time they work with young athletes and their parents.

Circulating such information is only the first step in alerting others in the school to eligibility and recruiting regulations and in sensitizing them to the developmental needs of young athletes. Athletic directors must also

- Publicize an open-door policy to everyone in the building, especially to young athletes, who can benefit from an increased involvement with them.

- Distribute to coaches and counselors the pamphlets and forms that are provided by the NCAA at the start of each school year regarding eligibility requirements and such specifics as the Clearinghouse. In addition to those provided, materials can be secured from the NCAA by writing:

NCAA Publications
6201 College Blvd.
Overland Park, Kansas 66211-2422

- Meet with Varsity Clubs and other student organizations to promote a knowledge of eligibility and recruiting regulations, to discuss sports competition from an adult perspective, and to emphasize the school's training rules and the value of academics. Athletic directors can influence young athletes significantly during such meetings by de-emphasizing the "win-at-all-costs" mentality and looking at sports as an important but supplementary learning experience during high school.

- Attend occasional meetings with other departments, especially the guidance department, to provide and explain updated information, to answer questions about NCAA legislation, and to promote sports as activities that complement, not obscure, the learning experiences of young athletes.

- Meet periodically with parent organizations, other than booster clubs, to alert parents to the realities of intercollegiate *and* interscholastic athletics. The principal's parent advisory committee and community groups such as Women's Clubs and Optimist's Clubs provide excellent forums for such discussions.

- Set aside time during scheduled coaches' meetings to review legislation of the NCAA and other regulatory organizations and to discuss changes as well as their implications for working with student athletes and their families.

- Regularly attend meetings with department chairs and other building administrators to represent coaches and young athletes during school planning activities. In fact, where excluded from the school's administrative hierarchy, athletic directors are encouraged to seek department chair status in the building. Athletic directors contribute as much, sometimes more, than anyone else in the building to the total development of students.

- Organize individual meetings with head coaches, perhaps once each semester, as an element in their total supervision to encourage them to reach out to college-bound athletes and their parents during the college selection process. During such meetings, discuss responsibilities and strategies with them and reaffirm such involvement as an essential part of their roles as coaches within the building.

Athletic directors complement the work of coaches, counselors, and others in the building by being available resources whenever sports-related information and discussion are appropriate for school personnel or parents. As indicated elsewhere in this book, they are central figures in the coalitions that are developed to assist young athletes with their transitions from high school to college. That everyone in these coalitions "speaks the same language" is essential.

SPEAKING THE SAME LANGUAGE: A GLOSSARY OF SPORTS TERMS

The athletic director probably is primarily responsible for providing information such as that included in Figure 6-2, "Important Terms." The glossary includes definitions of everything from "agents" and "blue-chippers" to "visits" to college campuses and "waivers" of the requirements of bylaw 14.3. It provides information regarding the NCAA's Clearinghouse and the "Student Release Form" and outlines the provisions of bylaw 14.3 as well as financial aid and recruiting restrictions.

The glossary is equally appropriate for parents, student athletes, coaches, and counselors. It contains valuable information about intercollegiate athletics and promotes a common language among everyone involved in helping high school athletes make the transition to college. Athletic directors should distribute it to counselors and coaches early in the school year and make it available to parents and young athletes as needed, probably whenever informational meetings are held.

THE COUNSELOR'S RESPONSIBILITIES

Like coaches, counselors have pre-season, in-season, and post-season responsibilities. Figure 6-3 provides a checklist that reminds counselors of the essential tasks they must perform at key times in the student athlete's high school career. These tasks must be performed for every young athlete who plans to continue his or her sports involvement in college.

The Counselor's Pre-season Responsibilities

One of the primary responsibilities for counselors who work with college-bound athletes is to assure their compliance with NCAA eligibility requirements. They can do this each time they meet with a student and parents to discuss registration decisions for the coming school year. To assure such compliance, counselors are dependent on the information provided by the school's athletic director, another reason for ongoing dialogue between the athletic and guidance departments.

Counselors must also encourage young athletes to explore potential careers by taking career inventories and having them interpreted by qualified persons and by developing a list of colleges that provide preparation for such careers. This is not to suggest that all high school students are prepared to make decisions about future careers, but at least they should explore their interests, improve their understanding of the occupational and career opportunities that are available to them, and identify the colleges that provide the variety they might need to accommodate several potential careers.

The Counselor's In-season Responsibilities

This is the time for counselors to check the academic progress of student athletes to assure future college eligibility. Most schools send notices of unsatisfactory progress to parents in the middle of grading periods. Anyone who has camped out in a counseling office for more than a few weeks realizes that some students find ingenious ways to intercept such notices before Mom and Dad see them. Counselors are advised, therefore, to call the parents of students who are in danger of failing or otherwise falling short of meeting eligibility requirements.

Ultimately, students who are having academic problems should accompany their parents to a meeting with the counselor. Generally, such meetings should be arranged with the parents and should be used to review eligibility requirements and to reaffirm college as an academic experience. Because coaches are especially influential with young athletes and can supplement the counselor's advice with relevant stories and suggestions, they should be invited to attend such meetings, particularly with student athletes who are having serious academic problems.

Counselors should also encourage student athletes to join their classmates processing college applications. As indicated earlier in this book, even the most highly recruited athletes can injure themselves during the season and suddenly need to adjust their plans for the future. This is a tough enough time for kids; it is *not* the time to suddenly start asking significant questions about future careers and appropriate college programs.

We hope that all young athletes in high school will realize their dreams and have the time to decide which of several college scholarship offers is best for them; however, such a possibility is unlikely for most youngsters. Some will be injured; others will realize at the end of the season that recruiters suddenly have lost interest.

Whatever the reason, student athletes should be encouraged by their parents as well as their counselors to apply to one or more colleges that satisfy their special requirements sometime early in the senior year. If something adverse should happen, at least the student will be prepared to get on with the rest of his or her life while adjusting to a future without organized sports.

Finally, for students who can continue playing a sport in college, counselors must encourage them to complete the "Student Release Form" from the Clearinghouse (Figure 2-6) to initiate the recruiting process. Students should be encouraged to meet with their counselors and coaches to discuss sections on the form before mailing it. The highly recruited athlete, for example, may want to select option 2 on the form to restrict the number of colleges that have access to his or her academic information. Less recruited athletes may want to select option 1. Each of these options should be discussed in a meeting with the coach and, probably, the counselor.

The Counselor's Post-season Responsibilities

This is the time to arrange meetings with coaches to discuss athletes who are eligible for athletic scholarships and to develop strategies for the highly recruited athletes. Some college coaches still try to sidestep the NCAA Clearinghouse by finagling information from counselors and other school personnel. Counselors must be aware of such tactics and avoid them, then inform the appropriate coach. Coaches can use such information when helping young athletes make decisions about the right college program.

This is also the time to talk to coaches about the less-recruited athletes who may be able to use their academic achievement to qualify for admission to highly selective schools. These students also require well-coordinated strategies, somewhat different from those for the highly recruited athletes but every bit as important. Finally, the school may have several athletes who want to play in college but have to seek admission to NCAA Division II or III programs, NAIA schools, or junior colleges.

Counselors and coaches have to devote equal time to them. Less-recruited athletes often require more time than highly recruited players because it takes more time to "sell" them to college coaches. Usually, more phone calls are required, and the coach and player must develop skill and highlight videotapes that exhibit the athlete's ability to play in college. Letters of recommendation from a variety of people are also important.

Sometimes the superior academic qualifications of less-recruited athletes will help them gain admission to some of the best schools in the nation. As indicated elsewhere in this book, I have worked almost every year with one or more Ivy League schools that have expressed interest in good athletes who also are outstanding students. Such students may not be good enough athletically to be highly recruited or strong enough academically to gain admission to an Ivy League school without their sports, but the combination of the two often results in admission and a uniquely rewarding college experience for qualified *student* athletes.

When working with such athletes, coaches and counselors must remember what the Ivy League schools and other selective colleges sometimes refer to as the "squeeze play." Some young athletes who are interested in selective schools may also be offered scholarships to other schools and asked to sign the National Letter of Intent. The Letter of Intent must be signed in some sports, usually those offered in the fall and winter months, prior to the official notification of admission by most Ivy League schools, which normally send letters of acceptance early in the spring of the year.

This process places some athletes in a bind, wondering if they should sign the Letter of Intent in late winter or hope to gain admission to the Ivy League school of their choice in early spring. Many of the Ivy League schools have accommodated this problem by informing qualified young athletes that they have been placed on the athletic department's "priority list," a list of high school athletes who qualify for admission and special consideration from admissions officers.

Ivy League sports programs, like most others in the country, seek to maintain a good relationship with their offices of admissions; they refuse to include on their priority lists, therefore, the names of youngsters who may be superior athletes but who clearly fall short of admissions criteria. Coaches and counselors are well advised, therefore, to recommend to Ivy League and other selective schools only those athletes who have both the athletic and the academic ability to compete against some of the finest athletes as well as some of the strongest students in the country.

Finally, counselors must make a final check of the transcripts of senior student athletes near the end of the first semester to make whatever changes are necessary for the second semester. Failure in one or more courses or inappropriate planning may have resulted in the inability to meet NCAA eligibility requirements. Registration changes may have to be made for the second semester to guarantee compliance.

At such times, it's normally a good idea to have others in the building (the athletic director, the athlete's coach, and the college counselor) check the transcript for accuracy and compliance with eligibility standards, then meet with the student's parents to review it once more and secure their signature(s) on the form provided in Figure 6-4. Such a process removes the onus of responsibility from one person, the counselor, and spreads it among everyone involved in the coalition.

Counselors can then put the form in the student's file for future reference and, depending on the preferences of others in the coalition, forward copies, especially to the athlete's parents. The more the recruiting process is regarded by everyone as a shared responsibility, the more successful it will be and the less likely it will be to involve misunderstandings and disagreements.

STUDENT ATHLETES AND THE COLLEGE CONSULTANT

Any discussion of open communication and shared responsibility must include the high school's college counselor, if it has one. College counselors are specialists in college identification and selection and can provide valuable insights during the athletic recruitment and college search processes. They should be included in coalition activities, especially during early meetings, when career objectives and academic programs are being explored by the athlete and his or her parents.

College counselors can

- provide easy reference to a wide range of college resource materials
- suggest interest inventories and career materials that promote a broader understanding of the purpose of college
- invest the college identification and selection processes with a strong sense of credibility for parents
- discuss the relative quality of different colleges and universities regarding specific academic and career programs
- provide unique insights into most colleges and their surrounding communities, including recreational and cultural opportunities, dorm life, fraternity and sorority activities, and even the ethnic composition of the student body

- capitalize on personal relationships with college admissions officers to promote the admissibility of marginal students

No one else in the school or community offers similar expertise—not even the school's most experienced counselor. Most college counselors visit scores of colleges and universities every year, so they have firsthand knowledge of the unique characteristics of the schools and personal relationships with key persons in the admissions offices. They are valuable resources when young athletes, parents, counselors, and coaches seek knowledgeable information about certain schools.

RECOGNIZING THE JUNIOR COLLEGE AS A REALISTIC ALTERNATIVE TO FOUR-YEAR SCHOOLS

Some high school athletes fall short of the physical or academic requirements of four-year schools; they fail to study appropriately or don't have the academic talents of their classmates, or they have yet to realize their full growth potential. Whatever the reasons, these students often require a junior college to improve their academic or athletic capabilities and to prepare for admission to a four-year school.

Other students are interested in two-year programs that provide excellent career opportunities and obviate the need for a four-year school. Such students are advised to attend junior colleges to satisfy their educational and career interests and play their sports on the college level. Counselors and college counselors can identify several schools that can provide such opportunities. They are sometimes the best match for youngsters who seek specialized training in vocational or career-oriented programs.

As mentioned in Section 2, admission to junior colleges is relatively easy compared with the requirements of most four-year schools, and they offer a wide range of athletic programs. Most of these programs involve excellent athletes, many of whom will transfer to major college programs. They also provide championship competition and annually award national championships in a variety of sports. They are excellent opportunities for many athletes who, for whatever reason, must seek alternatives to four-year schools.

HELPING STUDENT ATHLETES FIND THE RIGHT INFORMATION

How do young athletes and their parents find the information that enables them to make decisions regarding a junior college or the right four-year school? They follow Art Costa's advice by knowing what to do when they don't know what to do! They follow the right process by scheduling a preliminary meeting with the counselor and the coach to discuss their athletic and academic potential and to identify the range of college and career resources available to them.

Trusting the right process is essential if young athletes and their parents want to find answers to very difficult questions, and the right process must involve the counselor and the coach, the two people in the school who have the knowledge and the concern to be most helpful. In most schools, their knowledge is complemented by a wide range of additional resources:

- Many schools have college or career resource rooms that contain a variety of college materials: catalogues, bulletins, videotapes, vertical files, and volunteers who can assist students with the search process.

- Others have computer programs that print out lists of schools that match the unique qualifications of students.

- Some communities have private college consultants who meet with students and their parents to match students with colleges or universities that satisfy their educational, career, social, and personal requirements.

- Most athletic departments have materials from the NCAA and other regulatory organizations that explain eligibility requirements, scholarship opportunities, and ways to contact the organization for additional information.

The process will span several months; the initial identification of colleges should be done in the junior year, probably without much input from the coach. This is the time when student athletes and their parents focus on their status as students and consider a college experience irrespective of their athletic goals.

Later, probably after the final season of competition or, for athletes in spring sports, during the middle of the year, athletes and their parents should meet with the counselor and the coach to focus on the athletic as well as the academic opportunities of the college experience. The resources available through the school should be used throughout this process. One additional resource might even be considered.

STUDENT ATHLETES AND COMMERCIAL "SCHOLARSHIP FINDERS"

For the past several years at conventions and presentations throughout the country, I have emphasized that for every abused college athlete, there are a high school coach and counselor in the athlete's background who didn't do their jobs. Invariably, an abused student athlete goes to the wrong college or to the right college for the wrong reasons. Whenever this happens, the high school coach and the counselor failed to involve the athlete and his or her parents in the appropriate college selection process.

Whenever such a process is unavailable to athletes and their parents in the high school, they may look to college recruiters or other outside sources for the help they need. The clear bias of most college recruiters makes them undesirable as an exclusive source of information! Unfortunately, the limited services offered by some schools have created a void of information regarding the college search and selection processes for young athletes, and commercial organizations have filled it.

Predictably, many of these organizations are interested primarily in making money. They are interested in finding scholarships for young athletes, irrespective of the athlete's educational and career goals. Less reputable commercial organizations allow parents to believe mistakenly that all colleges provide fundamentally similar educational experiences and that distinctions among them are unnecessary. Parents who accept such services tend to believe that any college will be satisfactory and that the scholarship service will relieve the financial burdens that loom so large in the family budget. Fortunately, this is not true of all of them. Some recognize the academic needs of young athletes and try to work with families to find not just a scholarship but the appropriate college experience for the youngster. No matter how good the service, however, it will be unable to match the service provided by your high school personnel. Parents are encouraged, therefore, to start the process in their local high schools, where everyone has the best interests of young athletes at heart.

In those few instances where the high school provides inadequate services, parents may have to contact a commercial organization. I do not recommend any organization specifically but do suggest several criteria to keep in mind when making a selection:

- The organization should be relatively inexpensive, $300 to $500 being a reasonable maximum fee.

- All their informational materials should emphasize the importance of academics, including reference to ACT and SAT scores, class rank and grade point average, and educational and career goals, plus any other considerations that are important to the athlete, such as ethnic composition of the student body or size of the school.

- They should have a broad computer base, providing access to a wide number of colleges and universities. Some commercial organizations have computer access to as many as 2,000 colleges and universities; others are regional in their approach.

- The initial meeting with the representative of the organization should reveal genuine concern about the athlete as a total person, including his or her academic, social, personal, and religious needs. If the representative talks only about scholarships and financial aid, no matter how important such issues may be for the family budget, the service is not designed to meet the total needs of the athlete.

Again, some commercial organizations provide a worthwhile service. They may be important in their own right or they may be an important supplement for the high school coach who may maintain only regional or local contacts with college recruiters. College recruiters, like most hunters, tend to be territorial. So do high school coaches. The computer base of a reputable commercial organization may provide the needed broader picture.

ACCOMMODATING THE NEEDS OF THE STUDENT ATHLETE WITH LEARNING DISABILITIES

Athletes with learning disabilities require special attention. First of all, they require the assistance of coaches and counselors who recognize that they can be as successful in college as any other student, given the right program and the assistance they may need to compensate for their learning interferences. I had the good fortune over the years to enjoy the significant contributions of several athletes with learning disabilities.

All that was required of us as coaches was to make concessions to how such athletes learn, perhaps engaging them in every phase of modality learning to assure their understanding of our instruction. Some of them had short-term verbal memory loss, so we showed them the skills required and then walked them through each one. In the process of accommodating the needs of athletes with learning disabilities, our coaching staff discovered that *all* kids learn best when each of their modalities is engaged in the learning. It was a good experience for us as well as the kids.

Next, they require the kinds of programs in college that satisfy their learning needs. Students with learning disabilities learn as well as other students, often better because of their motivation and natural intelligence, but they require special programs in high school and in college that enable them to develop compensatory skills to promote immediate and lifelong learning. Some colleges have excellent programs; others have none. The college search and selection processes must include this very important consideration.

It must also acknowledge the existence of waivers and exceptions to the eligibility requirements of the NCAA and other regulatory organizations. The NCAA, for example, provides for council-authorized waivers to bylaw 14.3 "based on objective evidence that demonstrates circumstances in which a student's overall academic record warrants the waiver of the normal application of [regulation 14.3]. Such waivers must be initiated by a member institution that officially has accepted the student athlete for enrollment as a regular student."

Student athletes with learning disabilities may warrant such waivers, given the circumstances of their academic experiences in high school. Because each situation is different, coaches, counselors, and parents are encouraged to discuss such possibilities with college recruiters and the NCAA. Contact the NCAA for additional general or specific information by calling 913-339-1906 and asking for Legislative Services.

COLLEGE COACHES
AND HIGH SCHOOL PERSONNEL

Some college recruiters reflect an insensitivity that could distress Attila the Hun. After months of active recruitment, they can drop a young athlete faster than a baby can fumble a football. They can send folders full of letters, questionnaires, publicity materials, and informational brochures that convince students of their interest and, when the actual recruiting process begins, never contact them again. Such circumstances pose special problems for high school personnel and the parents of the athletes involved.

When these youngsters are dropped, someone had better be there when they fall. They can "hit bottom" so dramatically that it takes months to recover. Few adults handle rejection well—some teenagers not at all. Because the realization of our goals is a measure of our success, an adolescent's failure to realize one so significant as playing in college can provoke depressive reactions in many young athletes.

Counselors, especially, must be available to high school athletes when they experience such rejection. Certainly, their parents can provide support, and so can their coaches, but their counselors have the kind of training and experience that best qualifies them to deal with high school athletes who suddenly find themselves with no prospects for playing in college. This is just another reason for coaches and counselors to stay in contact throughout the recruiting process.

Finally, coaches must stay in touch with recruited athletes and their parents to assess the quality of treatment they have received from college coaches. High school coaches want to know if college personnel are abrupt, uncommunicative, or generally unresponsive to phone calls and letters. All recruiters are sensitive to the needs of the young athletes they actively recruit, but they sometimes can be unresponsive to athletes, parents, and even high school coaches when they are only moderately interested in a young athlete.

When this happens, high school coaches want to mention such behaviors to the recruiters. Generally, the recruiter will get the message, particularly if he or she wants to recruit athletes at the high school again at any time in the future. If the message does happen to go unheeded, a letter or phone call to the college's head coach will resolve the situation. His or her job is dependent on the recruiting tactics of assistant coaches and such feedback generally is appreciated.

LET'S WRAP IT UP

The 1983 NCAA Convention in San Diego, California, tackled an issue that, to this day, has yet to be resolved in the minds of some college coaches across the country. Many of them still roll up their sleeves and put on the gloves whenever anyone mentions intercollegiate eligibility requirements. Although other issues are involved, their arguments against raising eligibility standards focus ostensibly on its discriminatory effect on minority athletes.

A legitimate consideration, such discrimination affects not only socially and educationally disadvantaged athletes but the schools to which they might have applied. In essence, tougher eligibility requirements prevent many youngsters from pursuing intercollegiate athletics as viable postsecondary options, thereby reducing the pool of talented athletes available to recruiters. All those coaches prepared to "duke it out" on behalf of minority students, therefore, are concerned as much with their own programs as with the kids they represent.

No, I'm not condemning their duplicity, because most of them are reasonable people, convinced that they are fighting the good fight—an effort to help the socially disadvantaged. In many instances, that's exactly what they do—provide doors to futures that, under other circumstances, are closed to disadvantaged young athletes. No matter how sensitive or reasonable their arguments, however, the phrase "athletic parity" continues to echo long after they have finished talking.

Consider just one sport. There are approximately 300 Division I men's basketball programs in this country. Assuming that each school awards an average three scholarships a year, almost 1,000 young athletes will be signed by major basketball programs. The scramble to sign the best 50 to 100 high school basketball players in the country is intense. As indicated already in this book, "blue-chippers" are few and far between and inevitably attract swarms of college coaches.

Tougher eligibility standards further reduce this pool of athletes from which to draw. Coaches who *really are* concerned about missed opportunities for minority athletes, therefore, must also entertain visions of missed opportunities for their basketball programs. "Athletic parity" has been a recurring phrase in NCAA history for decades, and it's still an issue today.

If "academic integrity" is to parallel the rise of "athletic parity" in college, therefore, high school counselors and coaches will have to assure it. Counselors assure it when they take a more active role in meeting with student athletes, their parents, and coaches to discuss the role of sports in education. They assure it when they work hand in hand with coaches to promote the value of academics. And they assure it when they promote processes that inform high school athletes and their parents of NCAA and admissions requirements and that assist them with the college identification and selection processes.

They assure academic integrity when they use their influence on highly recruited athletes to steer them away from colleges with low graduation rates and watered-down courses. As mentioned in the previous section, many high school coaches already instruct college recruiters to contact them before calling a highly recruited player's home. They run interference for the families of blue-chippers who are likely to be barraged by phone calls and requests for visits. Impressionable players and parents are sometimes easily misled by recruiting tactics. Counselors must work with coaches to help these families make decisions that are as important as any they will make during high school.

Most important, counselors and coaches must gain access to information regarding college programs in order to distinguish the good from the bad. Then, working closely with their students, they must answer questions involving graduation rates, number of years to earn a degree, time commitments in and out of season, living arrangements, insurance coverage, and placement possibilities after graduation. Only high school counselors can provide this kind of objectivity for their students.

Fortunately, NCAA legislation requires college athletic programs to share their graduation rates with the public. Bylaw 14.3 continues, therefore, to impose reasonable expectations on all college-bound student athletes. Additional legislation now imposes expectations on the colleges to get their houses in order. We are moving in the right direction.

Even if some college coaches continue to disregard the most fundamental needs of freshmen athletes in the name of "athletic parity," therefore, high school counselors and coaches can let them know that someone is watching. It may seem like the tail wagging the dog, but at least the kids who play with it will be safer.

Figure 6-1

TO COUNSELORS:
For Your Information

The following list contains the names of students who recently were cut from one of our teams. We tried to accommodate as many of them as possible, but equipment and facilities limitations required that we limit the number of athletes on the team. Some of these students may require watching. You could be very helpful if some of the students on the list are unable to adjust to the coach's decision to cut them. Please intervene where appropriate—and thanks for your help.

TEAM:

COACH'S NAME:

NAMES OF STUDENTS:

Figure 6-2

IMPORTANT TERMS FOR COACHES, COUNSELORS, AND ATHLETES

If you are involved in the transition from high school to college sports or you assist student athletes with that transition, you may encounter some unfamiliar terms. It is important that you understand these terms in order to promote the transition and to avoid possible violations of NCAA requirements. Read the following list to familiarize yourself with significant terms and review it as appropriate before meetings or phone conversations. For more detailed information, refer to the *NCAA Guide for the College-Bound Student Athlete.* Copies are available in the Athletic and Guidance Offices.

1. *Agents*—High school and college athletes are in violation of NCAA rules if they agree (orally or in writing) to be represented by an agent while in high school or college.

2. *All-Star games*—High school athletes are permitted to participate in only two all-star games per sport.

3. *Blue-chipper*—A "blue-chipper" is any exceptionally gifted high school athlete who is being recruited by a significant number of major colleges.

4. *Booster*—High school athletes may not be contacted by boosters (persons who represent a school's athletic interests) or alumni for purposes of promoting their selection of certain schools. This restriction does not apply, however, to alumni who contact students as part of the college's regular admission program for all prospective students.

5. *Bylaw 14.3*—The NCAA legislation for Division I and II colleges (formerly Proposition 48) that requires high school student athletes to satisfy the provisions of a specific core curriculum, a minimum grade point average, and minimum ACT or SAT scores in order to participate in college sports. Bylaw 14.3 also specifies graduation from high school. Refer to other terms in this glossary for specific information.

6. *Clearinghouse*—The Clearinghouse is an extension of the NCAA coordinated by ACT to determine the eligibility of high school student athletes to be recruited and ultimately scholarshipped by athletic programs in Division I and II colleges and universities.

7. *Contacts*—Any face-to-face meetings between a college coach and you or your parents. High school athletes may not be contacted off the college campus on or before July 1 following the completion of their junior year. Refer to the *NCAA Guide for the College-Bound Student Athlete* for information regarding the number of contacts permitted.

8. *Core Curriculum*—A provision of bylaw 14.3 that requires student athletes to complete an academic program of at least 13 academic units, consisting of at least 3 years of English, 2 of mathematics, 2 of social studies, 2 of natural or physical science (including at least 1 lab class, if offered by the high school), 2 additional academic courses, and 2 more from the above or foreign language, computer science, philosophy, or nondoctrinal religion. Effective August 1, 1996, students first entering college will be expected to complete a core curriculum of 13 academic units, including 4 years of English. In addition, the 2 years of math must involve algebra and geometry.

Figure 6-2 (continued)

IMPORTANT TERMS FOR COACHES, COUNSELORS, AND ATHLETES

9. *Drug policies*—Each academic year, student athletes are required to sign a drug-testing consent form at the time of reporting for practice or prior to the Monday of the college's fourth week of classes, whichever occurs earlier. Anyone who tests positive during routine testing is ineligible for further participation, subject to appeal for reinstatement.

10. *Financial aid*—Student athletes who have met the requirements of Bylaw 14.3 may receive financial aid from the college that includes tuition and fees, room and board, and books. See the *NCAA Guide for the College-Bound Student Athlete* regarding the specifics of aid in other circumstances.

11. *Letter of Intent*—The National Letter of Intent is administered by the Collegiate Commissioners Association and involves a commitment from the student athlete to attend a specific school. For detailed information, contact the conference offices of the colleges of interest. It also is important not to sign an institutional or conference letter of intent prior to the National Letter of Intent signing date.

12. *Minimum College Admissions Scores*—Bylaw 14.3 requires that all student athletes score a minimum composite of 17 on the ACT and combined 700 on the SAT with a grade point average of 2.0 on a 4.0 scale. Effective August 1, 1995, these minimum scores will require a grade point average of 2.5 on a 4.0 scale. See "Sliding Scale" in this glossary.

13. *NAIA*—the National Association of Intercollegiate Athletics normally represents smaller schools but does provide financial aid for athletic purposes. Student athletes must meet two of the following three requirements: achieve an 18 on the ACT or a 740 on the SAT; earn an overall grade point average of 2.0 on a 4.0 scale; graduate in the top half of the class.

14. *NCAA*—The National Collegiate Athletic Association is the primary regulatory organization for intercollegiate athletics. Information can be secured from them by writing NCAA, 6201 College Blvd., Overland Park, Kansas 66211-2422, or by calling 913-339-1906.

15. *NCAA Divisions*—The NCAA is composed of three divisions. Division I is normally considered the "major college" division, the big schools that attract considerable media attention. These are the schools that give full scholarships and engage in widespread recruiting. Division I-AA schools are somewhat smaller, recruit on a smaller scale, and give fewer full scholarships but a sizable number of partial scholarships. Division II schools are similar to Division I-AA schools in their recruiting practices and the allocation of scholarships but on a somewhat smaller scale. Division III schools give no athletic scholarships, tend to recruit locally, and represent some of the most prestigious colleges in the country.

16. *Professionalism*—High school and college athletes are considered professionals if they are paid to compete in an athletic contest; commit in writing or orally to an agent or a professional sports organization; request that their names be placed on a draft list; use their athletic skills for pay in any form (TV commercials, e.g.); play on a professional sports team; or play on an amateur team and receive any payment or gratuity.

163

Figure 6-2 (continued)

IMPORTANT TERMS FOR COACHES, COUNSELORS, AND ATHLETES

17. *Prospective Student Athlete*—A player is a "prospective student athlete" once he or she starts the ninth grade of school. Prior to the completion of the junior year, high school student athletes may meet with college coaches, but only on the coach's campus. Refer to the definition of a "contact" regarding meetings anywhere else.

18. *Recruited Prospective Student Athlete*—A player is a "recruited prospective student athlete" when a coach or a representative of a particular school's athletic interests encourages the student to play for that school. Such encouragement normally occurs when the coach or booster provides transportation to the school or some kind of entertainment such as complimentary tickets to a game, calls the player's home, or visits the player anywhere other than the college campus. Be sure to review the definitions of "Boosters" and "Contacts" when discussing the whole issue of recruitment.

19. *Red-shirt*—An athlete is "red-shirted" when (s)he is withheld from actual competition for one year. The athlete may practice with the team during that time but, because of injury or coach's decision, (s)he will not play in games. Be advised that the athlete must complete his or her athletic eligibility within a six-year period once matriculated at the college. The red-shirt year must occur within this time frame.

20. *Sliding Scale*—The most recent provisions of bylaw 14.3 provide a sliding scale for equating grade point average with ACT or SAT scores. Please refer to the *NCAA Guide for the College-Bound Student Athlete* for specifics.

21. *Student Release Form*—The "Student Release Form" is the document used by high school student athletes and high school counselors to verify the academic eligibility of the athletes to be recruited and ultimately accepted to compete in Division I and II athletic programs.

22. *Visits*—Prospective student athletes are permitted by NCAA requirements only one expenses-paid visit to a particular college. Subsequent visits to that college must be paid for by the athlete. Student athletes are allowed a maximum of five such visits. In essence, they can visit only five schools during the senior year, regardless of the number of sports they may play.

23. *Waiver of bylaw 14.3 requirements*—Bylaw 14.3 requirements may be waived based on documented evidence demonstrating student achievement that warrants something other than the normal application of the bylaw. All appeals must be made by a member institution that has officially admitted the student as a regular student. Athletes, coaches, or counselors should contact the college or university in question for more information about the waiver process.

MORE QUESTIONS?
CONTACT THE ATHLETIC DEPARTMENT.

Figure 6-3

THE COUNSELOR'S RESPONSIBILITIES TO STUDENT ATHLETES

Use the following checklist to remind yourself through the year if you have met the needs of your counselees who are student athlete(s).

Pre-Season

DID I:

_____ Assure that each athlete explored career opportunities?

_____ See that the results were interpreted?

_____ Review transcripts to assure compliance with NCAA requirements?

_____ Help student athletes develop a list of potential colleges?

In-Season

DID I:

_____ See if athletes initiated the college application process?

_____ Periodically check grades to assure compliance with the NCAA?

_____ Notify parent(s) if athlete has academic problems?

_____ Meet with highly recruited athletes to discuss the schools that have contacted them?

_____ Assure that the athlete, if a senior, has initiated the NCAA's "Student Release Form"?

Post-Season

DID I:

_____ Talk with the coaches about athletes who are candidates for athletic scholarships?

_____ Modify each athlete's registration for second semester *as needed* to assure compliance with NCAA requirements?

_____ Work with any highly selective schools the athlete is interested in if he or she also is considering signing a Letter of Intent elsewhere?

_____ Meet with the athlete, his or her parents, the counselor, and relevant others to assure an appropriate process?

(This form is reprinted from Mike Koehler's *Football Coach's Survival Guide.* It also was used in the videotape, the *ABCs of Eligibility for the College-Bound Student Athlete,* marketed by the College Board.)

Figure 6-4

TRANSCRIPT VALIDATION

Please review the attached transcript to assure that it complies with the NCAA's eligibility requirements for Divisions I and II as specified in bylaw 14.3. A copy of the bylaw is attached. Review it as well for compliance with the eligibility requirements of any other regulatory organization, such as the NAIA. You should have copies of their requirements. If you don't, be sure to call the school's Athletic Department. Be sure to contact the student athlete's coach and/or counselor if you have any questions. Once you have completed your review of the transcript and are satisfied that it meets the eligibility requirements of the NCAA and other regulatory organizations, sign and date the form in the spaces provided.

I attest that I have reviewed my son's or daughter's transcript and am satisfied that (s)he meets the

eligibility requirements of _____.
(Name of organization)

PARENT'S NAME: _____

DATE: _____

Thank you for your help. Your signature on this form indicates that everyone involved with your child is promoting his or her best interests.

SEVEN

THE RESPONSIBILITIES OF STUDENT ATHLETES AND PARENTS

First, a quick story. I worked once with a young woman who took the recruiting bull by the horns so firmly and sold herself so well that she eventually was awarded a scholarship to play for one of the premier field hockey programs in the nation. She had been selected to the All-State team during both her junior and senior years in high school, but played in a midwestern state and went largely unnoticed by the East Coast colleges, the breeding ground for some of this country's top intercollegiate field hockey.

Unfortunately, she was coached by a woman who was employed full time elsewhere in the community, so the athlete was unable to get the push she needed from her coach to attract recruiters from East Coast schools. I found her on my doorstep one morning asking for the chance to talk about her dilemma.

We talked, and she listened—amazingly well. I suggested resumes, letters of recommendation from her coach and opposing coaches, letters from officials (many of whom had contacts with a variety of schools), highlight tapes of contests, phone calls (a couple of which were made by me), and skill tapes. Fortunately, she was able to accommodate all this while maintaining an excellent grade point average and class rank.

When all was said and done, she ended up visiting a top-notch East Coast school, impressing them with her commitment, and receiving a partial scholarship to play for them. She attended the school and, during her sophomore year, played for a team that went on to win the national championship. Her accomplishment made us both very happy. I was happy because I knew that I had played a very small part in the recruiting process. She was happy because—well, for a variety of obvious reasons.

THE FUTURE, LIKE CHARITY, BEGINS AT HOME

Her initial satisfaction resulted from the knowledge that she had taken control of her future, that, in spite of her coach's inability to help, she had taken the right steps to satisfy her athletic as well as her academic interests in college. Her situation was somewhat atypical in the sense that she found herself almost exclusively responsible for making phone calls and coordinating the information flow between the high school and the college coaches.

Fortunately, I was able to help her. Unfortunately, our nation's schools have a variety of young athletes, many of whom are girls, bumping into similar obstacles when they explore opportunities on the college level to complement academics with athletics. Such athletes and their parents will find direction in this section. Even those young athletes who enjoy the capable assistance of a knowledgeable coach will find help in the next several pages. They and their parents will discover that the coach and the counselor, no matter how experienced, are unable to do it all.

Young athletes and their parents have major responsibilities in the recruiting and college selection processes. They are, after all, the focus of the activity, the "products" sought by the colleges and the recipients of major admissions and financial aid concessions from them. This is serious business—far too important in the life of a young athlete to leave only to persons outside the home, no matter how experienced and concerned they may be.

THE FAMILY'S PRE-SEASON RESPONSIBILITIES

The word "family" is used in this section to emphasize the need for everyone to perform a role throughout the college identification and selection processes. Obviously, the young athlete is primarily responsible for his or her future and should follow up on most of these tasks. Any parent realizes, however, that most teenagers, especially active ones, spend more time foraging through the refrigerator than paging through college catalogues. Gentle reminders are required periodically; some of the gentlest are provided in this section.

Figure 7-1, for example, provides a checklist that parents can tape to the refrigerator door, the most likely place in the house to get a teenager's attention. It will also serve as a reminder to parents to see that these tasks are completed. Parents will be involved in many of them; they may even have to initiate one or more of the activities. The meeting with the counselor in the spring of the year, for example, should be organized by the parents in order to make a statement to both the young athlete and the counselor.

The statement is implicit, but it serves notice to everyone involved in the process that they will be watching as it unfolds; when parents become visible in the process, their children attribute more importance to it, and high school personnel become even more conscientious about their responsibilities. Another element of accountability has been introduced, and there's nothing wrong with that.

Young athletes must recognize, for example, that some career exploration is essential during the junior year. They also must recognize the importance of taking the SAT and the ACT at about the same time. Career and interest inventories can be taken some time during the first half to the middle of the junior year and admissions test results from the middle to the last half of the year, but both should be completed in the junior year.

Certainly, admissions test results are not determinative regarding college selection, but, like career information, they do provide valuable insights into the kinds of college programs that will satisfy the needs of student athletes. Combined with the college search process, they result in a list of colleges that provide an excellent starting point for the recruiting and "marketing" processes.

The marketability of a young athlete also is influenced by the quality of his or her transcript. Another element in the pre-season responsibilities, therefore, is to check with the counselor to ensure that the selection of senior year courses and the completion of the junior year courses continue to satisfy the eligibility requirements of the NCAA and other regulatory organizations.

Having accomplished this, the athlete and his or her parents are prepared to visit one or more campuses during the spring and summer of the junior year to decide upon one or more schools to apply to early in the senior year. Such schools, probably no more than one or two, should satisfy the student's educational, social, and personal requirements as identified in earlier meetings with the counselor and disregard any possibility of athletic participation in college.

Looking into Careers

Many student athletes are disinclined to take this important step. Inadequate time is usually a problem; most often, simple disinterest places it near the bottom of the student's priority list. Once they do it, however, students realize that career exploration provides surprisingly interesting and revealing information.

Because the process normally involves an initial interest inventory, students discover much about themselves, including information about their values, interests, even levels of introvertism and extrovertism. The information is then compared with similar information about persons involved in certain occupations and career areas. Favorable comparisons indicate the likelihood of a student's interest in selected jobs.

Interest inventories and career assessments are usually available through the school's guidance office. Student athletes should be encouraged to contact their counselors for specific information about the administration and interpretation of such inventories, which may include paper and pencil tests or interactive video experiences.

THE FAMILY'S IN-SEASON RESPONSIBILITIES

An anticipated future in intercollegiate athletics may fade for a variety of reasons. Sports pages across the country are full of stories about prep phenoms who are expected to sign with major universities. Such eventual commitments provide the sustenance that assures the survival of intercollegiate sports. What these stories fail to report is that the recruiters' search for sustenance is more a banquet than a bread line. Blue-chippers may be in short supply, but excellent athletes are abundant enough to enable recruiters to leave the table completely satisfied, never having touched most of the offerings. The media rarely relate the stories of the thousands of talented athletes who enjoy successful high school careers and a growing expectation to play in college, but who encounter injury or the unexpected disinterest of college recruiters.

Every athlete, therefore, no matter how highly recruited, should apply to one or two colleges early in the senior year to guarantee a school, even if it doesn't involve athletics. The concept that there is life beyond sports is much more than a cliché. Even professional athletes have limited careers and, when their playing days are over, often find themselves searching for vocations that provide not only a salary but a sense of fulfillment.

The entire career exploration process during the sophomore and junior years in high school convinces students that salary is but one aspect of the career decision-making process. Ask the person who is fortunate enough to find fulfillment in his or her life's work. A career is a daily opportunity to find personal growth, fulfillment, and a deep sense of individual satisfaction. Such a reward in life does not come easily; it involves careful planning and the mature awareness that, compared with the lifelong journey provided by a career, sports is only a whistle-stop along the way.

That is yet another reason why young athletes and their parents should discuss the list of colleges developed with the counselor and take the time during the pre-season to visit some campuses. "Pre-season" can include the freshman or sophomore years, ideal times for parents to introduce high schools students to the college scene. The traditional appeal and academic atmosphere of a college campus can provide enduring images for youngsters, the kind that can motivate for years to come.

Maintaining Academic Achievement

Primary among the in-season responsibilities is the need to maintain a level of academic achievement that is commensurate with the student's ability. A related responsibility involves periodic checking with the counselor to assure continued compliance with eligibility requirements. The form in Figure 7-2 will be very helpful in this regard. A strong academic emphasis throughout high school and the desire to achieve in college normally are sufficient to guarantee eligibility.

For those several students, however, who allow academics to take a back seat to athletics, parents must be constantly vigilant both at home and at school to guarantee the student's attention to coursework. This will mean periodic calls to teachers and to the counselor to secure updates on academic progress between grading periods and follow-up meetings with school personnel if the student is falling below reasonable levels of performance. Such meetings need not be confrontational with the student or unnecessarily threatening. They should be low-key, informal sessions that focus on ways to help the student complete assignments and perform up to par on tests, quizzes, and other assignments.

Such meetings often fail to materialize for a variety of reasons. Sometimes parents are fearful of provoking arguments at home with their children. At other times, they are reluctant to contact school personnel. Many times, they simply are unable to find the time to meet with teachers and counselors to discuss issues that seem so complicated at home. Whatever the reasons, the failure to have such meetings with counselors and teachers generally perpetuates the student's academic and, sometimes, behavioral problems.

Parents are encouraged, therefore, to contact school personnel at the first sign of a school problem, whether it be academic or behavioral. Teachers and, especially, counselors are trained to objectify such problems by diagnosing interferences and suggesting remediation. I have had several such meetings with parents. During the course of our discussions and after continued diagnosis of the issues, we have discovered everything from learning disabilities to regular adjustmental interferences that, once addressed, allowed students to perform at expected levels.

Such meetings can also involve coaches. Be careful not to impose on too much of their time, but early in a young athlete's high school career, a coach can work motivational miracles with reluctant students. The coach's early involvement also paves the way for later requests to have him or her contact college coaches to initiate a process for unrecruited athletes or to discuss future steps regarding highly recruited athletes.

THE FAMILY'S POST-SEASON RESPONSIBILITIES

Now's the time to have the meeting with the coach. He or she probably will contact you if the student is highly recruited. In the absence of such an invitation or if the student is not highly recruited, parents may have to suggest such a meeting by calling the coach, or using the letter in Figure 4-1 for highly recruited kids or Figure 7-3 for less-recruited athletes. This is a very important meeting because it identifies appropriate schools for your child and involves the reevaluation of your original list of schools.

If the young athlete is recruited by several schools, each will have to be compared with the original list or researched to determine if it satisfies the student's original specifications for a college. If the athlete is not being recruited, the meeting should focus on strategies for selling the athlete to appropriate schools, some of which will involve letters from the athlete and assistance from the coach.

Parent Involvement in the Recruiting Process

Exactly what can parents expect from the high school coach during this phase of the college selection process? First of all, they can expect and *seek* honesty. One of the first questions you, as a parent, must ask during this first post-season meeting is, "In your estimation, what level of competition, if any, is best for my son or daughter?" Then, be sure to set aside your normal, parental expectations for the absolute best for your child and *listen* to the coach's response. The absolute best for your child is an experience that enhances his or her growth and provides opportunities for self-expression, personal satisfaction, and individual fulfillment. Such experiences can be found at the nation's smallest university; in fact, some of the major universities are inappropriate for student athletes who require a personalized college environment.

Look at it this way. John Wooden, perhaps the greatest college basketball coach in history, continually emphasized one important fundamental principle for his players—balance. He said that it was critical every time a player shot a basketball or guarded an opponent. He also said that it was critical psychologically for all young people. Young athletes must constantly seek a balance between their academics and their athletics, their wants and their needs, and their individual desires and their social and team responsibilities.

Parents must do the same thing. I have three daughters and fell more than once from that tightrope that extends between expecting the best *from* them and promoting the best *for* them. I learned that sometimes what is best for them is to expect a little less from them, as long as the expectations are consistent with their ability levels. I'm not at all suggesting a blanket lowering of expectation levels.

We must always expect our child's best effort, but within the framework of his or her abilities, not according to our goals or needs as parents. This is an aspect of child rearing that warrants some serious soul-searching for many parents. Wanting the best for our children is different from wanting their best for us as parents. Certainly, each of us is proud of the accomplishments of our kids; but of which are we most proud—the accomplishments or the kids?

Parenthood is a paradox. The very love that binds us to our children must enable them to grow away from us. College is that first big step away from us; it should be one that promotes only the best for our children. Fortunately, most coaches have our children's best interests at heart, too, so we are well advised to listen to them when discussing athletics in college. College is a part of the journey of youth. Our jobs as coaches, counselors, and parents, therefore, is to prepare our youngsters for the journey.

ORGANIZING FOR SUCCESS

Academics still remains the most important initial consideration during that journey. Before seriously considering a college, therefore, young athletes should do a little soul searching themselves. A good first step is to develop an educational profile that summarizes the high school class rank and core grade point averages, admissions tests results, and a personal assessment of the skills required for success in college. Athletes are encouraged to discuss such a profile with their parents and counselors and use it to develop educational and career goals and ultimately select appropriate schools.

Figure 7-4 provides a profile that students and parents can use to make such assessments and to share with counselors during the college search and selection processes. The form provides space for new scores, changes in class rank, and personal growth in one or more areas. Students might begin using it sometime in the junior year, if only to focus on the most important elements in their educational lives.

Once such assessments are complete, students should start collecting information on the colleges that seem to satisfy their initial requirements. The folders might include letters from college coaches, brochures describing the schools, informational materials from the schools or coaches' offices, copies of letters the athletes have sent, and summaries of phone conversations.

Athletes should also develop personal profiles or resumes late in the junior year or early in the senior year to share with coaches, admissions officers, and other university personnel. Such profiles should be concise yet complete. Figure 7-5 provides a framework that students can use to develop their own resumes. It contains all the important information college coaches and other university officials need to assess a student athlete's ability to succeed at their schools.

Notice that the form provides space for the student's social security number and such additional specifics as the names of her or his conference, coach, and counselor. Coaches and admissions officers will require such information at some time in the future to secure additional information. They also will be referring to your student athlete during the admissions process by the social security number, so it's best to provide it on the resume to avoid potential problems.

Figure 7-6 provides a "Contact Reminder" that student athletes and parents can use to record the date and substance of contacts from college coaches and other university personnel. Athletes and their parents will find this form extremely helpful throughout the recruiting and college selection processes. It provides a quick summary of previous contacts before meetings or follow-up contacts. It reminds you if you have mailed follow-up letters, returned phone calls, or made visits to certain schools, and should be used in conjunction with the "Record of Contacts" provided in Figure 5-9.

Finally, be sure to update any and all information as the student's circumstances change. If he or she receives additional honors and awards, significant changes in grade point average, or new SAT/ACT scores, be sure to notify coaches and/or other university personnel. Such new information will keep the young athlete's name fresh in their minds and underscore his or her interest in their schools, and it may have an effect on admissions status.

LEAVING THE RIGHT IMPRESSION

The recruiting and college selection processes seek decisions that result in mutual advantage. The school admits and provides some form of financial aid to a student athlete who can help its athletic program, and the student athlete receives a scholarship or admission to a university that meets his or her educational and career needs. Because the process involves selling as well as buying, young athletes and their parents must do what they can to leave favorable impressions.

College coaches and other university personnel always respond favorably to thank-you notes. Figure 7-7 provides a model that young athletes can use for thanking coaches after phone calls, meetings, and visits to campuses. A close friend of mine has been a college recruiter for over twenty years, and he indicates often that he rarely receives thank-you notes from high school athletes. High school athletes are sometimes too preoccupied with finding or fending off recruiters to remember the simple courtesies.

Such courtesies may not be critical for the highly recruited athlete, but are essential for the young athlete who is trying to sell himself or herself to one or more colleges. A short note after an important phone call or meeting, therefore, can be very helpful when trying to establish the right relationship. The athlete should also remember to

- Dress well during meetings and visits to schools. Yes, a tie or a dress can do wonders to create favorable impressions, especially for college coaches who are surrounded by faceless hordes of jeans and sweatshirts. Good grooming is the personal equivalent of the salesperson's dictum: "Presentation is half the sell job." A friend of mine likes to say that it constantly amazes her that kids today know so much about sex and so little about soap. When they're out to sell themselves, looking good helps!

- Speak well, especially when seeking admission to a highly selective school. Samuel Johnson said that language is the dress of thought; using proper English and speaking slowly and convincingly creates the desired impression.

- Ask questions. Review the materials in Figures 4-10 and 4-11 with your young athlete before college visits or meetings with recruiters. Remember, particularly with a highly recruited athlete, the recruiting process is a two-way street. College coaches are trying to buy the athlete—and sell themselves. It is essential that your youngster ask the kinds of questions that will elicit an idea of the quality of the product you are considering. College coaches will be impressed with her or his maturity.

- Be sure your student asks questions to receive honest answers, not defensive reactions. Discuss this whole issue in your family, and rehearse the questions to be asked.

- Even the most gifted young athlete dampens recruiting fires when he or she is too cocky. Self-confidence shines much brighter than self-importance. Recruiters are looking for young athletes who can contribute coachability and teamwork as well as talent to their programs.

KEEPING ALL THE DOORS OPEN

This leads us to some additional considerations about the recruiting process and making and *maintaining* the right impression. Keep the following suggestions in mind throughout the entire process:

- Don't burn any bridges behind you. Whether the student athlete is highly recruited or unrecruited, it's best not to say no to anyone early in the recruiting process. The school rejected early may be the one that has the most to offer as you and your youngster begin to look closer at the colleges that are available to her or him. The exception is the student athlete who is receiving offers from every corner of the country, especially if he or she has completed the career and college search processes before the actual recruiting begins.

  Again, thank-you notes and follow-up letters are always appropriate. As the recruiting or selection processes unfold, the student can begin to narrow the list, but only in consultation with parents and the coach. I will discuss more of the college notification process later in this section.

- Recruiters want to know that they have a chance to buy the object of their interest. The widely recruited athlete who suddenly starts indicating—particularly to the media—an interest in only one or two schools might discover a sudden disinterest from the others. If they discover in conversation with other recruiters or by reading the papers that one of their prospects has expressed interest in another school, they will quickly direct their efforts elsewhere.

I worked with a young man one year who was recruited by scores of midwestern schools. Each had agreed to contact me whenever he wanted to share or receive information involving the athlete or his family. The process was going quite well until the athlete happened to mention to a local sportswriter that he was likely to go to one particular school. Within two or three weeks, many of the others either stopped calling or indicated to me that they were no longer interested in recruiting him.

Like any hard worker, a recruiter will devote himself or herself to the investment that promises the greatest dividends. Fortunately, my player ended up attending an excellent school and enjoying a very productive career. Had he not been as highly recruited, he might have found himself out in the cold, especially if the school he had mentioned to the papers failed to offer a scholarship. Remember, recruiters are notoriously fickle, so don't give them any opportunities to lose interest.

- Have your student athlete ask the coach, opposing coaches, and even officials to put in a good word periodically with schools that interest him or her. Recruiters who are "on the fence" may fall off on the right side if given a push from the right people.

- Finally, parents are discouraged from making comments about the college selection process before a final decision has been made. Expressions of interest and tentative decisions made to one recruiter sometimes find their way to other recruiters and can provoke disinterest in schools that were formerly interested.

REVIEWING THE NEEDS OF THE FEMALE ATHLETE

The needs of female athletes warrant special attention. Females and their parents generally have to be more aggressive than do their male counterparts. Again, the reasons have nothing to do with the unavailability of scholarships or the disinterest of women coaches. The need to win on the college level is a universal phenomenon, easily as appropriate for women as for men and characterized by the same levels of intensity and commitment to the sport.

The aggressiveness is required because of the relative inability of coaches to travel widely enough to watch female prospects in order to assess the degree of their talent. Much of this is true of several men's sports as well, although the media hype about major college football and basketball would have the uninitiated among us believe that hordes of recruiters representing a variety of sports also descend upon any youngster who can swing a racquet or dig a volleyball.

Such images, though painted with bright colors, arouse the fascination of the public but obscure the truth. Recruiting dollars are often scarce for "nonrevenue-producing" sports, especially among the women; many gifted high school athletes excite the local fans with their talents, but often go unnoticed by college recruiters unless someone attracts their attention.

Often, the person most capable of attracting such attention is the athlete herself. Following are a few ways she can do it:

- Write several coaches at the conclusion of her junior year competition. Introduce herself and provide information about her size, academic qualifications and interests, performance statistics, and awards and honors. She should be sure to mention her desire for college competition, reasons for believing she can participate successfully, and her reasons for wanting to go to college. The letter in Figure 7-8 is a good example of the desired informal and conversational tone.

- Have her coach write a similar letter at the same time, making reference to her academic and athletic abilities from the coach's perspective. The student's letter will discuss college from the standpoint of desire; the coach's letter will discuss it from the standpoint of willingness, ability, leadership, and talent.

- If the coach is unable or unwilling to write such a letter, don't worry about it at this point; the student athlete's letter will be sufficient to alert the college coaches to her interest and ability levels. It won't hurt, however, if an opposing coach writes a letter on her behalf—or if not an opposing coach, at least someone whom the colleges might acknowledge as an expert.

- After your youngster receives a response from the college, she might call the coach to seek answers to questions. During this conversation, she can ask the coach if it would be helpful to see a videotape of her performance during competition. If yes, she should mail one, providing information about her jersey color and number, if applicable, as well as a return address.

- During your athlete's senior year competition, send periodic letters including newspaper clippings that document her performance. The purposes of such letters are to show improvements in performance and to keep her name fresh in the minds of the college coaches.

- At the conclusion of the student athlete's senior year competition, she should write another letter reintroducing her to the coaches and including all her statistics. In this letter, she should mention her desire to compete on the college level and to prepare herself academically for a future career, and indicate that she or her coach will be calling within a week or two to secure additional information.

- Make the follow-up phone call in two or three weeks. Again, a high school coach is the most likely person to make the call, even an opposing coach if necessary. If no coach is available, however, the student herself can make the follow-up call. Whoever makes it, the caller should be sure to ask the college coach if he or she would like to see videotapes of the student athlete's performance.

- A word about these tapes: If you have the technology available to you, make one or more "highlight tapes" of your athlete's performance. Such tapes will illustrate exceptional performance throughout the season. Such tapes will require some editing of the season's game tapes. You will also want to make one or more "skill tapes" that demonstrate her special skills. Shooting jump shots, kicking or maneuvering a soccer ball, handling a field hockey stick, or fielding a grounder and getting the ball off quickly to first base are a few examples of such skills.

Coaches may also want to see actual tapes of competition, particularly against the toughest opponents. If the coach or school is unable to make such tapes routinely, a parent might want to shoot the games. Your student athlete will then have the additional advantage of using such "home-developed" tapes to analyze her own performance between contests.

Again, be sure to include a sheet that identifies the color of the athlete's jersey, her number, the name of the opponent, and any exceptional players on the opposing team who may not have been able to stop her! A return address and an indication of a plan to call and discuss the coach's evaluation of her performance should be included.

- Make such a phone call a week or two after the coach receives the tape or at a time designated by him or her. The recruiting process is sometimes slowed by the fact that the college season is longer than that of most high schools, so the college coach may need a few weeks beyond the high school season to make such an evaluation.

- After the evaluation is made, however, and if the coach is interested, be sure to visit the college. The coach may invite you for such a visit and pay the expenses, or he or she might express an interest in your student athlete but make no reference to an all-expenses-paid visit. If no visit is offered but an interest is expressed, you pay for the visit, family expenses permitting.

The visit will determine the young athlete's desire to play for that particular school, give her the chance to impress the coach with her enthusiasm, and reveal something about the coach, the athletic program, and the school. Remember, you're not only selling; you're buying. You'll need as much information as possible to make the right decision later on.

A final word: Although the foregoing steps are outlined for female athletes, they are equally appropriate for the unrecruited male athlete. They are provided in this section because they suggest a more aggressive college selection process.

SELECTING THE RIGHT COLLEGE OR UNIVERSITY

If two or more colleges have everything a young athlete wants and only one of them offers a scholarship, the choice among them is pretty easy. Rarely, however, is anything that simple! More often, student athletes have several desirable alternatives from which to choose. To consider the dimensions of this decision, let's look closely at the term "student athlete."

From the "student" standpoint, the athlete and his or her family should consider a range of factors, including the student's learning style, size of campus, average class size, access to professors, even ethnic composition of the student body and proximity to a major metropolitan area. Such factors will play a large part in determining the student's comfort levels and meeting his or her personal needs.

Often, a visit is essential for students to gain a "feel" for the college campus and the people with whom he or she will be living and working. Consider the size of the campus. Some colleges that claim to be "medium-sized" are located on small campuses. One midwestern school of approximately 8,000 students, for example, is located on only 77 acres. Students on the campus literally bump into each other between classes and have little access to their professors because of a high student:faculty ratio.

Other midwestern colleges and universities have large student populations but are located on 1,000- to 2,000-acre campuses and enjoy low student:faculty ratios. Many of these schools work to maintain a small-college atmosphere on a large university campus. Obviously, many of them are unsuccessful because of sheer numbers, but a lot of them have, in fact, accommodated the needs of youngsters who require a personalized education. A visit will reveal much of this.

From the "athlete" standpoint, I borrow once again from a conversation with George Kelly, the coaching legend at Notre Dame, a man involved in four national championship teams and someone who once enjoyed the reputation of being the nation's best recruiter. I asked him recently what are the one or two most important principles for young athletes and their parents to keep in mind during the recruiting process in high school. Without a moment's hesitation, he indicated that the most important principle relates to how much the college coach "cares" about the young athlete. He went on to define the attributes of "caring":

- The coach must be honest. He or she must avoid impractical promises, such as assuring immediate starting positions. Honesty requires coaches to indicate that they represent successful programs that enjoy associations with successful players, many of whom have gained experience and have developed the skills that make them starters. Uniquely talented youngsters may be told that they will be given every opportunity to start but that such a position is not guaranteed.

- The coach must focus on the value of the total college experience, not emphasize early promises about the college's statistics for developing professional players. The athlete's immediate future involves hours of work on the field or court and the accompanying burden of doing well in the classroom. Coaches who care focus on these tasks and indicate a willingness to help with both.

- Coaches who care, however, do not promise "intervention" in the student's academic affairs, aside from assuring the school's academic advisement program. The coach who makes guarantees regarding academic performance cares only about his or her win-loss record, not the student athlete.

- Finally, the coach who cares relates to a total person, not just an athlete. He or she responds to feelings and concerns, academic as well as athletic accomplishments, and the student's personal as well as athletic life.

Coach Kelly's second principle initially seems to be a contradiction of his first. He recommends that student athletes "choose the school, not the coach." Coaches resign and go to different schools; recruiters receive different coaching assignments within the same program. Once the athlete loses contact with that one coach, the entire college experience can change for the worse.

Coach Kelly recommends, therefore, that recruited student athletes and parents consider the recruiter as a representative of the athletic program and use that information when making a final decision, but that they look primarily at the academic, career, and social advantages offered by the school. Once gain, the"student"in the term student athlete is a primary consideration.

WHAT TO DO AFTER DECIDING ON A COLLEGE

Review Figure 4-12 for the criteria and a process to use in making your final selection. This final selection is often a difficult task. It is made easier, however, when all your questions have been answered, student athlete and parents have gathered enough information about the schools, and have taken the time to discuss such information with the coach and counselor.

Additional visits may be required at this time. Remember, your athlete can make as many as she or he wants, as long as you pay for them. The school can provide only one all-expenses-paid visit during the recruiting process. Parents may want to pick up the bill for more visits, however, if such visits help your family make a final decision.

Finally, however, your family will make a decision. Once you do, be sure to tell the coach, then notify the school you have selected as well as those you have rejected. The student athlete may want to call the coach of the school or to write (see the sample letter in Figure 7-9). It is brief but addresses all of the important points.

Finally, use the sample letter in Figure 4-8 to notify the schools the athlete has rejected. It avoids reference to the reasons for his or her choice, but thanks them for their interest and consideration throughout the recruiting process. It also provides the opportunity for the high school coach to make a pitch on behalf of some of next year's players.

Following the mailing of these letters, the student athlete may want to call the coach of the college he or she will be attending to discuss the next steps to be taken. Colleges routinely mail off-season workout programs and other informational materials, such as time tables regarding registration, first day of practice, and the school calendar.

LET'S WRAP IT UP

The media would have us believe that most of the recruiting process involves high school and college coaches. Certainly much of it does, but the responsibility of decisions resulting from any process must rest primarily with the person(s) most affected by them. The focus of the recruiting process is the student athlete. He or she is responsible, therefore, not only for the final decision but for much of what happens throughout the process.

This is not to say that student athletes and their parents should assume the entire responsibility, especially when high school coaches fail to provide the kind of help that they can provide best. As indicated earlier, many intercollegiate athletic abuses are traceable directly to the inability or the unwillingness of high school coaches and counselors to provide expert help during the recruiting process. With the right kind of information and assistance, offered in this book, you can help your high school athlete make college decisions for the right reasons. When everyone who should be involved in the process works cooperatively, a synergy is created that results in the best possible decision. A process for promoting such cooperative effort is the focus of the next section.

Figure 7-1

MY "DID I" LIST

Use the following checklist to remind yourself through the year of the tasks you need to perform to find the "right" college experience.

Pre-Season
DID I:

_____ Meet with my counselor in the spring of the junior year to discuss my college plans?

_____ Take the ACT and/or the SAT near the end of my junior year?

_____ See my counselor about a career inventory to find potential college majors?

_____ Meet with my counselor to make sure my senior year courses comply with NCAA rules and regulations?

_____ Review my transcript at the end of my junior year to be sure I am in compliance with bylaw 14.3?

_____ Develop a list of colleges with my counselor?

_____ Visit a representative sample of college campuses?

_____ Identify a school or schools I can apply to that meet my academic and career needs in the event I don't play a sport in college?

In-Season
DID I:

_____ Apply to at least one school that will meet my needs if I don't play a sport?

_____ Double-check with my counselor to assure compliance with the NCAA?

_____ Maintain good academic standing?

_____ If highly recruited, meet with my coach to deal with persistent recruiters?

Post-Season
DID I:

_____ Meet with my coach to assess my potential to play in college?

_____ Meet with my coach to deal with persistent recruiters?

_____ Review the NCAA rules regarding recruiting?

_____ Make college visits?

_____ Assure the right program of study in the schools that have expressed an interest in me?

_____ Meet with my counselor, coach, and parents to make a final decision?

_____ Discuss the proper application procedure with college coaches?

(This form is reprinted from Mike Koehler's *Football Coach's Survival Guide*, published by Prentice Hall. It also was used in the videotape, the *ABCs of Eligibility for the College-Bound Student Athlete*, marketed by the College Board.)

Figure 7-2

A LITTLE HELP FROM THE COUNSELOR

TO: (Name of Counselor)

FR: (Parents' Names)

RE: Academic Eligibility for College

As you probably know, (Student's Name) is a student athlete and has enjoyed the long-time dream of playing a sport in college. As parents, we realize that college sports is extremely competitive and that relatively recent changes in eligibility standards have reaffirmed the importance of proper academics in high school. We understand such requirements and would like to do what we can to assure our child's compliance with them.

Would you be so helpful as to complete the attached form and return it to us by mail? We also would appreciate your help by meeting with (Child's Name) to discuss his/her progress, to clarify these requirements, and to provide a periodic academic boost. You are an important person in our child's life; your intervention should be very helpful.

Our address and phone number are:

CORE COURSES COMPLETED:

1. _____   _____   _____   _____

2. _____   _____   _____   _____

3. _____   _____   _____   _____

4. _____   _____   _____   _____

5. _____   _____   _____   _____

CUMULATIVE GPA AND CLASS RANK: _____   _____
                                         (GPA)   (Rank)

ADMISSIONS TEST SCORES:

ACT Composite: _____   *SAT Composite:* _____
Subtest scores: Subtest scores:

_____ _____ _____ _____   _____ _____

Figure 7-3

LETTER TO COACH FROM PARENTS
The Unrecruited Athlete

Date

(Coach's Name
Address
City, State Zip)

Dear (Coach's Name):

Now that the season has concluded, we'd like to meet with you to thank you for all you have done for (student's name) and to discuss some of her/his future plans. Although (student's name) had a great season and really enjoyed playing for you, we feel fairly confident that he/she probably won't receive a scholarship to continue the sport in college. We know how competitive they can be.

Our student has, however, explored the whole college issue and has developed a list of schools that meet his/her academic and career interests. Maybe she/he can continue playing for one of the schools, or for another that might provide the same opportunities. Because of your years of experience dealing with these issues, we would like to meet to discuss what, if anything, can be done to help (student's name) continue with the sport next year. He/she has even considered walking on.

We realize that you are busy and promise not to take too much of your time. Please check your calendar and give us a call regarding the particulars of a meeting. We would like to bring (student's name) with us, if that meets with your approval.

In advance, thanks for your help, and we look forward to seeing you in the near future.

Sincerely,

(Parents' Name)

Figure 7-4

EDUCATIONAL PROFILE

To the Student Athlete:

Use this profile to keep track of your academic progress through school. It will help during future planning activities.

NAME: _____

ACT:

  Composite: _____

  Subtest Scores: _____   _____   _____   _____

SAT:

  Composite: _____

  Subtest Scores: _____   _____

CLASS RANK:

  _____ of _____   _____ of _____   _____ of _____
  (5th sem.)   (6th sem.)   (7th sem.)

GPA IN CORE COURSES:

	5TH SEM.	6TH SEM.	7TH SEM.
MATH	_____	_____	_____
SCIENCE	_____	_____	_____
SOCIAL STUD.	_____	_____	_____
ENGLISH	_____	_____	_____

ASSESSMENT OF ACADEMIC STRENGTHS:

	JUNIOR YEAR	SENIOR YEAR
ACADEMIC COMMITMENT	_____	_____
SOCIAL MATURITY	_____	_____
COMMUNICATION SKILLS	_____	_____
ORGANIZATION SKILLS	_____	_____

Rate the above skills "High," "Medium," or "Low," then discuss your rating with your parents and counselor. This will give you an idea of a few things you might do between now and the time you leave for college. The above information will also be important when you make decisions about the program of study you will pursue in college.

Figure 7-5

RESUME

Student Athlete's Name: _____

NAME	GPA:
ADDRESS	CLASS RANK
CITY, STATE ZIP	ACT SCORE
PHONE NUMBER, INCLUDING AREA CODE	SAT SCORE
SOCIAL SECURITY NUMBER	HT. ____ WT. ____
DATE OF BIRTH	CONFERENCE _____

NAME OF HIGH SCHOOL:

HIGH SCHOOL COACH:

COACH'S HOME PHONE:

GUIDANCE COUNSELOR:

COUNSELOR'S SCHOOL PHONE:

SCHOOL FAX NUMBER:

ACADEMIC INTEREST IN COLLEGE:

   1.

   2.

   3.

HONORS AND AWARDS:

WORK EXPERIENCE:

ATHLETIC STATISTICS/PERFORMANCES: (if appropriate)

Figure 7-6

CONTACT REMINDER

NAME OF COACH	SCHOOL REPRESENTED	NATURE OF CONTACT	DATE

Figure 7-7

THANK-YOU NOTE

Date

(Coach's Name
Address
City, State Zip)

Dear (Coach's Name):

I want to take just a minute of your time to thank you for the recent visit to your campus. I enjoyed having the opportunity to meet the coaches and several of your players, to walk the campus, and to accept your hospitality. The trip was everything I expected it to be—and more. I'm not surprised that your school and athletic program enjoy such widely recognized reputations. My coach is right; your program is classy.

My parents asked me to thank you, too. They say they enjoyed a weekend of peace and quiet, and they appreciate your generosity!

Thanks again for the time you spent with me. I will be getting back to you soon regarding my decisions for the future. In the meantime, if you have any questions, please call me or my coach at your convenience.

Sincerely yours,

(Student's Name)

Figure 7-8

LETTER FROM JUNIOR ATHLETE
TO COLLEGE COACH

Date

(Coach's Name
Address
City, State Zip)

Dear (Coach's Name):

I would like to take this opportunity to introduce myself to you. I am currently a junior at (name of high school) and, with the completion of this current season, have played softball for three years, starting at shortstop for the last two. I am 5'9" and weigh 145 pounds and can also play first base and catcher. I have been All-Conference for the past two years and was recently selected to the All-Area team.

My coach's name is Sandra Miller; she has encouraged me to write this letter. She indicates that she plans to write one as well. Regarding my statistics: I committed only two errors this season and batted .425, with 23 triples and 19 home runs. I currently own five school records in softball and also play basketball and field hockey.

I rank 23 in a class of 389 and have a 3.4 grade point average on a 4.0 scale. My career goals are as yet undefined, but I am interested in math and science, so I probably will want to go into engineering. I am looking forward to college as an opportunity to pursue my educational and career goals and would love to continue playing softball on the college level, especially with your program.

I would appreciate hearing from you and am available in the event you are interested in additional information. Please forward whatever materials I need at this point to further express my interest in your program.

Thanks for the time, and I look forward to hearing from you.

Sincerely yours,

(Student Athlete's Name)

Figure 7-9

LETTER OF ACCEPTANCE

Date

(Coach's Name
Address
City, State Zip)

Dear (Coach's Name):

Writing this letter gives me a great deal of pleasure because it enables me to confirm my decision to attend your school next year and to be a member of your (name of sport) program. Everyone involved in the decision, including my parents, my coach, and my counselor, agrees with me that the academic and athletic programs at your school satisfy all my needs as a student athlete. You have been particularly helpful throughout the process; I want to thank you for your help and understanding.

I am forwarding a copy of this letter to my high school coach for her/his records and would appreciate hearing from you at some time in the future regarding the next steps.

I know I've made the right decision, and, believe me, I'll do what I can to justify your confidence in me. Again, thanks for your help, and I look forward to hearing from you.

Sincerely,

(Student's Name)

cc: (High School Coach's Name)

EIGHT

DEVELOPING COALITIONS OF ATHLETES, PARENTS, COACHES, AND COUNSELORS

INTRODUCTION

Back in the 1950s, prominent psychologist Abraham Maslow and a variety of writers wrote about the social benefits of "synergy." They defined synergy as a combination of individual actions creating a total output that is *greater* than the sum of the individual actions. In simpler terms, high synergy creates a situation in which 2+2=7. High synergy results when the elements in the group are mutually cooperative. Low synergy results when the elements are mutually antagonistic, as when 2+2=3.

Synergy can be potentially dangerous as when two otherwise benign drugs combine to create a malignant substance. Maslow, however, applied the concept to social institutions and preferred to think of the positive implications of mutual cooperation. This section follows Maslow's theory. Coalitions—groups of athletes, parents, coaches and counselors—create positive synergy whenever each contributes his or her special strengths to the needs of student athletes.

According to Maslow: "[Consider] the possibility of arranging social institutions ... in such a fashion that the people within the organization are coordinated with each other and are perforce made into colleagues and teammates rather than into rivals." Because "teammates" has been an important word throughout this book, let's use it once again to describe the relationships among parents, athletes, coaches, and counselors in the social institution we call the school.

DEFINING TEAMWORK

Teammates create more positive synergy than rivals. Successful teams coordinate the activities of individuals in such a way that the total output of the team is greater than the individual outputs of the members. Obviously, some teams are more successful than others in this regard. No matter what the field of endeavor, collective effort alone is insufficient to guarantee success. "Teams" are much more than groups of people.

Only a relatively few sports teams continue year after year to win championships; only a minority of schools across the country consistently receive recognition for educational excellence; only a few business organizations continue each year to dominate industry. The others have their ups and downs, and struggle year after year to win enough of whatever it is they need to survive.

Successful teams engage members in mutually cooperative, complementary, and satisfying activities that promote a continuing sense of commitment to team goals and objectives. Each member's involvement simultaneously satisfies his or her individual needs while it contributes to the goals of the team. Such involvement promotes person-al *and* collective relevance and is constantly motivating to members because it satisfies their intrinsic needs.

Look at it this way. To the extent that our rivals are *teammates*, we promote circumstances that are low in synergy. When every member of a basketball team aspires to be the high scorer, no one makes the assists or sets up the screens that are so critical to a team's success. When halfbacks care only about running the ball and fail to block for each other, the entire team suffers. When a school's administration isolates teachers and fails to promote their mutual interaction in professional growth programs, the school disregards its normative values and the students suffer.

Examples of low synergy are everywhere, in a wide variety of organizations. No group is a team until it guarantees individual satisfaction through mutual cooperation. This is just as true in the high school's efforts to assist student athletes as in the variety of sports teams they represent. Some people seek involvement with the team to satisfy selfish needs. When vested interests are the *exclusive* reason for their participation, the entire team experiences low synergy.

If the athlete wants only a scholarship or a guarantee to start his or her freshman year and if the parents want only the relief of an expected financial burden, they seek the help of high school personnel for the wrong reasons. If high school coaches want only the thrill of working exclusively with blue-chippers and if counselors want someone else to deal with NCAA regulations, high school personnel do little to satisfy the needs of athletes and their parents. Neither contributes to team-coalition synergy. What is required initially is a mutual acceptance of the team's goals and the team commitment to achieve them.

WHAT ARE THE COALITION'S GOALS?

Coalitions must function as teams. For purposes of this book, a coalition is defined as *a group of people, including a student athlete and his or her parents, coach, and counselor, working cooperatively to identify and select a college that will satisfy the student's educational, career, personal, social, and athletic interests and needs.* Coalitions will be expected to meet periodically with others in the school or community, including experts such as college counselors and athletic directors, who can further the academic and athletic interests of the student.

Aspects of this goal have been discussed throughout this book; this section focuses on it exclusively. When athletes, parents, coaches, and counselors work cooperatively to realize such a goal, one result will be the opportunity for more college athletes to find satisfying and fulfilling lives. As important, the current accumulation of intercollegiate abuses, fermented by vested interests, will disperse and draw less media attention.

DEVELOPING COALITIONS

Increased synergy enhances the coalition's power. Each of us, therefore—athlete, parent, coach, and counselor—provides potential power to coalition activities. Such potential is actualized only when we meet to achieve consensus, to leave our vested interests at home, and to develop a process that is satisfying as well as cooperative. This section considers the steps in the process.

Figure 8-1 contains a decisional flowchart that provides a graphic example of the first few steps. Two additional flowcharts follow. At the end of this section, a composite will be provided that consolidates all three flowcharts and abstracts much of what we have discussed throughout the entire book. Each flowchart involves a series of diamonds, which suggest the need for a decision, and a rectangle representing complementary function for each diamond.

The flowchart reflects decisions that must be made by the athlete, his or her parents, or the high school's personnel—and the nature of the activities that result from the decisions. The text will discuss how one decision influences another and who is responsible for each of the activities. The figures containing the flowcharts are provided for use during in-service activities with coaches, counselors, college counselors, and athletic directors.

The flowcharts might also be distributed during meetings with young athletes and their parents to illustrate the interrelationships that exist among them, the high school coach, and the counselor. The flowchart and the checklists provided earlier in the book can be combined to create an informative and useful handout to be distributed to athletes and their parents early each year—in the freshman year to introduce families to coalition activities, in succeeding years to remind them of their importance.

Necessary First Steps

Figure 8-1 outlines five decisions that affect young athletes and their parents almost from the start of high school:

DECISION 1—THE DISTRIBUTION OF INFORMATION. The first decision involves the distribution of needed information throughout the student's high school career, but primarily during the junior and senior years. The information that is distributed and the process for distribution should include the following:

• A brochure comparable to the one provided in Figure 3-1 outlines the tasks to be completed each year. These tasks range from the development of an academic four-year plan in the freshman year, to the identification of appropriate colleges in the junior year, to specific coalition activities in the senior year. The brochure is most appropriate in the freshman year when coaches, counselors, and parents are emphasizing to young athletes the importance of academics.

Time to distribute: Early in the freshman year

Person(s) responsible: Athletic department

• The school's training rules should be reemphasized each year, in such a way that athletes and parents understand the reasons for them and the consequences of violating them.

Time to distribute: In the fall of each year

Person(s) responsible: Athletic department

• Athletic codes or pledges should be distributed at the start of each year. Athletes and parents should be asked to sign them. Again, such a process is educational for the athletes. Coaches should use the time when they distribute such pledges as opportunities to discuss the value and the goals of sports competition.

Time to distribute: In the fall of each year

Person(s) responsible: Athletic department

• This also is the time to distribute information about health insurance and doctor's permission and to indicate when such forms should be returned to the athletic department.

Time to distribute: In the fall of each year

Person(s) responsible: Athletic department

• Information about eligibility and recruiting requirements should be distributed not only to athletes and their parents but to coaches and counselors. Such information should refer to both high school and college requirements, and it should accommodate the periodic changes in the requirements of the NCAA and other regulatory organizations.

Time to distribute: As needed

Person(s) responsible: Athletic and guidance departments

• Obviously, everyone involved in the coalition will require information about college athletics. Information about terms (see Figure 6-2) enables everyone to speak the same language.

Time to distribute: As needed

Person(s) responsible: Athletic department

• Finally, this book contains a variety of informational materials that should be shared with student athletes, their parents, and high school personnel at critical times of the year. To help with the gathering and distribution of such information, this book provides four appendixes—each an informational booklet that can be provided to entering freshmen, highly recruited athletes, unrecruited athletes, and female athletes.

Time to distribute: The junior and senior years of the athlete

Person(s) responsible: Individual coaches

Generally, the first three booklets should be shared with the athletes and their parents during the junior and senior years. As you will see, they relate to the eligibility and recruiting processes and suggest ways to promote the interest of college coaches.

Decision 2—Transcript Review. The second decisional area involves the review of transcripts to guarantee academic eligibility. Discussions of eligibility should include high school as well as NCAA standards. Such information should be given to athletes and their parents at meetings in the fall. Review of each athlete's transcript, however, should be undertaken periodically to assure compliance with local, state, and intercollegiate requirements. Following is a suggested format:

• Review the academic records of student athletes at the end of each grading period to assure compliance with local and state eligibility requirements. This need not be done exhaustively. Usually, counselors must check the records only of those students who fail courses to determine if they are eligible to continue playing. In those states that have tougher requirements, the job of checking transcripts may require more time, more people, and a well-coordinated process.

Timing: At the end of each grading period

Person(s) responsible: Guidance and athletic departments

• Routinely check the student athlete's transcript at the end of the freshman, sophomore, and junior years to assure compliance with the standards of the NCAA and other regulatory organizations. When parents assume this responsibility, they are dependent on the athletic department for updated information from the NCAA and the other organizations. See Figure 7-2 for the appropriate form.

Timing: At the end of each of the first three years of school

Person(s) responsible: Student athletes and their parents

• Check the student athlete's transcript at the end of the sophomore and, particularly, the junior years to assure continued progress toward the completion of eligibility requirements. See Figures 2-2 and 6-4 for additional information.

Timing: End of sophomore and junior years

Person(s) responsible: High school counselor, student athlete, and parents

• Validate the transcript prior to any recruiting activity and just before the end of the senior year for compliance with the requirements of the Clearinghouse.

Timing: The student's senior year

Person(s) responsible: High school counselor

DECISION 3—CAREER EXPLORATION. A necessary preliminary to the identification and selection of the right college, the exploration of personal interests and possible careers must be done at some time during high school. As indicated earlier, the process may not reveal one *right* career area, but it will open the athlete's eyes to the world of work and reaffirm the importance of an appropriate academic experience in high school and in college.

Timing: Any time during high school, but particularly in the junior year

Person(s) responsible: Counselor, career consultant, student athlete, and parent(s)

DECISION 4—COLLEGE EXPLORATION. Student athletes must use the information they have gathered from career exploration experiences to develop a list of colleges that satisfy their personal, social, educational, and vocational interests. Even the most highly recruited athlete must apply to one or two of the schools on the list early in the senior year, then await future recruiting decisions to be made in conjunction with his or her coach, counselor, and parents.

Timing: Late winter or spring of the junior year

Person(s) responsible: High school counselor, college consultant, student athlete, and parents

Notice that most of the foregoing tasks are conducted irrespective of athletics. These are the responsibilities of *students.* Young athletes must not wait until the conclusion of competition in the senior year to make college decisions, particularly if such decisions are dependent on recruiting activity. They may *never* be recruited—for a variety of reasons. They probably *will* want to go to college, so they should plan accordingly.

The Intermediate Steps

Figure 8-2 illustrates the intermediate steps of the college selection process for student athletes:

DECISION 5—IS THE ATHLETE GOING TO PLAY IN COLLEGE? The first of these steps involves the student athlete's decision. I have discovered over the years that some of my finest athletes recognized their limitations as players and, even though they might have received scholarships to Division II colleges, chose not to play intercollegiate sports. They opted instead to devote all their time to academics. On the other hand, if the athlete is talented and highly recruited, the decision probably has been made much earlier.

Timing: After completion of senior season or some time during the senior year, probably earlier if the athlete is highly recruited

Person(s) responsible: Student athlete, parents, and—sometimes—the coach

Concluding the athletic relationship warrants special mention. Sometimes this is done in the locker room or a meeting room after the final game. It can be a very emotional time for everyone, especially for the seniors, most of whom realize they probably will never play the game again in the same way. Coaches must be very sensitive to this fact and use the time to abstract everything that has happened for the past four years and, especially, the most recent season.

They should personalize the experience as much as possible for each senior and discuss with the entire team the contribution each of them has made to the program and the lessons they have taught everyone through their hard work. This also is the time to acknowledge the growth each player has experienced and reaffirm the values of cooperation, team membership, commitment, and hard work.

The conclusion of the athletic relationship can have significant carry-over value for the rest of the athlete's life. It is the time for the coach to let the seniors know that he or she is available to them at any time in the future, because of the special bond they have created. It is the time to encourage, even challenge, each player to integrate the values he or she has developed during the season and reflect them over a lifetime.

Decision 6—The High School Coach's Involvement. If the student athlete decides to continue his or her sport on the college level, this is the time to introduce the athletic component to coalition activities by gathering together the people who can answer critical questions and provide information and expertise. The high school counselor's and coach's perspectives are critical if the student athlete is to find the proper balance between athletic and academic needs in college.

A meeting involving the student athlete, his or her parents, the counselor, and the coach is essential at this point to coordinate the athletic and academic interests of the student. This meeting is an extension of the meeting that occurred in the locker room at the end of the season. It is another opportunity to let the athlete and his or her parents know that college is much more than sports competition and, for that matter, that sports competition is much more than playing a game.

Timing: After the completion of competition in the senior year or some time during the senior year—probably earlier if the athlete is highly recruited

Person(s) responsible: Primarily the coach, but also the coalition, which can be organized at this point by any of the four primary parties involved

Decision 7—Is the decision to play in college realistic? This is a very sensitive area and requires considered honesty from the coach and genuine objectivity from the athlete and parents. Often, both predispositions are difficult to achieve, but all parties must make an honest effort if the student athlete is to seek realistic and satisfying goals. If the decision seems unrealistic to the coach or counselor, they will have to reopen the question of the student's goals and seek to provide objective evidence of their perceptions, including reference to the opinions of college coaches.

Timing: Sometime during the student athlete's senior year

Person(s) responsible: Everyone in the coalition

The final steps in the process involve finding the right school for the unrecruited athlete or assisting the highly recruited athlete with his or her ultimate decision.

The Final Steps

Figure 8-3 illustrates the final steps in the process:

DECISION 8—IS THE ATHLETE HIGHLY RECRUITED? If the answer to this question is yes, the student athlete and his or her parents, in conjunction with the coach and counselor, must compare the schools making scholarship offers with the list of schools already developed during the college exploration process. Sometimes this process is surprisingly simple, if scholarships are offered by the two or three schools that were identified earlier as having exactly the academic and career program the student athlete wants.

The coalition must still consider offers coming from other schools, which may have something different to offer. The decision is uncomplicated, however, when the athlete and his or her parents are already familiar with college selection materials and processes. It also tends to be an abbreviated process because most student athletes accept offers from the schools that are highest on their lists.

The case for marginally recruited athletes is somewhat different. Student athletes who receive one, two, or three scholarship offers sometimes have to make decisions regarding the desire to play in college or the need for a specific academic program. Some athletes opt for the academic program; most others, however, because their educational and career alternatives have not been finalized, accept one of the scholarship offers—generally the one that meets their personal and social preferences.

If the answer to the question is no, the coach and the athlete will need to resurrect the athlete's list of colleges and contact the coaches of the schools in which the athlete is most interested. This involves considerably more difficult tasks for the coach than overseeing the recruiting of blue-chippers. Selling the marginal athlete requires numerous letters and phone calls; it requires persistence from the coach and a willingness to accept rejection from the athlete and his or her parents.

Timing: The student athlete's senior year

Person(s) responsible: Generally, the coalition but particularly the athlete and the high school coach

DECISION 9—IS THE SCHOOL SELECTED? If, for some reason, the answer to this question is no, the coalition might have to meet a final time to review the selection criteria and help the family make a decision. At this point in the process, Figure 4-11 can be extremely helpful. The family should be urged to consider it during discussions at home or in meetings with the high school coach and counselor.

The inability of some athletes to make decisions among scholarship offers often results in the cancellation of some of the offers. Colleges want to sign recruits, and if the indecision of a prospect suggests disinterest, they will offer the scholarship to a more willing, if somewhat less-talented player. The high school coach is often the most influential person when families are unable to make such decisions, and his or her involvement at this point is very important.

If the answer to the question is yes, the time has come to notify all the schools that have been involved in the process. This task is another that must be handled sensitively by the high school coach. He or she can expect a continuing relationship with many of the colleges that have been involved in the process. Because the ability to "sell" future athletes to these same schools depends upon the strength of the relationship, the colleges that have been rejected must be thanked for their interest and congratulated on the merits of their programs, as well as those accepted. See Figures 4-8 and 7-9 for sample letters.

A Look at the Whole Process

Figure 8-4 provides an illustration of the entire process. Coaches, counselors, and athletic directors are encouraged to reproduce this figure for distribution to student athletes and parents at informational meetings. It is an excellent complement to Figure 3-1 and abstracts the process, including the checklists outlining the varying responsibilities of everyone in the coalition. For additional information, refer to the appendixes at the end of the book.

SETTING UP
COALITION MEETINGS

Before concluding this section, we had better discuss logistics. Nothing can destroy relationships any faster than an inability to find time to see each other. Sometimes these logistical problems provide excuses to the one or two people in the coalition who might not want to meet. I have avoided much of this by sending the counselor, the athlete, and his or her parents a letter that requests from them a list of alternative times they will be available for such a meeting. Figure 8-5 provides a sample. Notice that in the letter I provide an indication of the times I will be free and ask each party to try to align their schedules with mine. Sometimes this can be a problem, however, so I also ask them to indicate their most convenient times. I also include a return envelope to make the process as convenient as possible for them.

This process usually identifies two or three days for the coalition to meet. We may not need all three, or we may need more, depending on the needs of the student athlete and his or her family, but this process gets us off to a good start and can always be used again in the event more meetings are required.

FOLLOWING UP
AFTER THE STUDENT GOES TO COLLEGE

The high school athletic department that genuinely cares about young athletes works with them while they're in school and wonders about them afterward. Specifically, the athletic director, the coach, and the counselor wonder if the coalition activities were successful:

- Is the athlete satisfied with his or her academic program in college?
- Is athletics a satisfying complement to that program?
- Is athletic involvement somehow unsatisfying? In what ways?

Other questions are warranted as well:

- Did high school prepare the athlete adequately for athletics in college?
- What additional kinds of information did the athlete need to make the transition more comfortable?
- What kinds of realities experienced in college were surprising, even shocking?
- How might meetings with parents and high school personnel have better prepared the athlete for such realities?
- What options are available other than meetings to anticipate those realities?

Athletic departments should send copies of the letter in Figure 8-6 to the parents as well, asking them to respond to the same questions from a parental perspective. The combined responses of former students and parents provide valuable information regarding the effectiveness of coalition activities. As important, for the price of one or two stamps, athletic departments and coaches can realize significant public relations benefits, the kind that promote parental and community support for athletics.

LET'S WRAP IT UP

Because this section provides an abstraction of several earlier sections, the reproducibles are useful for informational meetings with student athletes, their parents, and high school personnel who assist students with college and career selection. Figure 8-4 is particularly helpful as an overview of the process and a complement to the checklists that outline the responsibilities of student athletes, parents, coaches, and counselors.

If high schools are to influence the direction of intercollegiate athletics, parents and schools must coalesce the knowledge, energy, and experience of athletes, their parents, coaches, and counselors. Once we work together to seek a satisfying and productive academic and athletic experience for college-bound student athletes, the tactics of unprincipled college recruiters will have less effect on young athletes as they select colleges.

Young athletes will be more inclined to seek college for the academic, social, and personal benefits it provides and merely complement them with athletics. This is an uphill battle, considering the vested interests of college recruiters, and it is complicated even further by the almost hypnotic influences that high school and college sports have on young athletes. "Love of the game" is but one of them.

Its promises, real or imagined, can be even more dramatic. The promise of continued local recognition is a strong enticement for adolescents. The promise to escape a bleak and sometimes savage environment is overwhelming to many inner-city kids. The potential to make millions of dollars is a distant but intriguing notion to most youngsters. And the promise to reinforce a self-concept that is tied to success in sports is hard to refuse.

Most of these promises are only implicit in the desire or the invitation to play a sport in college. They are nonetheless real, and the fact that they are rarely discussed explicitly makes them subtle but powerful interferences in the college selection process. Attempts to identify and overcome such interferences are more successful when persons involved in the process coalesce their knowledge and experience.

Figure 8-1

NECESSARY FIRST STEPS

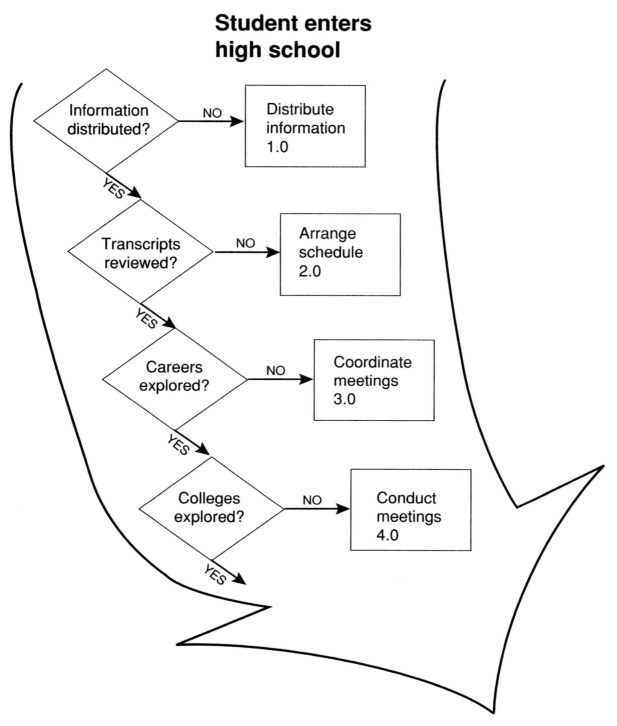

Student enters high school

To Intermediate Steps

199

Figure 8-2

INTERMEDIATE STEPS

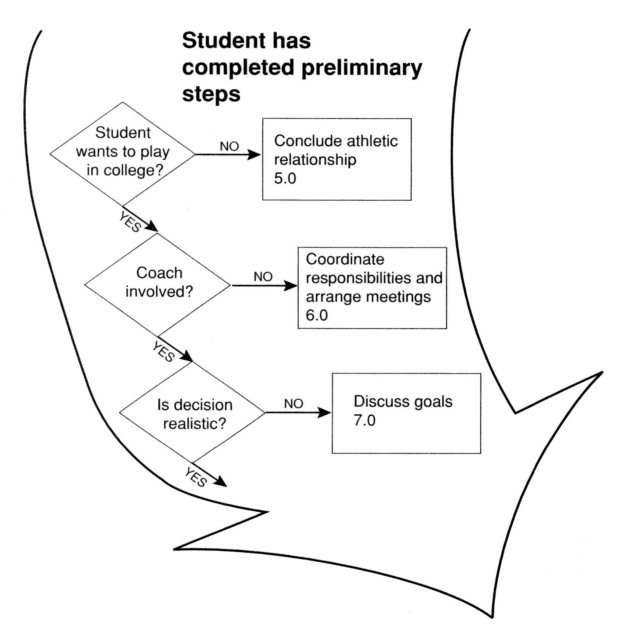

Student has completed preliminary steps

Student wants to play in college?
NO → Conclude athletic relationship 5.0
YES

Coach involved?
NO → Coordinate responsibilities and arrange meetings 6.0
YES

Is decision realistic?
NO → Discuss goals 7.0
YES

Student athlete prepared for Final Steps

Figure 8-3

FINAL STEPS

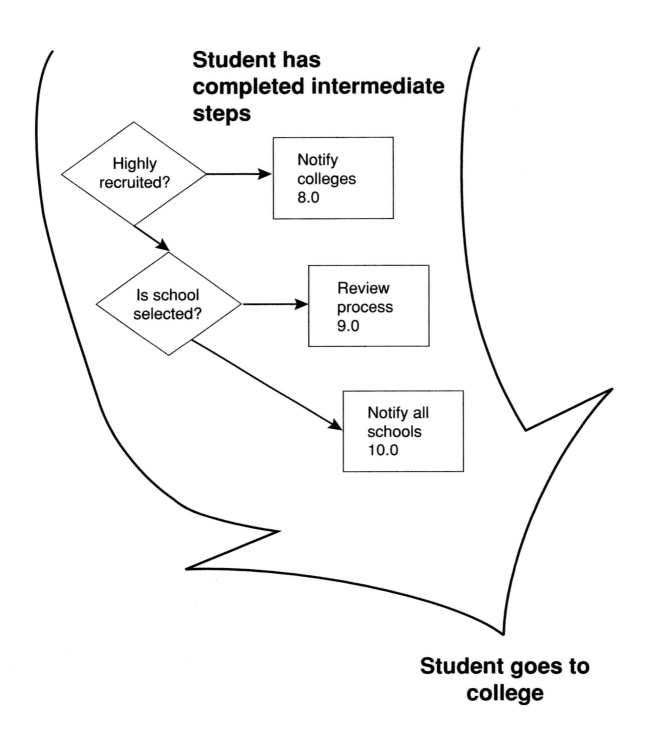

Student has completed intermediate steps

Highly recruited?

Notify colleges 8.0

Is school selected?

Review process 9.0

Notify all schools 10.0

Student goes to college

© 1996 by Michael D. Koehler

Figure 8-4

THE WHOLE PROCESS

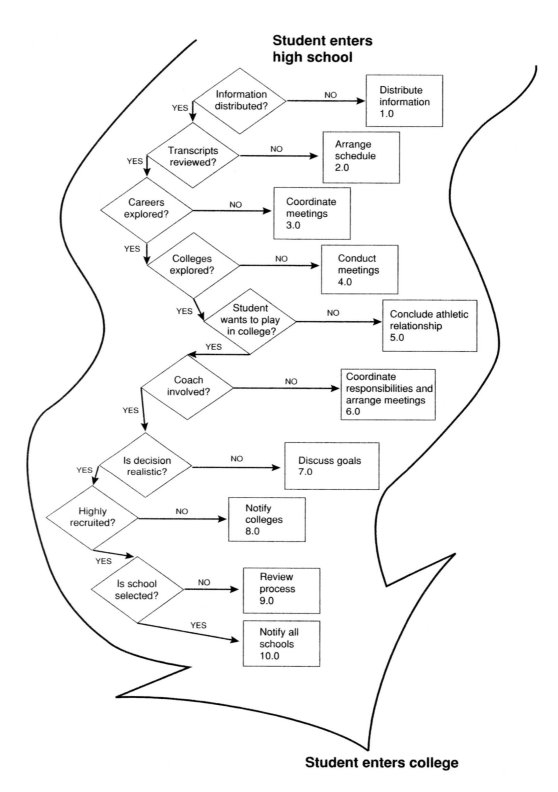

Student enters high school

Information distributed? — NO → Distribute information 1.0

YES ↓

Transcripts reviewed? — NO → Arrange schedule 2.0

YES ↓

Careers explored? — NO → Coordinate meetings 3.0

YES ↓

Colleges explored? — NO → Conduct meetings 4.0

YES ↓

Student wants to play in college? — NO → Conclude athletic relationship 5.0

YES ↓

Coach involved? — NO → Coordinate responsibilities and arrange meetings 6.0

YES ↓

Is decision realistic? — NO → Discuss goals 7.0

YES ↓

Highly recruited? — NO → Notify colleges 8.0

YES ↓

Is school selected? — NO → Review process 9.0

YES → Notify all schools 10.0

Student enters college

Figure 8-5

SAMPLE LETTER OF INVITATION
FOR COALITION MEETING

Date

(Name of Person(s)
Address
City, State Zip)

Dear (Person's Name):

The time has come for what may be the first of several meetings to discuss the college selection and recruiting processes for your son/daughter. We have a range of topics to discuss, so I suggest we meet sometime in the near future. Trying to coordinate such meetings over the phone invariably results in the frustration of "telephone tag," so I thought I'd send this letter before I call to arrange the meeting(s).

Please indicate on the spaces provided the days and times you will be available to meet with me and the other parties who can make a contribution to the success of the process. I will look at the times provided by everyone and call with a specific suggestion regarding our first meeting. We can then discuss the dates and times of future meetings, as they may become necessary.

Thanks for your time, and please feel free to use the stamped, self-addressed envelope to send me your reactions:

DATE: TIME OF DAY:

1. _____   _____

2. _____   _____

3. _____   _____

4. _____   _____

5. _____   _____

6. _____   _____

7. _____   _____

Thanks again for your help. I look forward to meeting with you.

Sincerely,

Figure 8-6

FOLLOW-UP LETTER
TO STUDENT ATHLETE AND PARENT(S)

Date

(Appropriate Name
Address
City, State Zip)

Dear (Athlete's/Parent's Name):

Now that college is a daily reality for you, we wonder how you're doing! I remember it as one of the happiest times of my life; I hope it is much the same for you. Because we had a hand in your decision, we would appreciate some feedback to a few questions. The information you provide will enable us to do an even better job with tomorrow's student athletes.

Please take just a moment or two to respond to the following questions:

1. Are you satisfied with your academic program in college?

2. Are you satisfied with the athletic program in your school? If not, why?

3. Do you feel the meetings we had here in high school helped with your decision?

4. What kind of additional information would have been helpful?

5. What kinds of experiences have you had in college that were surprising, even shocking?

6. What options other than meetings might we have explored to anticipate those realities?

We wish you the best, and hope you'll stay in touch. Thanks for the help with this letter. Please use the stamped, self-addressed envelope to return it to us.

Sincerely,

Athletic Director

NINE

FINANCING THE STUDENT ATHLETE'S COLLEGE EDUCATION

INTRODUCTION

The issue of "play for pay" is a recurring controversy among sports fans. Many in the growing legion of sports critics "out there" agree that paying college athletes for their time and talent seems to be a reasonable response to the lowering of eligibility standards or the time demands during practice or in the off-season. The issue has grown so big that compromises like "need-based athletic aid" are echoing through the halls of ivy and the offices of intercollegiate officials.

In part, a concession to the argument favoring "play for pay," such responses must be considered in a broader perspective if intercollegiate athletics is to continue being perceived "… as an integral part of the educational program and the athlete as an integral part of the student body." (Statement of Basic Purpose in *NCAA Manual*) In other words, is "play for pay" a response to the symptoms of an illness affecting intercollegiate athletics, or does it respond to the illness itself?

Too often, our government, both on the state and federal levels, and our social institutions spend a great deal of time treating the symptoms of social issues and avoiding the issues themselves. Your family doctor will be quick to tell you that it's less complicated treating symptoms than diagnosing and treating underlying illnesses. She or he will also tell you that, in some instances, patients die.

It may be unfair or inaccurate at this stage in the evolution of intercollegiate athletics to say that it's dying, but it's certainly reasonable to suggest that *something* is rotten on the inside, and it doesn't take a team of prominent social psychologists to make a diagnosis. Any fair-thinking spectator of the sports scene—whether a fan, an athlete, a coach, or a parent—recognizes that the two vested interests identified in Section 1 of this book—the overemphasis on winning and money—*can be* pathogenic; they *can* cause an underlying illness.

Isn't it interesting, therefore, that one of society's suggested "cures" (play for pay) for an illness affecting intercollegiate athletics (the overemphasis on money) does more to strengthen the disease than to cure it? When we treat symptoms, that can happen. This section avoids that tendency by recognizing the intrinsic value of a college education and identifying intercollegiate athletics as only a complement to that education.

FINANCING WHAT?

A prominent professional sports official once said to me, "Mike, isn't it incredible that Notre Dame and Michigan are playing in front of hundreds of thousands of fans and bringing in hundreds of thousands of dollars for both schools, and the players are the only ones not getting any of the money?" My response was, "Isn't it equally incredible that most major schools are bringing in hundreds of thousands of dollars from revenue-producing sports and breaking even each year—if they're lucky!"

The fact is, many of them, perhaps most, are losing money each year. I'm the first to admit that gender equity is both desirable and justifiable. The fact remains, however, that it has strained athletic budgets across the country—so much so that most major athletic programs are struggling to stay alive financially.

What this means is simple. To expect such schools to pay their athletes a fair wage, whatever that means, for the athletic talents they bring to the campus is not only unrealistic financially but shortsighted as a way to combat one of its vested interests, an overemphasis on money. The question remains: What are we seeking to finance for college-bound student athletes? Are we financing a hiatus between high school and the pros that promotes an almost exclusive focus on athletics and money? Or are we financing an academic experience—also involving a sport—that prepares someone for a life of work that promotes fulfillment for the individual, security for his or her family, and the potential to earn hundreds of thousands of dollars more than if the athlete had not gone to college? Furthermore, I believe that financing a college education is not just an investment in the future but a reflected desire to provide for the immediate educational, personal, and social needs of students.

Sometimes, such an investment involves sacrifice. Parents often give up simple pleasures to find the money to help their children pay college expenses. Students often maintain two and sometimes three jobs during the school year as well as the summer to meet personal expenses and to help with tuition costs. Rarely do such families complain; they realize the importance of their sacrifice.

This section, then, reemphasizes the intrinsic value of a college education and suggests that young athletes and their parents have access to processes *right now* that can help finance it. Understanding those processes is important if we are to benefit from them. A knowledge of general terms is the logical first step.

UNDERSTANDING THE GENERAL TERMS AFFECTING FINANCIAL AID

With the exclusive input of Joe Russo, the Director of Financial Aid at the University of Notre Dame, this section provides a list of terms that introduces parents and young athletes to a general overview of what it means to finance a college education. According to Joe, the following concepts apply:

- *Student-Expense Budget*—In essence, this is the cost of attending a given college for one academic year. It includes both the direct and indirect expenses of attendance.

- *The Direct Expenses*—These expenses normally involve tuition and fees, room and board.

- *The Indirect Expenses*—These expenses normally involve the purchase of books and supplies, incidental expenses, and transportation to and from the campus one or more times.

- *Family Contribution*—This is the amount of money the family is expected to pay to meet the student's total college expenses, which are a combination of the direct and indirect expenses. The family contribution is a fixed sum as determined by the Federal Methodology. It will be the same at any college to which the student applies, regardless of the variability of the costs of the different colleges.

Student-expense budgets vary, depending on the tuition and room and board rates of different colleges. The student's financial need, therefore, as determined by the federal need-analysis formula, is the difference between the total costs of attending a given college and the family's expected contribution. This financial need, which can be different for the same student, depending on each school's expense budget, becomes the basis for the family's search for financial aid.

- *Financial Aid*—This is any type of assistance used to help a student meet college costs. It is divided into two categories:

  —*Gift Aid*—normally consists of scholarships, grants, and/or athletic grants-in-aid.

  —*Self-Help Aid*—normally involves loans and/or work assistance.

- *Financial Aid Package*—A financial aid package is offered to students who evidence a financial need, and consists of some combination of gift aid and self-help aid. Figure 9-1 provides a reproducible that can be distributed to student athletes and their parents to explain much of the foregoing information.

Student athletes and their parents should realize that an athletic grant-in-aid normally covers all the *direct expenses* and some of the *indirect expenses* relating to college costs. This may not be enough for some families to cover the total costs of going to a particular college. The NCAA and other regulatory organizations, therefore, permit student athletes to apply for Pell Grants and academic awards to supplement funds.

Under current regulations, Federal Pell Grants are awarded as "entitlements" by most colleges and universities, as elements in the total financial aid process. Academic awards, under certain circumstances, may also be permitted above and beyond athletic grants-in-aid. Families are encouraged, therefore, to initiate the financial aid process during the student's senior year in high school to identify the different interpretations of some schools. A knowledge of a few specific terms will be helpful at that time.

SPECIFIC TERMS RELATING TO FINANCIAL AID AND ATHLETIC SCHOLARSHIPS

Families are likely to hear most of these terms during the financial aid process. A knowledge of them is likely to avoid problems. These terms are borrowed from the *NCAA Guide to Financial Aid.* Figure 9-2 lists the most relevant terms and is an excellent reproducible to give student athletes and parents who seek additional information about the financial aid process. Although the following list uses some of the exact language of the *NCAA Guide,* not all of the terms have been included. For detailed information, therefore, coaches, counselors, athletic directors, and parents are encouraged to refer to a copy of the *NCAA Guide to Financial Aid.*

- *Academic Honor Award*—normally made for outstanding academic achievement to student athletes in Division II and III programs. They must be awarded independently of athletics and should be consistent with the amounts normally awarded to nonathletes.

- *Athletics Aid*—any financial aid given to a student athlete that is based on athletic ability.

- *Countable Aid*—aid, no matter what the amount, that must be included in the individual and institutional limits set by NCAA regulations.

- *Counter*—a student athlete who receives institutional financial aid that must be included in the college's sport-by-sport limits for such aid. The limits are established by the college's NCAA membership division.

- *Equivalency Sports*—sports that can award full grants-in-aid or divide the equivalent of one full grant-in-aid among two or more student athletes, in effect creating partial scholarships. It's important to note that in Division I schools, all sports are equivalency sports except football, men's and women's basketball, and women's volleyball, tennis, and gymnastics. In Division II schools, all sports are equivalency sports.

- *Financial Aid Agreement*—a written statement that annually informs a student athlete of the exact amount of financial aid the college is offering. The agreement is finalized when the student athlete signs it and returns it to the college's office of financial aid.

- *Individual Limits*—the restrictions placed on the amount of aid intercollegiate student athletes can receive and still keep their eligibility. Four groups of student athletes are affected by such restrictions—those who:

  —Receive athletic aid from a college.

  —Were recruited and receive any aid from the college.

  —Were recruited and receive athletic aid that is administered outside the college.

—Receive financial aid that is administered outside the college and is based on participation in high school, whether the athlete was recruited or not.

- *Legitimate Loans*—loans that involve repayment schedules and are available to all students. Perkins and Stafford Student Loans are the most common. They do not have to be counted toward a student athlete's individual limits or the college's sport-by-sport limits for financial aid.

- *National Letter of Intent*—a document attesting to a student athlete's commitment to attend a particular college. The process is administered by the Collegiate Commissioners Association.

- *Outside Financial Aid*—aid that is not administered by the college the student athlete attends. It must involve:

  —Aid given by the student athlete's parents, legal guardians, or someone upon whom they are legally dependent.

  —Aid having nothing to do with athletic ability.

  —Aid awarded through an established and continuing program. See bylaw 15.2.5.3 in the *NCAA Manual.*

  —Aid derived from an established and continuing program that recognizes outstanding high school graduates and allows athletics to be a major criterion. (See bylaw 15.2.5.4.)

- *Pell Grant*—a federal grant available to students who meet prescribed criteria. Student athletes and their parents are advised to discuss the specific amounts with financial aid personnel at the colleges they are considering.

- *Recruited Student Athlete*—one of the student's goals is to participate in a college's athletic program and a member of the athletic department or a representative of the athletic interests of the college does any of the following:

  —Provides an official visit.

  —Arranges an in-person, off-campus meeting with the athlete or parents or legal guardian(s).

  —Telephones the athlete or her or his family more than once to encourage sports participation at the college.

- *Representatives of Athletic Interests*—people who seek to help a particular college's athletic program (boosters). Colleges are responsible for the activities of these individuals if they:

  —Belong to an organization that promotes the college's athletic program(s).

  —Make financial contributions directly to the college's athletic department or indirectly through a booster organization.

  —Help recruit student athletes (even if the athletic department did not request their assistance).

  —Provide benefits to enrolled student athletes.

  —Promote the athletic program in other ways.

- *Student Athlete*—a student who is recruited to enroll in a college and intends to participate in its intercollegiate athletics program. An unrecruited student becomes a student athlete as soon as he or she reports for an intercollegiate squad within the college's athletic department. Simply having participated in high school sports does not apply.

These definitions are important for student athletes and their parents if they are to understand the language of the recruiting process. Many of the definitions explain the NCAA requirements for colleges engaged in recruiting, one of which involves "boosters." Because this requirement is potentially as serious for student athletes as for colleges, it warrants special mention.

BEWARE OF THE BOOSTER

As suggested in the previous list, boosters (Representatives of Athletics Interests) can provide a significant service to college athletic programs. The financial contributions they make often result in major equipment and facilities needs for sports programs. Boosters make such contributions for a variety of reasons. Some have a personal affiliation with the university or some of its personnel, perhaps having played for it at some time in the past. Others maintain a sense of loyalty to an alma mater.

Others choose to affiliate with a college athletic program by contributing money in order to identify with its successes and to claim a "liaison" with them. And still others become deeply involved because of one or more vested interests. They may own a local business and benefit from the revenues produced during home contests, or they may seek the contrived satisfaction that results from doing "favors" for outstanding young athletes.

Most boosters offer their support to share their own good fortune and to maintain their personal affiliation with a favorite college. Some, however, have selfish reasons or work in collaboration with unprincipled coaches or "agents," enhancing their self-images by working behind the scenes to "buy" young athletes for certain sports programs. Because such persons clearly violate the principles of amateurism and tend to be indistinguishable among the college's sports fans, the NCAA has ruled that no booster can be involved in the actual off-campus recruiting process.

Although boosters are permitted to write letters and make phone calls at other times during the student athlete's junior and senior years, athletes and their parents are advised to avoid contact with boosters, no matter what their promises or involvement with the university. It's not always that easy to identify someone who promotes the university's athletic interests but in an unofficial capacity. Families, therefore, should be alerted to NCAA regulations involving recruiting.

SIGNING THE NATIONAL LETTER OF INTENT

The National Letter of Intent is not administered by the NCAA. It is coordinated by the Collegiate Commissioners Association and represents the student athlete's commitment to attend a particular university. At one time a commitment to one school within a particular conference, the letter now represents a national commitment. According to David

Thompson, the Assistant Commissioner of the Atlantic Coast Conference and an overseer of the National Letter of Intent, "Let's put it this way, it would be as difficult for an athlete to alter his or her commitment between two different conferences as within the same one."

Virtually every Division I and II school in the country subscribes to the National Letter of Intent, which is signed at different times of the year, based on the sport involved. For specific signing periods, young athletes and their parents are encouraged to read the *NCAA Guide for the College-Bound Student Athlete*. In fact, any young student athlete asked to sign a National Letter of Intent is strongly encouraged to sit down with his or her parents and read the document very carefully.

To quote David Thompson again, "It's a four-page document that should be read in its entirety. Many families fail to do this. As a result, some don't completely understand what they're committing to." Thompson went on to suggest that student athletes and their parents should then be encouraged to ask questions and seek additional explanations about the Letter of Intent before signing it.

In essence, the National Letter of Intent is the culmination of all the planning the family has experienced within the past several months. It is not only a commitment to a particular school, therefore, but a statement from the athlete and his or her parents that they have planned well and are prepared to make a decision that assures the academic and athletic best interests of the student athlete. It represents a relatively binding decision.

The relativity of the decision involves the opportunity to transfer to another school but only after one academic year or if the student is "mutually released" from his or her commitment by both schools involved in the transfer. If mutually released, the student athlete must still pay the penalty of sitting out of competition for one year and losing that year of eligibility. Students can also appeal to the Letter of Intent Steering Committee for release from the commitment without penalty.

If a student fails to honor the commitment and attends a school other than the one he or she committed to, that student can be penalized by sitting out of competition for up to two years and losing both years of eligibility. The Letter of Intent involves a very serious commitment and should not be taken lightly. Because it represents the student athlete's one, final decision, it is the only form that should be signed throughout the recruiting process.

Student athletes are not permitted to sign any kind of commitment, not even the National Letter of Intent, until the official signing period. Again, student athletes and their parents are encouraged to talk to their coaches, even to call the Collegiate Commissioners Association for additional information about the National Letter of Intent. As important, they are encouraged to accept it as the culmination of months of careful planning, their commitment to the one, best school that satisfies the educational and athletic needs of the student.

AN INTERVIEW WITH JOE RUSSO, DIRECTOR OF FINANCIAL AID, UNIVERSITY OF NOTRE DAME

Joe Russo has been involved in university administration for over thirty years, having served as the Director of Financial Aid at Notre Dame since 1978. He is the editor of the

Journal of Student Financial Aid and a member of several national committees, including the NCAA Committee on Financial Aid and Amateurism. In that capacity, Joe was responsible for helping to write a section of the *NCAA Guide to Financial Aid*. He is a frequent speaker at national conventions (he and I have teamed up several times). There may be no one more qualified to validate the substance of this chapter than Joe Russo.

Mike: "What one, two, or three things must student athletes and their parents know about financial aid as it applies to them? What can we tell them that will make this chapter useful?"

Joe: "Well, as the best preface for my answer, I'm inclined to say to young athletes, 'What a great opportunity your athletic talent can provide for you to further your education. Having the opportunity to further your education is a real privilege, and it recognizes your talent and outstanding achievements. It will continue to require your disciplined approach to your studies and, most important, to your development as a young adult.'"

Mike: "Joe, excuse me for interrupting, but I asked Lorna Straus a related question a while ago, one dealing with eligibility, and she gave me fundamentally the same answer. I hope everyone out there can begin to look at a college education the way we do."

Joe: "You know how much I agree with that. Like Lorna, I'm proud to be associated with a university that believes it, too. What's another thing they absolutely have to know? NCAA policies require that the amount of assistance awarded has to be determined on an annual basis. That's one; another one is that the rules governing financial aid differ among the three divisions in the NCAA, among different schools, and certainly among the students who apply for the aid."

Mike: "Without my getting into the specifics of that statement, which are almost impossible to explain in one chapter, I agree that their understanding of those issues is critical."

Joe: "Absolutely. The provisions among Divisions I, II, and III are very different."

Mike: "And even then, it will differ among schools. Right?"

Joe: "Right. Then, we start trailing off into confusion."

Mike: "What a great way to put it! That's exactly what it does."

Joe: "Well, maybe that's the point."

Mike: "How do you mean?"

Joe: "Well, we have the NCAA stipulation of tuition, fees, room and board, but we also have the "cost of attendance" factors that are determined by the individual school's financial aid office. This latter concept includes transportation and other expenses related to attendance. These factors, therefore, vary not only from individual student to individual student but from school to school, so there are two moving targets."

Mike: "In other words, one student athlete can be recruited by five schools and have five different financial offers."

Joe: "Yes, that's true, and, as you know, that's also true of all students. That's a fact in the world of financial aid, no matter who is involved."

Mike: "It does get complicated, doesn't it?"

Joe: "You bet, and not only do the aid offers differ but what's expected from the family can differ. There's a third moving target. So you've got three moving targets here, all for the same student."

Mike: "So the bottom line is to get answers. Because the needs of athletes are treated so differentially, would you advise prospective student athletes to call financial aid offices for specific information?"

Joe: "Their best bet is to get involved in the financial aid process, and they can do that by talking to their coaches and, most of all, to their high school counselors to get the forms and explanations of them."

LET'S WRAP IT UP

Perhaps that's the best place to conclude this section. The financial aid process is complicated enough without further discussions of NCAA restrictions regarding summer school, work, qualifiers versus nonqualifiers, academic awards, government grant programs, and loans. Fortunately, these considerations are accommodated by financial aid offices once the student athlete initiates the process by submitting the necessary forms.

Like Joe Russo, financial aid administrators are committed to finding equitable ways to meet the financial needs of all students. They all work very closely with coaches and families to identify a financial aid package that makes a college education possible for qualified student athletes. In addition, they are in the best position to assure compliance with all pertinent regulations. At some time in the process, therefore, they become ex-officio members of the coalition that works on the student athlete's behalf.

The most important people in this process, however, are the student athlete and his or her parents. Their initial focus on college as an opportunity to promote the educational, personal, and social development of the student is the force that sustains the sense of direction for everyone involved in the recruiting and college selection processes. Such a focus obscures "play for pay" as a critical consideration. "Play for pay" focuses primarily on the needs or wants of the athlete.

"Playing the price" may be a better catch phrase. Young men and women who use their athletic talents to further their educations realize the best of both worlds. They play a sport that gives them a great deal of pleasure and recognition, and they receive an education that is personally and professionally fulfilling. The returns on the college "investment," therefore, promote not only financial security but the personal development that brings genuine happiness in life.

Figure 9-1

FINANCIAL AID AT A GLANCE

Student athletes and parents: Use the following information to give you a better idea of financial aid in college. If you have questions, call your counselor.

- *Student-Expense Budget*—In essence, this is the cost of attending a given college for one academic year. It includes both the direct and indirect expenses of attendance.
- *The Direct Expenses*—These expenses involve tuition and fees, room and board.
- *The Indirect Expenses*—These expenses normally involve the purchase of books and supplies, incidental expenses, and transportation to and from the campus.
- *Family Contribution*—This is the amount of money the family is expected to pay to meet the student's total college expenses, which are a combination of the direct and indirect expenses. It will be the same at any college to which the student applies, regardless of the variability of the costs of the different colleges.

Student-expense budgets vary, depending on the tuition and room and board rates of different colleges. The student's financial need, therefore, as determined by the federal need-analysis formula, is the difference between the total costs of attending a given college and the family's expected contribution. This financial need becomes the basis for the family's search for financial aid.

- *Financial Aid*—This is any type of assistance used to help a student meet college costs. It is divided into two categories:
  - —*Gift Aid*—normally consists of scholarships, grants, and/or athletic grants-in-aid
  - —*Self-Help Aid*—normally involves loans and/or work assistance
- *Financial Aid Package*—A financial aid package is offered to students who evidence a financial need and consists of some combination of gift aid and self-help aid.

	COLLEGE		
	A	B	C
TUITION	$ 5,000	$ 9,200	$12,000
R&B	4,100	3,300	4,400
BOOKS	550	480	500
PERSONAL	600	600	600
TRAVEL	300	550	150
TOTAL	$10,550	$14,130	$17,650

(The above constitutes three different student-expense budgets, each consisting of direct and indirect expenses.)

Assume a family contribution of $7,000.

COLLEGE		
A	B	C
$10,550	$14,130	$17,650
− 7,000	− 7,000	− 7,000
$ 3,550	$ 7,130	$10,650

This, too, can vary:

	COLLEGE		
	A	B	C
GRANT:	$2,000	$2,500	$2,000
LOAN:	1,000	4,000	3,200
WORK:	550	550	550
	$3,550	$7,050	$5,750

The above constitutes three different packages, only one of which meets all the needs.

SEE YOUR COUNSELOR FOR MORE INFORMATION

© 1996 by Michael D. Koehler

Figure 9-2

FINANCIAL AID
AND THE STUDENT ATHLETE

TO: *Student Athletes and Their Parents:*

Following are some terms that may apply to your future situation regarding financial aid for college expenses. Your familiarity with them will help during planning activities and meetings with college coaches.

- *Athletics Aid*—any financial aid given to a student athlete that is based on athletic ability.

- *Countable Aid*—aid, no matter what the amount, that must be included in the individual and institutional limits set by NCAA regulations.

- *Counter*—a student athlete who receives institutional financial aid that must be included in the college's sport-by-sport limits for such aid. The limits are established by the college's NCAA membership division.

- *Equivalency Sports*—sports that can award full grants-in-aid or divide the equivalent of one full grant-in-aid among two or more student athletes, in effect creating partial scholarships. It's important to note that in Division I schools, all sports are equivalency sports except football, men's and women's basketball, and women's volleyball, tennis, and gymnastics. In Division II schools, all sports are equivalency sports.

- *Individual Limits*—the restrictions placed on the amount of aid intercollegiate student athletes can receive and still keep their eligibility. Four groups of student athletes are affected by such restrictions—those who:

  —Receive athletic aid from a college.

  —Were recruited and receive any aid from the college.

  —Were recruited and receive athletic aid that is administered outside the college.

  —Receive financial aid that is administered outside the college and is based on participation in high school, whether the athlete was recruited or not.

- *Legitimate Loans*—loans that involve repayment schedules and are available to all students. Perkins and Stafford Student Loans are the most common. They do not have to be counted toward a student athlete's individual limits or the college's sport-by-sport limits for financial aid.

- *National Letter of Intent*—a document attesting to a student athlete's commitment to attend a particular college. The process is administered by the Collegiate Commissioners Association.

- *Outside Financial Aid*—aid that is not administered by the college the student athlete attends. It must involve:

  —Aid given by the student athlete's parents, legal guardians, or someone upon whom they are legally dependent.

  —Aid having nothing to do with athletic ability.

  —Aid awarded through an established and continuing program. See bylaw 15.2.5.3 in the *NCAA Manual.*

  —Aid derived from an established and continuing program that recognizes outstanding high school graduates and allows athletics to be a major criterion. (See bylaw 15.2.5.4.)

215

Figure 9-2 (continued)

FINANCIAL AID
AND THE STUDENT ATHLETE

- *Pell Grant*—a federal grant available to students who meet prescribed criteria. Student athletes and their parents are advised to discuss the specific amounts with financial aid personnel at the colleges they are considering.

- *Recruited Student Athlete*—one of the student's goals is to participate in a college's athletic program and a member of the athletic department or a representative of the athletic interests of the college does any of the following:

  —Provides an official visit.

  —Arranges an in-person, off-campus meeting with the athlete or parents or legal guardian(s).

  —Telephones the athlete or her or his family more than once to encourage sports participation at the college.

- *Representatives of Athletic Interests*—people who seek to help a particular college's athletic program (boosters). Colleges are responsible for the activities of these individuals if they:

  —Belong to an organization that promotes the college's athletic program(s).

  —Make financial contributions directly to the college's athletic department or indirectly through a booster organization.

  —Help recruit student athletes (even if the athletic department did not request their assistance).

  —Provide benefits to enrolled student athletes.

  —Promote the athletic program in other ways.

- *Student Athlete*—a student who is recruited to enroll in a college and intending to participate in its intercollegiate athletics program. An unrecruited student becomes a student athlete as soon as he or she reports for an intercollegiate squad within the college's athletic department. Participation in high school sports does not apply.

SEE YOUR COUNSELOR OR COACH
FOR ADDITIONAL INFORMATION

TEN

ACADEMIC ADVISEMENT IN COLLEGE

INTRODUCTION

Academic advisement for athletes started almost thirty years ago at the University of Texas and, a short time later, at schools like Notre Dame and some of the Big Ten schools. The cynics among us would suggest that they were developed to assure the continuing eligibility of athletes. My discussions with directors of academic advisement programs, however, suggest more altruistic motives.

Many of them were developed to respond to the growing need for some kind of support system for college athletes. With the gradual but relentless time demands being placed on college athletes, it was becoming increasingly evident to authorities that something had to be done to help student athletes with their personal and academic adjustment to the expectations of college.

Although currently mandated by the NCAA for Division I athletes, academic advisement started well before NCAA and governmental mandates for reform. It was introduced by schools that recognized the college athlete's need for academic assistance to compensate for the time and energy demands of their sports. Such programs have grown considerably over the years and now provide help for athletes in a variety of areas of their personal, academic, and professional development.

217

Some high school athletes are well advised to consider the quality of the academic advisement programs at colleges when choosing the"right"school. Some provide only a cursory attempt at advisement. Others work closely with student athletes to assist them with the transition to college, the demands of their academic programs, their personal problems, the need to meet graduation and eligibility requirements, and the processes involved in finding employment after graduation.

This section outlines the characteristics of good programs and explains the steps student athletes must take before and during college to assure academic and athletic success. Student athletes and their parents are encouraged to read this section before visiting college campuses, to assess the quality of the schools'academic advisement programs. The quality of the program may not be the single most important criterion in the selection process, but it is a very important one.

PREPARING THE HIGH SCHOOL ATHLETE FOR LIFE IN COLLEGE

Some of the preceding sections discussed college eligibility and graduation requirements, the demands of competitive sports, and the criteria that young athletes use to select"best"schools. Student athletes and their parents are advised to review Figures 3-9, 3-15, 4-5, and 4-11 to identify topics that require discussion before they decide on a college and eventually enroll.

The young athlete who perceives college as an athletic hiatus between high school and the pros is an unlikely candidate for the pros and a likely dropout from college. His or her unwillingness in high school to explore potential careers and to develop an academic orientation for coursework poses a serious obstacle to an eventual adjustment to the academic, personal, and social demands of most campuses. Without such an adjustment, young athletes inevitably miss out on the promise of a future career in professional sports—or anywhere else.

They are advised to discuss the topics listed in Figure 10-1 with their parents, counselors, and coaches well before leaving for college. The reproducible was developed by Marybeth Kravets, a prominent college consultant, and identifies several considerations before young athletes leave for school. A copy should be shared with student athletes and their parents along with the suggestion that they discuss it at home.

Starting College on the Right Foot

Well-conceived programs of academic advisement provide for the orientation needs of entering student athletes. Specifics are discussed later in this section. For now, let's focus on a few of the reasons why young athletes experience adjustment problems during their first few months in college. Much of this information is used with the permission of Dr. Roger Grooters, the former Director of Academic Advisement for Athletes at the University of Nebraska. Dr. Grooters helped develop one of the best programs in the nation at Nebraska and has since relocated to Florida State University, where he is maintaining another excellent program. Much of his success is attributable to a knowledge of the reasons for the poor adjustment of students during their first year of college, which includes recognition of the following:

- Almost a third of the nation's first-year college students either drop out or transfer to another school during their freshman year. A significant number of these students will leave during their first six weeks of school.

- A major reason for dropping out involves academic boredom and inappropriate course selection. Often, first-semester freshmen attack their courses the same way they hit the training table. Many invariably take on too much and underestimate the difficulty of their programs. Many first-semester freshmen should be encouraged to take a full-time but reduced load to accommodate the demands of their classes as well as the personal, social, and athletic adjustments they will have to make.

- Dropping out also results from the stress of transitional experiences. The move from high school to college represents for most students their first big step away from home. In some instances, the loneliness they experience can cause depressive reactions. Many will benefit from periodic contact with campus support services.

- Many first-year students enter college with unrealistic expectations. Jethro, Jed's energetic but shortsighted nephew on the Beverly Hillbilly's, was convinced that his sixth grade education qualified him to be a brain surgeon. Many entering freshmen—if not quite as bad as Jethro—set their sights on unrealistic professional programs that lead to almost immediate academic problems.

  In many instances, the students with the most unrealistic goals are those guilty of the least preparation; they somehow failed to engage in career exploration during the junior year in high school. Entering college students must meet with their advisors early to understand the relationship of their aptitudes and academic achievement with the expectations of the programs they have selected.

- A fourth reason that students drop out during the freshman year involves incompatibility with the college. Some student athletes feel that they just "don't fit in." While much of this may be normal, especially during the first month of school, such incompatibility may result from poor planning in high school. Families wanting to avoid similar problems are encouraged to review relevant sections of this book, particularly those dealing with the college selection process.

- The final reason for dropping out involves inadequate academic preparation in high school. While this can be a significant interference during the first several weeks of college, students can overcome the problem if they believe in themselves and follow the eight principles contained in Figure 10-2. Because Dr. Grooters developed this format while at Nebraska, it's not surprising that he entitled them the "Big Eight" academic success tips. Because you may want to reproduce the material, I have omitted "Big Eight" from the title, although I do so reluctantly. (Nebraska is my alma mater.) Parents are encouraged to discuss each of these tips with their students before loading the car for that first trip to college. A preliminary discussion of them can avoid many unnecessary problems during the first several weeks at school.

CHARACTERISTICS OF GOOD PROGRAMS OF ACADEMIC ADVISEMENT FOR ATHLETES

Generally, the effective programs of academic advisement for student athletes involve at least three components: Personal, Academic, and Professional. Following is a discussion of the aspects of each component.

The Personal Component. This component is primarily responsible for the student athlete's initial and continuing adjustment to the personal, social, and educational expectations of the college. The following elements tend to be representative of most good programs:

- *Orientation*—Student athletes generally are involved in a series of presentations and activities that introduce them to the campus, outline graduation and eligibility requirements, explain the purposes and operation of the academic advisement program, explain the services available to all students in the college, identify and discuss relevant NCAA policies, explain expectations of the conference, especially as they relate to the NCAA and other regulatory organizations, and promote discussion of the uniqueness of the first several weeks of college.

- *Personal Counseling*—Individual counseling experiences are usually available to student athletes who have problems with the transition to college life, experience serious academic problems and require academic assessments, suddenly find themselves unable to manage stress, or require special assistance with personal crises.

- *Minority Assistance*—Many programs acknowledge the need to provide discovery experiences in multiculturalism. Because of the unique ethnic mix of most sports programs and because many athletes come from culturally isolated parts of the country, several academic advisement programs provide seminars that promote cultural awareness for all students and career exploration for minority groups.

- *Drug Awareness*—Although the use of steroids and other illegal drugs seems to be declining on many college campuses, the problem is still significant enough to warrant drug awareness activities that inform student athletes about the dangers of alcohol and drug use, promote the skills to deal with temptation, and provide support programs that reinforce good intentions or that intervene in cases of drug use.

- *After Graduation*—Let's admit it, most student athletes receive preferential treatment from their coaches and almost daily recognition from others on the campus. Because fewer than one percent of them will find careers in professional sports, graduation marks the end of a very ego satisfying time in their lives. Several academic advisement programs help student athletes understand that "life after sports" can provide different but equally satisfying recognition. Often, such programs involve presentations from former players who have successfully made the transition.

The Academic Component. This component assures an appropriate academic orientation and the kinds of processes that enable student athletes to work up to their academic potential. Good programs integrate many of the following characteristics:

- *Tutoring*—Perhaps one of the most important components of any academic advisement program, tutoring is often the one intervention that enables student athletes to realize their academic potential. Tutoring is especially effective if some kind of academic assessment is completed for each student athlete, one that includes grades in high school, admissions tests results, and reading and writing strengths. With such information, individual tutors can capitalize on strengths and help overcome academic weaknesses. A good tutoring program, therefore, provides subject-matter tutoring as well as assistance with organizational and study skills.

- *Supervision*—To guarantee that student athletes are furthering their own educational interests, most effective programs of academic advisement monitor both the attendance and the grades of student athletes. Academic advisement counselors are in frequent, sometimes weekly, contact with professors to receive updates on the attendance and coursework of student athletes. Students who fall behind in either area are contacted by the counselors and, if necessary, their coaches to "reaffirm their good intentions."

- *Computer Instruction*—Many student athletes, particularly those from disadvantaged backgrounds, are unfamiliar with the benefits of computers and word processors. Many programs of academic advisement provide computer labs that introduce student athletes to the facilities and provide instruction on the use of computers. They also provide software packages and a support staff to help resolve problems and provide additional instruction as needed. This is a very important element in any good program.

- *Assistance with Reading and Writing*—Generally housed in a lab facility, this component involves one of the primary and most important areas of intervention for student athletes; it focuses on the improvement of reading rate and comprehension, and the improvement of writing organization and rhetoric. It also seeks to reduce reading and writing anxiety, improve note-taking skills, and promote creative thinking.

The Career Component. This final feature in a good program of academic advisement anticipates graduation by providing the following elements for student athletes:

- *Degree Progress*—Student athletes sometimes require help with the registration process. Some require assurances that they are maintaining eligibility and satisfying the academic requirements of their majors. To assure adequate progress, good academic advisement programs communicate routinely with each student athlete's advisor. Normally, such information is kept in a file to record cumulative progress.

- *Career Exploration*—Student athletes are encouraged to reconsider the same kinds of issues and experiences they explored in high school. The closer they get to graduation, however, the easier it becomes to identify career areas that interest them. In fact, most have identified specific career interests by their sophomore years when many schools require a specific academic commitment from them.

  To promote such planning early in college, academic advisement programs often offer Career Nights, Career Fairs, and information about internships and opportunities to visit local businesses to observe specific jobs.

- *Career Orientation*—The task of finding a job involves the development of a personal resume, a cover letter to express interest in the job, processes for finding employment opportunities, skills for effective interviewing, and opportunities for postgraduate or professional study. The high school student athlete who considers the importance of these characteristics in his or her school's program of academic advisement reaffirms the value of a college education and enters college for the right reasons. This aspect of the college selection process, therefore, is very important for both its long-range and its short-range benefits.

- *Job Placement*—This is one of the ultimate reasons for deciding to go to college and one of the most important criteria during the selection process. Basking in the sun on a sugar-white beach while reading Chaucer's romp through the *Canterbury Tales* may have short-term benefits, but if it doesn't involve a job at the end of four years, it can become an exercise in frustration.

  Good programs of academic advisement maintain a relationship with the university's placement office to assist student athletes with job identification. In addition, many of them supplement placement efforts by exploring their alumni network for help from former players and other graduates.

Additional Services

In addition to much of the above, some programs of academic advisement help graduating student athletes find postgraduate scholarships and grants, many of which are provided by the NCAA and other regulatory organizations. In many instances, their services are also available to student athletes after graduation to provide additional assistance with job searches.

Perhaps their most important service, however, is the assurance that student athletes new to the campus have "a place to go" and "someone to turn to" when the college experience becomes a problem. Good programs of academic advisement, therefore, are much more than neatly contrived processes to keep student athletes eligible for their respective teams. They are well-conceived support systems that make life easier and more predictable for a group of students who have committed so much of their time and energy to their respective schools.

LET'S WRAP IT UP

This section, although brief, provides very important information, particularly for the student athlete who may have experienced occasional academic problems in high school. For that matter, the information is helpful to any student athlete who anticipates normal adjustment problems during the first five to six weeks of college and recognizes the value of academic advisement and career exploration and placement.

Although the NCAA stipulates that all Division I schools must offer or make available academic counseling to all student athletes, most programs of academic advisement have exceeded those expectations by providing personal and career counseling as well. In effect, most of them provide a support program for many of the developmental as well as the adjustment problems of college students.

Some critics of intercollegiate athletics object to these kinds of programs for student athletes, condemning them for coddling an already pampered segment of the college population. Such critics fail to realize that college athletes are expected to spend almost as much time engaged in activities involving their sports as in their classwork. To make such a time commitment and still realize the personal and social benefits of a college experience, they need support services that help them realize their academic as well as their athletic potential.

Student athletes and their parents are encouraged, therefore, to evaluate the quality of such programs when they visit campuses and gather information to make a final college decision. This information may not be determinative, but it probably will figure heavily in the degree of success student athletes experience in the classroom as well as in their sports.

Figure 10-1

BEING A SUCCESSFUL STUDENT ATHLETE

There are many demands and pressures on the student athlete. All too often they result in failure—academic, athletic or both. Students must be prepared for the intense pressures they will experience.

1. Every expert agrees on one thing—put academics first!

2. Have realistic expectations; recognize that a future in sports is uncertain and even if you do become a professional, life as a pro is short!

3. Do your homework with as much effort as you put into your sport!

4. Try to get involved in other aspects of college life. It will add to your experience and prepare you for the world after college!

5. Learn to manage your time wisely! The student athlete is asked to play two roles and must find a balance between athletics and academics. Balance includes commitment, discipline, and responsibility to your coach, to your sport, and to yourself!

Problems You May Face

Eligibiliy—You must maintain a minimally acceptable grade point average and take a minimum number of credits to maintain good academic standing and be eligible to play a sport.

Financial Problems—College athletes rarely have time to work part time while in school. Most financial aid packages cover only basic educational and living expenses. Little is given for everyday expenses, clothes, or entertainment.

Personal Pressures—Coaches, teammates, parents, fans, media—all exert pressure—but no one exerts more pressure than you do yourself. Learn to handle this before you get to college.

Career Selection—Don't put this decision off for the future; take the time to pursue ideas, talk to career planning counselors at your school, set some goals.

Academic Pressures—Get help from the particular services offered at your school. Most schools have tutors available; maintain an ongoing relationship with your advisor and professors. Use the libraries, learning skills centers, counseling center, or health center. Get help before the problem becomes too great to overcome.

Advising—Get academic advice and information from the proper academic office—not from the coach or from listening to other players.

Used with permission from Marybeth Kravetz, College Consultant, Deerfield High School, Deerfield, IL.

Figure 10-2

SOME POINTERS FOR ACADEMIC SUCCESS

Student Athletes: The following pointers have been well researched by Dr. Roger Grooters, one of the nation's foremost directors of academic advisement, and have been proven to contribute to academic success in college. Read them carefully and apply them throughout college but especially during your freshman year. With use, they will become habits, the kind that carry over into everything you do in life.

1. *Organization*—Get organized! Read and periodically refer to the syllabuses your professors distribute in your classes. Also use the attached daily/weekly planner to provide regular reminders of work to be completed.

2. *Reading Materials in Advance*—Read assignments before class meets. Sometimes it's even a good idea to read the summaries of chapters before you read the chapters. That will give you a good idea of what is to come. As you read, list questions about confusing material, then be sure to ask about it in class.

3. *Class Attendance*—Go to class! This sounds pretty obvious, but you're about to discover that college provides more free time than some high school kids can handle. The freedom you experience in college can provoke some bad habits, so maintain the good habit of going to class regularly. And when you get there, you might as well participate. That's why you jot down all those questions when you read class assignments.

4. *Take Good Notes*—Learn good note-taking skills and record much of what you hear in class. That's why you have to be there! Then take your notes back to the dorm or the library and break down the key concepts, so you understand how everything fits together. Talk to your high school teachers about this skill before going to college and get pointers from them.

5. *Develop Exam Strategies*—Find some exams used previously in your courses and study them, even try to take them. They are usually available in department offices, in fraternities, or directly from the professor. Scan each exam before you take it to determine where you should put your priorities.

6. *Review and Rehearse*—Take just a few moments to review class notes on a daily basis. Overlearn the material before quizzes and exams! Look at your notes until you know what you're about to read before you turn the page. You'll be surprised how helpful this can be.

7. *Develop Your Writing Skills*—Understand what the professor wants in the paper and develop an outline. Then write the first draft on a word processor and look it over very carefully for changes. Write the final draft and have someone look it over for you, preferably someone in the academic advisement program.

8. *Get to Know Your Professors*—Visit them periodically so they know you. See them in their offices to ask about clarification of class materials and to let them know how serious you are about succeeding. You may feel funny saying such things, but they like to hear it!

SEE YOUR COUNSELOR AND TEACHERS FOR MORE POINTERS.
GOOD LUCK IN COLLEGE!

Figure 10-2 (continued)

DAILY/WEEKLY PLANNER

DIRECTIONS: Use the following calendar to record assignments and their completion dates. Each time you receive an assignment in class, write down the due date on this calendar, then indicate those times during the day when you will work on it. Include tests and quizzes and the amount of time you plan to devote to each one. Make approximately 50 extra copies of this form before going to college. You'll want to develop one each week.

For the Week of: _____

HOUR	MONDAY	TUESDAY	WEDNESDAY	THURSDAY	FRIDAY	SATURDAY	SUNDAY
8							
9							
10							
11							
12							
1							
2							
3							
4							
5							
6							
7							
8							
9							
10							

Especially important tasks for this week:

226

ELEVEN

"SPORTS FOR WHAT?"

INTRODUCTION

Those of us involved in American sports seem to have lost our moorings. Our values regarding the benefits of participation have become so divergent and so influenced by money that we seem unable to agree on the fundamental purposes of sport, let alone on the solutions to its problems. Section 1 of this book discussed my grandfather, Jim Thorpe, as America's prototypical student athlete. The focus of this section reminds me again of his situation, this time of his fundamental problem.

To review it, let me borrow from a recent article I wrote for *The College Board Review.* With the return of my grandfather's medals, the story of his ordeal came to an end, but thousands of young athletes can still learn from it. The most important lesson may involve the fact that, without competitive sports, Jim Thorpe might never have experienced tragedy, and his name certainly would not have echoed for decades, even centuries through time. Instead, he probably would have hunted and fished for most of his life in humble but relaxed anonymity.

Erich Fromm once said, "Sickness consists essentially in wanting what is not good for us." Jim Thorpe sublimated his personal, social, and intellectual development in a world that was essentially not good for him. He spent his last days reminiscing not about the 198 points he scored during his final year at Carlisle, but about carefree days fishing

227

with his twin brother, Charlie, along the red clay banks of the North Canadian River in southwestern Oklahoma.

Hunting and fishing and boyhood friends represented permanence in his life and, unlike professional sports, pleasures that never disappointed him. His slow drawl and down-home humor came more naturally when he hunted or fished, and they helped describe the real Jim. Jim Thorpe's satisfactions were found in the simplicity of his pleasures, not the magnificence of his gifts. His life is a lesson for all of us.

FINDING THE INTRINSIC PLEASURES OF SPORT

How do we get more student athletes to learn that lesson? How do we help them look beyond the whimsical promises of scholarships, professional sports, gold chains, and media hype to enjoy the intrinsic satisfactions of sport? How do we possibly battle the powerful influence of television's continuing message that kids simply need the right pair of shoes or the right sport drink to "be like Mike?"

For that matter, how do we battle a total media blitzkrieg that seeks only sensationalized stories of million-dollar salaries and frenetic lifestyles, creating role models of people who differ only physically from the rest of us? Think about it. The role model kids once found in the courage and dignity of a family member or a literary character has given way to the "role muddle" now found in taunting, slam dunking, and steroid abuse.

This is not to say that all college and professional athletes are bad role models; many of them are good ones. The point is, the behaviors of the good role models relate less to sports than to their personalities, their willingness to work with kids, to donate their time to charity, to love their parents, to *be* good parents, and to live upstanding lives. The personal behavior of good role models transcends their athletic ability and elevates them above the guy who may be a little taller or a little faster.

The same is true of the rest of us. Our society is full of nonathletes who actually live the values that many of us believe are still appropriate in our society: hard work, commitment, courage, and consideration. Their behavior, however, is too dull for media coverage. Real courage, the kind we see reflected in the behaviors of ordinary people every day, isn't newsworthy.

Fortunately, such behaviors are more immediately visible at home or in school than on sports pages. One of the answers to society's concerns, therefore, is to use the role models that are closer to home—parents, coaches, counselors—to combat media influences and to provide a daily reaffirmation of the values that lead student athletes toward fulfilling and satisfying futures.

To elaborate, consider the convincing argument of Total Quality Management (TQM). The brainchild of W. Edwards Deming, a popular American businessman and a force behind the resurgence of Japan as an economic power, Total Quality Management suggests a very important principle to keep in mind when we consider our place within the framework of American sport.

Through TQM, Deming suggests that up to 90% of the problems experienced in any system are the fault of the system. He suggests that, rather than seek out others to blame for system failures, the persons responsible for the system find the nearest mirror and ask themselves what they are doing to contribute to the problem. I suspect that this principle offers the logical starting point for each of us as we consider ways to combat the vested interests of athletics in this country.

As far back as 1927, Amos Alonzo Stagg said, "Most of the evils that have beset the game from time to time have been the direct result of student and alumni management, but the blame lies on the faculty doorstep." To be consistent with TQM, we might extend the comment to include the doorsteps of parents, coaches, and counselors as well. If Stagg were still coaching today, he'd probably criticize coaches who use the promise of scholarships as motivators, parents who use their children's athletic accomplishments as substitutes for their own, and counselors who refuse to learn the basics of NCAA eligibility.

Each of us, therefore, should look into Deming's mirror to examine how we might be contributing to the problem. If the system needs correction, each of us must acknowledge that we are very much a part of it, and we must do what we can to focus our attention and the hopes and dreams of young athletes on the intrinsic pleasure of the games they play.

GOOD SPORTSMANSHIP: A GROWING OXYMORON?

A sports psychologist at the University of California indicated recently that our society is experiencing in sport a "spiral of violence," that "aggression pays…. If the leagues really wanted to vanquish it entirely, they could, but I think it is seen as spice." In essence, taunting, chest bumping, and "trash-talking" have become the ganglike symbols that characterize the turf warfare of basketball and football, and the mutual respect that formerly dignified even bitter opponents has given way to bench-clearing brawls that leave everyone in the dirt.

In just two recent years, the National Basketball Association (NBA) experienced twenty-one fights and thirty-six game suspensions. In just one year, baseball had seventeen brawls and twenty-nine suspensions. Fortunately, the professional leagues are seeking to sanction both the players and the team each time brawls occur. The fundamental problem, however, remains. Many fans enjoy watching fights, and heightened levels of competitive intensity give it to them.

In such circumstances, all of us—fan and player alike—have to find the nearest mirror and reflect on our values and rethink the purposes of sport in this country. Are American sports a more tolerable equivalent of the flamboyant and violent spectacles of earlier times? Are they, in fact, concerned only with money and winning, or do they still impart the values that many of us believe to be so important for the youngsters who play them?

THE LESSONS OF SPORTS PARTICIPATION

Parents are probably the first to applaud the intervention of sports in the lives of their children. Like so many of us, they are convinced that athletic participation teaches youngsters of all ages positive values of team membership, hard work, and commitment.

Well, the good news is that, in many instances, participation in sports does just that. The bad news is that such positive influences seem to be changing.

In a recent article in the *Journal of the American Medical Association,* studies indicate that school sports really don't do much to alter the negative behaviors of youngsters. A study at the University of Pittsburgh, for example, studied approximately 500 12- to 16-year-olds who indicated to researchers that they had not drunk alcohol, smoked, or carried a weapon in the previous thirty days.

One year later, 9% to 15% of them had either carried a weapon, drunk, or smoked. The startling and relevant part of the study, however, indicated that, while only 7% of the nonathletes admitted to drinking, 17% of the boys who played one or two team sports now indicated that they were drinking. The percentage rose to 23% when the boys played more than two team sports. Among the girls, 27% of the former nondrinkers within one sport and 22% of the cheerleaders admitted drinking.

At about the same time, a study at the University of California in Los Angeles (UCLA) surveyed approximately equal numbers of athletes and nonathletes and discovered that the athletes drank more at one sitting and had more incidents of sexually transmitted diseases than nonathletes. An official at the university warned readers that the results of the study may not be generalizable. He also indicated, however, that such results should warn us against blanket acceptance of the notion that sports create self-disciplined students.

You and I should not assume that involvement in team sports causes teenagers to increase their involvement with alcohol or sex. The natural aggressiveness of many young athletes might result in such behaviors without their involvement in athletics. No matter what the cause, however, these studies indicate the predispositions of many young athletes to engage in the very behaviors that sports are supposed to curtail.

Such studies suggest the need for all of us, therefore, to constantly reevaluate the purposes of sport and to monitor our behaviors as well as those of our young athletes. Team sports place youngsters in mutually dependent circumstances and increase their influence on one another. When a sport becomes "something for its own sake," it increases the potential for abuse. Such abuse occurs in many different ways.

The High School Breeding Ground

Chicago prep sportswriter Tayor Bell discussed in a recent column how high school students, especially in their senior years, transfer to other high schools only to be on championship teams or to increase their media exposure for scholarships. Bell cited one prep basketball player who moved from a small town in South Carolina to play for a prominent Chicago team, one likely to vie for the state championship.

He mentioned another who moved from Tennessee to a nationally recognized prep school in Virginia for similar reasons. He also mentioned a youngster who moved from one school in the Chicago area to another school that is expected to compete for the Chicago-area basketball championship and traditionally is highly recruited by college football coaches. The young man left his mother to move in with his father, making the transfer legal according to the rules of the Illinois High School Association (IHSA).

Is it ethical, and does it send the right message to this young athlete and to the many others who read of his situation? Said the Executive Director of the IHSA:

"Something like this goes contrary to the spirit of residence of parents as the legitimate place where kids ought to go to school. [In such circumstances] the rule isn't accomplishing what it was intended to and needs to be evaluated."

Perhaps a lot of what we do in American sport has to be reevaluated. Consider just one more example.

Sacrifice for What?

Let's call him Tom. This is a true story. Tom was talented both on the football field and in the classroom. He was one of those kids who enhanced his natural talents with hard work and sacrifice. While other kids were wandering rapturously through the shopping mall after school, Tom was lifting weights and hurrying home to study for tomorrow's test. While classmates were lighting up cigarettes in cars on the way home after school, Tom was trudging toward the practice field for scrimmage and wind sprints.

The good news is that his hard work paid off. During his senior year in high school, Tom grew to 6'1" and 195 pounds, ran the 40-yard dash in 4.4 seconds, and became an All-City selection in football. He also ranked in the top five percent of his class, scored a 26 on the ACT, and was accepted to Harvard and the University of Chicago.

The bad news is, well, to quote him: "Everyone told me that hard work would make everything work out for me, but now I think that I have worked hard and sacrificed everything for nothing." You see, Tom wasn't offered a scholarship to play football for a major university. Tom, his coach, and his parents simply couldn't understand such recruiting disinterest. Even the newspaper that reported this story included the headline, "His Hard Work Doesn't Pay Off."

Certainly this story is only marginally tragic. Every day, the newspapers are full of others that describe athletes who can't read or who receive career-ending injuries, youngsters who experience intense emotional or physical pain. The tragedy of this story, however, involves a youngster who transformed his athletic and academic talents into a success story—by some parents' standards, a fairy tale. Because he failed to receive an athletic scholarship to college, however, he was convinced that somehow he had failed—or had been cheated.

Tom's pain was self-inflicted, and, ironically, it was aggravated by the people in his life who seemed to care most about him. The newspaper didn't help either. It only reported Tom's situation, but its emphasis on hard work not paying off helped perpetuate the misconception that the only reward at the end of a high school athletic career is a scholarship. We owe young athletes much more than this.

MORE TO THINK ABOUT

We owe them an education, and not just for the physical commitment they make to us as coaches and sports programs. We owe it because it satisfies our needs as well as theirs. When athletic participation results in well-educated high school or college graduates, they contribute more to society and make better decisions as citizens and parents. These are the biggest reasons to reconsider a recommendation that has been made recurrently in this book.

Among others, Joe Paterno, the head coach of the Penn State Nittany Lions, has suggested repeatedly that student athletes be declared ineligible for varsity competition during their freshmen years. In a special section of *USA Today,* he reasoned that student athletes need a year to "establish some priorities, adapt to changing academic challenges, and become comfortable in an environment free of the pressures of big-time college athletics."

I emphasized in Section 10 of this book the need to help young athletes adjust to their first big step away from home. Many youngsters have a tough time adjusting to significant transitions in their lives, even without the added daily pressure of competing with gifted students at almost every turn. They need time to adjust to academic and athletic expectations and to realize not only the challenges but the opportunities that accompany their efforts to earn a college degree.

The elimination of freshman eligibility would help satisfy the educational needs of most student athletes in two very important ways. The first is the most obvious. As indicated by Joe Paterno and scores of other coaches and high school and university officials, student athletes would have the time to adjust to college expectations. Such an argument seems too strong to warrant defense, even though it is constantly attacked by proponents of "athletic parity" on the university level.

As indicated in Section 1, "athletic parity"—the need to field teams of roughly equivalent ability—and "academic integrity"—the need to educate student athletes—have been argued for decades within hearing distance of the NCAA. The response of NCAA conventions and officials over the years has been dependent more on which way the political wind is blowing than on sheer force of reason. The argument, therefore, invariably reminds me of Voltaire's quote, "In long disputes, both parties are wrong."

The arguments have gone something like this. If university programs are to maintain athletic parity, freshman student athletes must be permitted to play. If university programs are to maintain academic integrity, schools must maintain minimal eligibility requirements, hence Proposition 48. Perhaps the time has come to consider a compromise position, one that might shorten the dispute and meet the needs of more student athletes.

A reasonable corollary to Paterno's recommendation for freshman ineligibility, therefore, is to create NCAA legislation that allows nonqualifiers (high school student athletes who are academically ineligible to receive athletic scholarships to college) to be recruited and scholarshipped by university programs but to be barred from practice or competition until the university has established their eligibility *by educating them.*

In essence, we would allow currently academically ineligible athletes to receive scholarships to universities that admit them but to continue to restrict them from competition until they become eligible within the NCAA's framework. Such a standard would represent a reasonable departure from the current NCAA position of refusing to educate disadvantaged or other athletes because they are uneducated.

The current claims of many coaches that disadvantaged nonqualifiers can succeed in a university classroom are undoubtedly correct. I am one example, and there are many others. Why not allow such coaches—and the universities they represent—to give scholarships to such youngsters *and bring them up to standard,* in effect, "put their money where their mouth is?" This would allow programs to try to recruit the athletes they need to maintain athletic parity, and it would satisfy the demands of others that universities maintain academic integrity. The onus of responsibility would be on the athlete and the university's sports program, where it belongs. Most important, it would compensate for the disadvantaged status of many young athletes and provide them the educational opportunities that promote their academic as well as their athletic potential. Again, it may be correct to say that we owe it to them—and to ourselves as a society of enlightened citizens.

LET'S WRAP IT UP

This section, and much of this book, provides some unique perspectives on interscholastic and intercollegiate athletics. They are perspectives avoided by spotlight-seeking congresspersons, university boosters, or some college coaches, many of whom are blinded by their own self-interests.

The perspectives come from parents, high school coaches, and counselors, those persons sitting in the shadows of American sport, behind-the-scenes forces who wield far more power than many in the spotlight seem willing to acknowledge. These are valuable perspectives, because they are shared by all of us who develop and influence the "blue-chippers" and other young athletes who attract college coaches and sometimes lure them to the brink of abuse.

This is a book for all of us, parents, athletes, high school coaches, counselors, athletic directors, school administrators—anyone who seeks the best interests of young athletes, no matter how highly recruited they may be. It reaffirms one basic principle: The more we work together, the more we meet the needs of our young athletes and influence the future direction of American sport.

LOOKING FOR AN ATHLETIC SCHOLARSHIP TO COLLEGE?

If you are a highly recruited
high school athlete,
you need this booklet!

HOW TO USE THIS BOOKLET

As a highly recruited student athlete, you probably need help sorting through the pile of letters, questionnaires, and phone messages that fill your days. While you may find all that attention complimentary, it can begin to wear on you, and, worst of all, it can get you thinking about college for all the *wrong reasons*. When college coaches are knocking down your door, you tend to overlook academics and think only about the athletic aspects of college.

This can be a mistake. College is, first of all, an experience that prepares you for the world of work and that is educationally, socially, and personally fulfilling in its own right. It can be one of the happiest times of your life and should not be restricted to athletic competition. Certainly, athletics will play a large part in your decision. That's one of the reasons for this booklet. But, as you will see when you complete this booklet, your selection of a particular college involves several considerations, only one of which involves sports.

Read the following discussion and refer to the forms that are mentioned. Use or modify them to suit your purposes. Some require that you meet with your counselor or coach to gather the right information. Make these appointments as necessary. You probably already know that these two people can provide some very important answers for you.

Additional answers can be found in the book, *Advising the Student Athlete*, published by Prentice Hall, Englewood Cliffs, NJ 07632 or the videotape, the *ABCs of Eligibility for the College-Bound Student Athlete*, marketed by the College Board, 45 Columbus Ave, New York, NY 10023.

A DISCUSSION OF THE FORMS

The first form, "My Did I List," is one of the most important because it outlines the important steps you must take to identify and ultimately choose the right college. It suggests the process you must follow in your junior year and provides a checklist so you can mark your progress through your last two years in high school. Once you have completed this list, you will be prepared to make a college decision for the right reasons.

The second form, "Form 48-H and the Clearinghouse," explains what happens when you fill out the Student Release Form to secure permission to be recruited and ultimately to receive an athletic scholarship to college. This is an important step to take early in your senior year, so be sure to see your counselor for more information.

The next two forms, "Watching Out for Improper Recruiting" and "Contacts and Visits," provide important considerations about recruiting and NCAA requirements. Read both forms very carefully. If, for some reason, you violate an NCAA requirement, even mistakenly, you can jeopardize your eligibility to play a sport in college. Discuss these two forms at home and with your coach and counselor. They can provide additional information.

"A Peek at the Pros" gives you some idea about the possibility of playing a professional sport. Disregard the form if you are recruited in a sport that doesn't have a professional level. If your sport does provide opportunities for play *and pay* beyond college, read this form very carefully. It underscores the importance of academics in college and discusses the incredible competition for positions on the professional level.

The "Player Information Sheet" and the "Resume" are important during the early stages of the recruiting process. The Player Information Sheet should accompany videotapes that you send to college coaches for evaluation of your performance. The Resume should be included in early mailings to college coaches, maybe even during your junior year. It serves as an excellent way to introduce you to coaches.

"Financial Aid and the Student Athlete" introduces you and your parents to important terms in the financial aid process. Read it before the recruiting process gets into full swing. You and your parents will want to be familiar with many of these terms in order to understand scholarship offers, even to ask the right questions during campus visits or meetings with recruiters.

The next two forms, "Questions to Ask During Your Visit" and "Questions to Ask After Your Visit" are extremely important and should be read very carefully before you visit a college campus. Notice that each of the forms addresses issues that go well beyond athletics—the kind that can influence the quality of your college experience. The answers to the questions on these two forms will be among the most important elements in your eventual decision to attend a particular college.

Write something similar to the "Thank-you Note" every time you return from a college visit. Such a note impresses coaches with your sincerity and expresses basic consideration.

If after all is said and done, nothing much gets done, you may need the form, "Selecting Your One, Best College." You hope to be able to choose from among a number of great colleges. Although this can be a wonderful advantage, it can also interfere with your ability to make a final decision. If you are having a problem making a decision or narrowing down your list, use this form. It provides the objectivity you may need to complete the process.

Once you have made a decision, write something similar to the form, "Letter of Acceptance." Then be sure to write or call the other schools that have recruited you. It's only fair that you let them know of your decision. Be sure, however, that both your commitment and your acceptance to your number-one school have been finalized. You don't want to be discouraging others if your chosen school hasn't yet finalized your admission or financial aid package.

Finally, read the last two forms, "Staying in College" and "Some Pointers for Academic Success," to orient yourself to the world of college. The expectations and the opportunities are considerably different from those you experienced in high school. These two forms are designed to give you a head start before you arrive on a college campus. You'll find some very helpful information in them.

When you review these materials, you will be well on your way to one of the most enjoyable and rewarding experiences of your life. It can also be one of the most successful, if you recognize that athletics is only part of your total college experience. Consider every aspect of college before you make your final decision and discuss it with your parents, your high school coach, and your counselor. Their input can identify elements that you may have forgotten. Good luck with the process and best wishes for several years of memorable experiences!

MY "DID I" LIST

Use the following checklist to remind yourself through the year of the tasks you need to perform to find the "right" college experience.

Pre-Season

DID I:

_____ Meet with my counselor in the spring of the junior year to discuss my college plans?

_____ Take the ACT and/or the SAT near the end of my junior year?

_____ See my counselor about a career inventory to find potential college majors?

_____ Meet with my counselor to make sure my senior year courses comply with NCAA rules and regulations?

_____ Review my transcript at the end of my junior year to be sure I am in compliance with bylaw 14.3?

_____ Develop a list of colleges with my counselor?

_____ Visit a representative sample of college campuses?

_____ Identify a school or schools I can apply to that meet my academic and career needs in the event I don't play a sport in college?

In-Season

DID I:

_____ Apply to at least one school that will meet my needs if I don't play a sport?

_____ Double-check with my counselor to assure compliance with the NCAA?

_____ Maintain good academic standing?

_____ Meet with my coach to deal with persistent recruiters?

Post-Season

DID I:

_____ Meet with my coach to assess my potential to play in college?

_____ Meet with my coach to deal with persistent recruiters?

_____ Review the NCAA rules regarding recruiting?

_____ Make college visits?

_____ Assure the right program of study in the schools that have expressed an interest in me?

_____ Meet with my counselor, coach, and parents to make a final decision?

_____ Discuss the proper application procedure with college coaches?

(This form is reprinted from Mike Koehler's *Football Coach's Survival Guide,* published by Prentice Hall. It also was used in the videotape, the *ABCs of Eligibility for the College-Bound Student Athlete,* marketed by the College Board.)

FORM 48-H AND THE CLEARINGHOUSE

HIGH SCHOOL PROCEDURE:

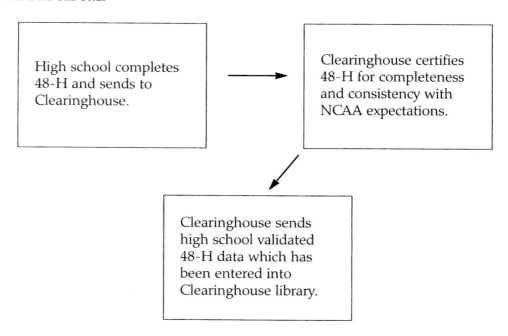

High school completes 48-H and sends to Clearinghouse. → Clearinghouse certifies 48-H for completeness and consistency with NCAA expectations. → Clearinghouse sends high school validated 48-H data which has been entered into Clearinghouse library.

STUDENT ATHLETE PROCEDURE:

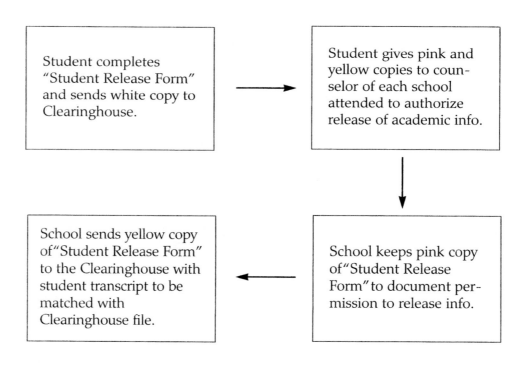

Student completes "Student Release Form" and sends white copy to Clearinghouse. → Student gives pink and yellow copies to counselor of each school attended to authorize release of academic info. → School keeps pink copy of "Student Release Form" to document permission to release info. → School sends yellow copy of "Student Release Form" to the Clearinghouse with student transcript to be matched with Clearinghouse file.

WATCHING OUT FOR IMPROPER RECRUITING

High school athletes being recruited by one or more colleges must always be alert to improper tactics used by some recruiters. Most college coaches are honest men and women who are interested in you as a total person. Some few, however, are interested in you only if you can help their athletic programs. Such coaches are to be avoided. Fortunately, they are pretty easy to spot. If you are being contacted by one or more college coaches, keep these pointers in mind:

WATCH OUT FOR:

- The coach who "bum raps" other schools and coaches. Some coaches try to make their own light shine brighter by blowing out everyone else's. When they resort to this tactic, their own light isn't very bright in the first place. You want to know this.

- The coach who talks only about how great his or her program is. It may be a good one, but if that's the only thing he or she talks about, you are being recruited only to *keep* it good. College for you is much more than helping someone else maintain his or her reputation.

- The coach who promises you a starting position right away. Obviously, there are some entering freshmen who are good enough to be first string right away, but they are few and far between. Listen to the recruiter who is honest with you now, because only then will he or she be honest later.

- The coach who doesn't give an oral commitment to a four-or five-year scholarship. The NCAA allows only a one-year, renewable scholarship, but honest recruiters can promise more than one year. Make sure the recruiter makes such a verbal commitment to you, your parents, and your coach.

- The coach who puts you in contact with a "booster" from the college. The NCAA permits *no* contact with boosters. If you even talk to one, you jeopardize your future.

- The coach who promises easy admission, easy professors, or an easy schedule. He or she has no interest in you as a student.

- The coach who says that his or her school's academic program in your field of study is the best in the nation. Have your counselor check this out for you.

- The coach who promises to let your best friend "walk on" with the team. Rarely is such a coach concerned with the best interests of your friend. He or she is using your friend only to get to you.

There are other tactics to watch out for. Whenever you have a question or a concern, be sure to talk to your coach.

CONTACTS AND VISITS

High school athletes are as bound by NCAA rules and regulations as any college player. Your ignorance of these requirements could jeopardize your athletic future. Read the following NCAA rules carefully and share them with your parents. Be sure to talk with your counselor or coach if you have questions or need explanations.

CONTACTS WITH COLLEGE COACHES

- High school athletes can be contacted by a college coach only after the completion of their junior year. A contact is a any face-to-face meeting involving even a simple "hello."
- High school athletes can receive letters from college coaches, faculty members, and students, but not until after September 1 of the junior year.
- "Contacts" are prohibited with university boosters at any time.
- College coaches may contact you at home or at school but as restricted by NCAA rules. Refer to the *NCAA Guide for the College-Bound Student Athlete* for specific information.
- During any contact, you may not receive T-shirts, college mementos, or financial inducements to sign with a particular university.

VISITS TO COLLEGE CAMPUSES

- The NCAA allows "prospective student athletes" one expenses-paid visit to five different universities. Select your visits very carefully; you are allowed only five of them. Remember, this restriction applies even if you are being recruited in more than one sport.
- You may not receive an official visit until you provide the college authorities with an official high school transcript and a score from the PSAT, PACT, plus SAT, or ACT taken on a national test date. See your counselor for information about the Clearinghouse and the Student Release Form.
- Each visit may not last more than 48 hours.
- You may visit any campus at any time beyond your five official visits if *you* pay all the expenses for each visit.

SEE YOUR COACH OR COUNSELOR FOR COPIES OF QUESTIONS TO ASK DURING AND AFTER YOUR CAMPUS VISITS. THEY ARE VERY HELPFUL.

A PEEK AT THE PROS

Coaches and counselors often hear young athletes talk about futures in professional sports. A life as a professional athlete certainly is an exciting and profitable goal; it simply isn't as possible as most people think. Take a moment to consider the following observations:

Professional Football

Each year, approximately 265,000 seniors play high school football, and about 215 rookies earn a spot on a professional team. Simple mathematics tells us that .0008 of one percent (eight one-*thousandths* of one percent) of high school seniors ultimately will play professional football. Those are not very good odds. Then consider these statistics: A couple of years ago, a prominent university official indicated that about half of all professional football players end their careers with no money; 85% of them are divorced; and their life expectancy is about 56. Even if a young athlete does beat the odds to become a professional, he can expect these kinds of circumstances and a career that lasts only three to four years.

Professional Tennis

There are approximately 30,000 senior boys and 30,000 senior girls playing high school tennis each year. Only 100 professionals in men's and women's tennis earn as much as minimum-salary professionals in the NBA or NFL. The odds of making big money in professional tennis are three-thousandths of one percent for high school seniors.

Professional Basketball

The NCAA tells us that approximately 158,000 high school seniors play basketball each year and that almost 70 rookies make the pros. Again, consider the odds. Only .0004 of one percent (four one-*thousandths* of one percent) of high school basketball players can expect to play for a professional team. Look at it another way. If we have eight seniors per year on our high school basketball team, and if our school had started when our *nation* did, we would still have to wait half a *century* for our first professional basketball player.

Other Sports

Professional baseball, soccer, and track and field offer the same kinds of odds. Of the hundreds of thousands of young athletes who play these sports each year, only a handful ever play professionally. What does all this mean to you?

**Keep your goals but be realistic. Your chances are better to be a doctor
or a lawyer than to be a professional athlete. Your future will be
influenced much more by what you do in the classroom than
by your athletic ability. Play hard but**

HIT THE BOOKS!

PLAYER INFORMATION SHEET

The accompanying videotape illustrates the performance of:

Player Name: _____. The video is a:

    highlight tape _____

    tape of a game/contest _____ against (Opponent): _____

Relevant information: (As appropriate)

    Player's Position: _____

    Player's Number: Offense: _____ Defense: _____

    Color of jersey: _____

    Player Size:

        Height _____

        Weight _____

Relevant Game/Contest Statistics:

Academic/Career Information:

    ACT score(s): _____

    SAT score(s): _____

    Class rank: No. _____ of _____ No. in class

    Cumulative grade point average on a 4.0 scale: _____

    Educational and career goals:

If you require additional information regarding this athlete, feel free to contact me at your convenience. When you have completed your review of the tape, please return it to:

(Coach's name, address, and phone number)

Thanks for your interest, and I look forward to talking to you.

(Signed)

RESUME

Student Athlete's Name: _____

NAME	GPA:
ADDRESS	CLASS RANK
CITY, STATE ZIP	ACT SCORE
PHONE NUMBER, INCLUDING AREA CODE	SAT SCORE
SOCIAL SECURITY NUMBER	HT. ____ WT. ____
DATE OF BIRTH	CONFERENCE _____

NAME OF HIGH SCHOOL:

HIGH SCHOOL COACH:

COACH'S HOME PHONE:

GUIDANCE COUNSELOR:

COUNSELOR'S SCHOOL PHONE:

SCHOOL FAX NUMBER:

ACADEMIC INTEREST IN COLLEGE:

   1.

   2.

   3.

HONORS AND AWARDS:

WORK EXPERIENCE:

ATHLETIC STATISTICS/PERFORMANCES: (If appropriate)

FINANCIAL AID
AND THE STUDENT ATHLETE

TO: *Student Athletes and Their Parents:*

Following are some terms that may apply to your future situation regarding financial aid for college expenses. Your familiarity with them will help during planning activities and meetings with college coaches.

- *Athletics Aid*—any financial aid given to a student athlete that is based on athletic ability.

- *Countable Aid*—aid, no matter what the amount, that must be included in the individual and institutional limits set by NCAA regulations.

- *Counter*—a student athlete who receives institutional financial aid that must be included in the college's sport-by-sport limits for such aid. The limits are established by the college's NCAA membership division.

- *Equivalency Sports*—sports that can award full grants-in-aid or divide the equivalent of one full grant-in-aid among two or more student athletes, in effect creating partial scholarships. It's important to note that in Division I schools, all sports are equivalency sports except football, men's and women's basketball, and women's volleyball, tennis, and gymnastics. In Division II schools, all sports are equivalency sports.

- *Individual Limits*—the restrictions placed on the amount of aid intercollegiate student athletes can receive and still keep their eligibility. Four groups of student athletes are affected by such restrictions—those who:

  —Receive athletic aid from a college.

  —Were recruited and receive any aid from the college.

  —Were recruited and receive athletic aid that is administered outside the college.

  —Receive financial aid that is administered outside the college and is based on participation in high school, whether the athlete was recruited or not.

- *Legitimate Loans*—loans that involve repayment schedules and are available to all students. Perkins and Stafford Student Loans are the most common. They do not have to be counted toward a student athlete's individual limits or the college's sport-by-sport limits for financial aid.

- *National Letter of Intent*—a document attesting to a student athlete's commitment to attend a particular college. The process is administered by the Collegiate Commissioners Association.

- *Outside Financial Aid*—aid that is not administered by the college the student athlete attends. It must involve:

  —Aid given by the student athlete's parents, legal guardians, or someone upon whom they are legally dependent.

  —Aid having nothing to do with athletic ability.

  —Aid awarded through an established and continuing program. See bylaw 15.2.5.3 in the *NCAA Manual.*

  —Aid derived from an established and continuing program that recognizes outstanding high school graduates and allows athletics to be a major criterion. (See bylaw 15.2.5.4.)

FINANCIAL AID
AND THE STUDENT ATHLETE
(continued)

- *Pell Grant*—a federal grant available to students who meet prescribed criteria. Student athletes and their parents are advised to discuss the specific amounts with financial aid personnel at the colleges they are considering.

- *Recruited Student Athlete*—one of the student's goals is to participate in a college's athletic program and a member of the athletic department or a representative of the athletic interests of the college does any of the following:

  —Provides an official visit.

  —Arranges an in-person, off-campus meeting with the athlete or parents or legal guardian(s).

  —Telephones the athlete or her or his family more than once to encourage sports participation at the college.

- *Representatives of Athletic Interests*—people who seek to help a particular college's athletic program (boosters). Colleges are responsible for the activities of these individuals if they:

  —Belong to an organization that promotes the college's athletic program(s).

  —Make financial contributions directly to the college's athletic department or indirectly through a booster organization.

  —Help recruit student athletes (even if the athletic department did not request their assistance).

  —Provide benefits to enrolled student athletes.

  —Promote the athletic program in other ways.

- *Student Athlete*—a student who is recruited to enroll in a college and intends to participate in its intercollegiate athletics program. An unrecruited student becomes a student athlete as soon as he or she reports for an intercollegiate squad within the college's athletic department. Simply having participated in high school sports does not apply.

SEE YOUR COUNSELOR OR COACH
FOR ADDITIONAL INFORMATION

QUESTIONS TO ASK *DURING* YOUR VISIT

Before you decide to make your first visit, it's a good idea to think carefully about the kind of information you are going to need to eventually make a decision. Once you do, you'll be able to ask the right kinds of questions. Following are some good ones to get you started.

ASK THE RECRUITER:

1. What position (event) do you want me to play (perform), and how many others are you recruiting for the same position?
2. What is your philosophy of offense? Defense? Are you considering any changes?
3. Will I be red-shirted?
4. If I need a fifth year, will you finance it?
5. What happens to my scholarship if I'm injured or ineligible?
6. Whom do I see if I have academic problems?
7. Has drug use been an issue at your school? Athletic program?
8. Are all injuries handled by a team insurance policy?
9. If injured, may I use my family doctor? Who determines my fitness to compete after an injury?
10. What is expected of players during the off-season?

ASK OF THE PLAYERS AT THE SCHOOL:

1. What does your typical daily schedule look like? In-season? Off-season?
2. Approximately how many hours a night do you study?
3. What generally are the attitudes of professors in different fields of study? In my field of study? Toward athletes?
4. How do you like the living arrangements?
5. Do you have an academic advisor? Is he/she any good?
6. Are the coaches available to help if you have academic problems?

ASK OF NONATHLETES AT THE SCHOOL:

1. What do you think of the quality of the education you are receiving at this school?
2. If you had to do it all over again, would you choose this school to attend? Why or why not?
3. What is the general opinion of athletes on this campus?

ASK OF SCHOOL OFFICIALS/ADMISSIONS OFFICERS:

1. What are the different graduation rates for athletes? In my sport?
2. About how long does it take someone in my sport to earn a degree from this school?
3. What is the placement rate and the average starting salary for graduates in (your field of study)?
4. What is my eligibility for additional financial aid?

LET'S TALK! BRING YOUR PARENTS IN!

QUESTIONS TO ASK *AFTER* THE VISIT

You will have to ask yourself several important questions *after* you have visited your schools in order to decide ultimately on the right school. These questions will provide a good start. Take the time to think about your answers, and be sure to talk to me, your counselor, and your parents about answers that may be difficult for you. Remember, you want the right athletic *and* academic experience, so *all* these questions are important.

1. Did any of the recruiters have bad things to say about the other schools that are recruiting me?

2. Did any of the recruiters promise that I'd compete right away, even be a starter? (If they did, they may have been less than honest.)

3. Would I attend this school if I had no intention of competing in my sport?

4. Do the coaches and players seem to care genuinely about each other?

5. Will I be successful academically in this school? Athletically? How do I measure up to everyone else?

6. Were the coaches and players I met honest, available to me and others, friendly, genuinely interested, or did they seem phony?

7. Were the coaches interested in academics? Did they ask me about my educational and career interests? Were they knowledgeable about my intended program of study? If not, did they introduce me to someone who might answer my questions?

8. Will I fit in with the rest of the student body at this particular school? Will I be comfortable associating with them for four or more years?

9. How will I feel if one or more of the coaches leaves? Will I still be happy with the school? My sports participation?

10. Does the school satisfy all the requirements that I identified earlier with my parents and counselor? *This probably is the most important question.* Give it a lot of thought, and be sure to talk it over with me, your counselor, and your parents.

TALK TO ME *ANYTIME*—ABOUT *ANY* OF THESE QUESTIONS.

THANK-YOU NOTE

Date

(Coach's Name
Address
City, State Zip)

Dear (Coach's Name):

I want to take just a minute of your time to thank you for the recent visit to your campus. I enjoyed having the opportunity to meet the coaches and several of your players, to walk the campus, and to accept your hospitality. The trip was everything I expected it to be—and more. I'm not surprised that your school and athletic program enjoy such widely recognized reputations. My coach is right; your program is classy.

My parents asked me to thank you, too. They say they enjoyed a weekend of peace and quiet, and they appreciate your generosity!

Thanks again for the time you spent with me. I will be getting back to you soon regarding my decisions for the future. In the meantime, if you have any questions, please call me or my coach at your convenience.

Sincerely yours,

(Student's Name)

SELECTING YOUR ONE, *BEST* COLLEGE

Now that you've taken the time to study a range of colleges for the academic program and setting that's right for you, the time has come to make a decision. Because there are so many excellent schools "out there," you and your family probably will need help making such a decision. This form should help. It asks that you respond to a series of questions involving different aspects of your decision with the name of the college that is the single best answer. Obviously, academic considerations are the most important, so they receive the highest numerical value. Be honest as you complete this form, and be sure to discuss areas of disagreement with your parents, explaining your reasons with as much objective information as you can find.

1. (Worth 10 pts.) Which college meets all the program requirements I developed earlier with my counselor and parents? College: _____

2. (Worth 9 pts.) Which school meets all the other characteristics I desire in a school, such as geographical location, size, etc.? College: _____

3. (Worth 8 pts.) Which school would I attend if I had no intention of playing a sport? College: _____

4. (Worth 7 pts.) Which school had the best graduation rate and job placement possibilities after graduation? College: _____

5. (Worth 6 pts.) Which school satisfies my playing needs best: offensive philosophy, position, likelihood of playing, etc.? College: _____

6. (Worth 5 pts.) Will my schedule of sports activities provide enough time to do well in my academic program? College: _____

7. (Worth 4 pts.) Which school offers the best financial package? College: _____

8. (Worth 3 pts.) Are the professors accepting of athletes, and are relationships among teammates and coaches positive? College: _____

9. (Worth 2 pts.) Are the living arrangements to my liking? Will they promote study? College: _____

10. (Worth 1 pt.) Are injuries handled appropriately, insurance costs met? College: _____

Now add up the numerical value for each college.
The one with the highest number *may be* your one, best school.
At any rate, this process has given you something to think about
and discuss at home. Contact your coach and counselor
if you need more help.

GOOD LUCK!

LETTER OF ACCEPTANCE

Date

(Coach's Name
Address
City, State Zip)

Dear (Coach's Name):

Writing this letter gives me a great deal of pleasure because it enables me to confirm my decision to attend your school next year and to be a member of your (name of sport) program. Everyone involved in the decision, including my parents, my coach, and my counselor, agrees with me that the academic and athletic programs at your school satisfy all my needs as a student athlete. You have been particularly helpful throughout the process; I want to thank you for your help and understanding.

I am forwarding a copy of this letter to my high school coach for her/his records and would appreciate hearing from you at some time in the future regarding the next steps.

I know I've made the right decision, and, believe me, I'll do what I can to justify your confidence in me. Again, thanks for your help, and I look forward to hearing from you.

Sincerely,

(Student's Name)

cc: (High School Coach's Name)

STAYING IN COLLEGE

Getting into college is one thing; staying is another! Obviously, high school counselors give a lot of attention to college admissions requirements, SAT and ACT test results, recommendations, interviews, personal essays, and student resumes. We should also take a moment to mention what it takes to *stay* in college—not to shake you up or to apply any more pressure for your senior year but to make sure you don't get any surprises when you leave for college next year.

Good Academic Standing

Students in good academic standing generally maintain at least a C average (2.0 on a 4.0 scale) while in college. That means that for every D they might receive in one subject, they have to receive at least a B in another. Those students who fall below a cumulative C average after a semester or two are put on academic probation by the university. In essence, they are required to get their cumulative grade point back up to a C average, or they subject themselves to dismissal from the university for academic reasons.

Graduating from College

Think about it. If you maintain a C average throughout college, you will graduate at the bottom of your class. Obviously, this isn't all bad. Thousands of students do it every year. The point is, if you want to graduate in the middle or near the top of your class, you will have to maintain at least a B or a B+ average in college. And if you plan to keep a scholarship while in school, you will have to satisfy the academic requirements of the university to maintain "good academic standing."

The best way to earn the required grade point average in college to maintain good academic standing is to develop the necessary study habits in high school. If you develop the right study habits now, you won't have any problems in college. Talk to your teachers, counselor, or coach if you need some help in this area.

SOME POINTERS FOR ACADEMIC SUCCESS

Student Athletes: The following pointers have been well researched by Dr. Roger Grooters, one of the nation's foremost directors of academic advisement, and have been proven to contribute to academic success in college. Read them carefully and apply them throughout college but especially during your freshman year. With use, they will become habits, the kind that carry over into everything you do in life.

1. *Organization*—Get organized! Read and periodically refer to the syllabuses your professors distribute in your classes. Also use the attached daily/weekly planner to provide regular reminders of work to be completed.

2. *Reading Materials in Advance*—Read assignments before class meets. Sometimes it's even a good idea to read the summaries of chapters before you read the chapters. That will give you a good idea of what is to come. As you read, list questions about confusing material, then be sure to ask about it in class.

3. *Class Attendance*—Go to class! This sounds pretty obvious, but you're about to discover that college provides more free time than some high school kids can handle. The freedom you experience in college can provoke some bad habits, so maintain the good habit of going to class regularly. And when you get there, you might as well participate. That's why you jot down all those questions when you read class assignments.

4. *Take Good Notes*—Learn good note-taking skills and record much of what you hear in class. That's why you have to be there! Then take your notes back to the dorm or the library and break down the key concepts, so you understand how everything fits together. Talk to your high school teachers about this skill before going to college and get pointers from them.

5. *Develop Exam Strategies*—Find some exams used previously in your courses and study them, even try to take them. They are usually available in department offices, in fraternities, or directly from the professor. Scan each exam before you take it to determine where you should put your priorities.

6. *Review and Rehearse*—Take just a few moments to review class notes on a daily basis. Overlearn the material before quizzes and exams! Look at your notes until you know what you're about to read before you turn the page. You'll be surprised how helpful this can be.

7. *Develop Your Writing Skills*—Understand what the professor wants in the paper and develop an outline. Then write the first draft on a word processor and look it over very carefully for changes. Write the final draft and have someone look it over for you, preferably someone in the academic advisement program.

8. *Get to Know Your Professors*—Visit them periodically so they know you. See them in their offices to ask about clarification of class materials and to let them know how serious you are about succeeding. You may feel funny saying such things, but they like to hear it!

SEE YOUR COUNSELOR AND TEACHERS FOR MORE POINTERS.
GOOD LUCK IN COLLEGE!

SOME POINTERS FOR ACADEMIC SUCCESS *(continued)*

DAILY/WEEKLY PLANNER

DIRECTIONS: Use the following calendar to record assignments and their completion dates. Each time you receive an assignment in class, write down the due date on this calendar, then indicate those times during the day when you will work on it. Include tests and quizzes and the amount of time you plan to devote to each one. Make approximately 50 extra copies of this form before going to college. You'll want to develop one each week.

For the Week of: _____

HOUR	MONDAY	TUESDAY	WEDNESDAY	THURSDAY	FRIDAY	SATURDAY	SUNDAY
8							
9							
10							
11							
12							
1							
2							
3							
4							
5							
6							
7							
8							
9							
10							

Especially important tasks for this week:

A–21

LOOKING FOR AN ATHLETIC SCHOLARSHIP TO COLLEGE?

If you need to sell yourself
to college recruiters,
you need this booklet!

HOW TO USE THIS BOOKLET

If you are interested in playing a sport in college but have discovered, for whatever reason, that colleges are not actively recruiting you, you may need to sell yourself to them. This booklet suggests the process and provides many of the forms to do just that. Before you start all this, however, be sure to be as objective as possible about your ability to compete on the college level. Get evaluations from others about your ability, and remember throughout the process that, above all, college is much more than a place to continue your sport.

It is, first of all, an experience that prepares you for the world of work and that is educationally, socially, and personally fulfilling in its own right. It can be one of the happiest times of your life and should not be restricted to athletic competition. Certainly, athletics will play a large part in your decision. That's one of the reasons for this booklet. But, as you will see when you complete this booklet, your selection of a particular college involves several considerations, only one of which involves sports.

Read the following discussion and refer to the forms that are mentioned. Use or modify them to suit your purposes. Some require that you meet with your counselor or coach to gather the right information. Make these appointments as necessary. You probably already know that these two people can provide some very important answers for you.

Additional answers can be found in the book, *Advising the Student Athlete*, published by Prentice Hall, Englewood Cliffs, NJ 07632 or the videotape, the *ABCs of Eligibility for the College-Bound Student Athlete*, marketed by the College Board, 45 Columbus Ave, New York, NY 10023.

A DISCUSSION OF THE FORMS

The first form, "My Did I List," is one of the most important because it outlines the important steps you must take to identify and ultimately choose the right college. It suggests the process you must follow in your junior year and provides a checklist so you can mark your progress through your last two years in high school. Whether you have to sell yourself or you're a highly recruited athlete, college is, first and foremost, an educational experience. Once you have completed this list, you will be prepared to make a college decision for the right reasons.

The second form, "Form 48-H and the Clearinghouse," explains what happens when you fill out the Student Release Form to secure permission to be recruited and ultimately to receive an athletic scholarship to college. Even if you're not sure you will be recruited eventually, this is an important step to take early in your senior year, so be sure to see your counselor for more information.

"Financial Aid at a Glance" introduces you and your parents to important terms in the financial aid process. Read it before the recruiting process gets into full swing. You and your parents will want to be familiar with many of these terms to understand possible scholarship offers, even to ask the right questions during campus visits or meetings with recruiters. It might even convince you that an athletic scholarship is not that important to you and open the door to the next two forms.

"Thoughts About NAIA and NCAA Division III Schools" and "Thoughts About Junior Colleges" suggest some very interesting information about colleges that provide a wide range of athletic and academic opportunities. Read these forms very carefully. Each provides different, sometimes very appealing alternatives to schools that provide athletic scholarships.

Whether you seek a college that does or does not offer scholarships, you and your parents will want to meet with your high school coach to get his or her help with the process. Use the letter in "Letter to Coach from Parents" as a model for the development of your own. You can modify according to your own unique situation. This meeting with your coach is very important. He or she probably will become very instrumental as your college search unfolds.

The "Player Information Sheet" and the "Resume" are important during the early stages of the recruiting process. The Player Information Sheet should accompany videotapes that you send to college coaches for evaluation of your performance. The resume should be included in early mailings to college coaches, maybe even during your junior year. It serves as an excellent way to introduce you to coaches.

Sometimes at this stage of the process, college coaches indicate an inability to offer a scholarship, but they do offer the opportunity to "walk on." Walking on means that you become a nonscholarshipped member of the team, that you receive all mailings and have your name included on the team roster and, sometimes, that you have the chance to earn a scholarship eventually. If this happens, be sure to read the form "So You Want to Walk On?" to identify the implications of this decision.

If one or more coaches do become interested in recruiting you, read "Watching Out for Improper Recruiting" and "Contacts and Visits." They provide important considerations about recruiting and NCAA requirements. Read both forms very carefully. If, for some reason, you violate an NCAA requirement, even mistakenly, you can jeopardize your eligibility to play a sport in college. Discuss these two forms at home and with your coach and counselor. They can provide additional information.

Even if a scholarship is still in doubt, the next two forms, "Questions to Ask During Your Visit" and "Questions to Ask After Your Visit," are extremely important and should be read very carefully before you visit a college campus. Notice that each of the forms addresses issues that go well beyond athletics—the kind that can influence the quality of your college experience. The answers to the questions on these two forms will be among the most important elements in your eventual decision to attend a particular college.

Write something similar to the "Thank-you Note" every time you return from a college visit. Such a note impresses coaches with your sincerity and expresses basic consideration. These kinds of qualities are the very characteristics many coaches are seeking in their athletes. Such a thank-you note, therefore, is not only a reflection of your good breeding but another reason for coaches to express interest in you.

When the process has been completed, whether you have been offered a scholarship or not, and you experience problems making a decision, use the form, "Selecting Your One, Best College." You hope to be able to choose from among a number of great colleges. Although this can be a wonderful advantage, it can also interfere with your ability to make a final decision. This form provides the objectivity you may need to complete the process.

Once you have made a decision, write something similar to the form, "Letter of Acceptance." Recognize that such a letter can be used even if your college selection doesn't involve a scholarship. Also be sure to write or call the other schools that have recruited you. It's only fair that you let them know of your decision. Be sure, however, that both your commitment and your acceptance to your number-one school have been finalized. You don't want to be discouraging others if your chosen school hasn't yet finalized your admission or financial aid package.

Finally, read the last two forms, "Staying in College" and "Some Pointers for Academic Success," to orient yourself to the world of college. The expectations and the opportunities are considerably different from those you experienced in high school. These two forms are designed to give you a head start before you arrive on a college campus. You'll find some very helpful information in them.

When you review these materials, you will be well on your way to one of the most enjoyable and rewarding experiences of your life, even if it doesn't involve an athletic scholarship! It can also be one of the most successful, if you recognize that athletics is only part of your total college experience. Consider every aspect of college before you make your final decision and discuss it with your parents, your high school coach, and your counselor. Their input can identify elements that you may have forgotten. Good luck with the process and best wishes for several years of memorable experiences!

MY "DID I" LIST

Use the following checklist to remind yourself through the year of the tasks you need to perform to find the "right" college experience.

Pre-Season

DID I:

_____ Meet with my counselor in the spring of the junior year to discuss my college plans?

_____ Take the ACT and/or the SAT near the end of my junior year?

_____ See my counselor about a career inventory to find potential college majors?

_____ Meet with my counselor to make sure my senior year courses comply with NCAA rules and regulations?

_____ Review my transcript at the end of my junior year to be sure I am in compliance with bylaw 14.3?

_____ Develop a list of colleges with my counselor?

_____ Visit a representative sample of college campuses?

_____ Identify a school or schools I can apply to that meet my academic and career needs in the event I don't play a sport in college?

In-Season

DID I:

_____ Apply to at least one school that will meet my needs if I don't play a sport?

_____ Double-check with my counselor to assure compliance with the NCAA?

_____ Maintain good academic standing?

_____ If highly recruited, meet with my coach to deal with persistent recruiters?

Post-Season

DID I:

_____ Meet with my coach to assess my potential to play in college?

_____ Meet with my coach to deal with persistent recruiters?

_____ Review the NCAA rules regarding recruiting?

_____ Make college visits?

_____ Assure the right program of study in the schools that have expressed an interest in me?

_____ Meet with my counselor, coach, and parents to make a final decision?

_____ Discuss the proper application procedure with college coaches?

(This form is reprinted from Mike Koehler's *Football Coach's Survival Guide,* published by Prentice Hall. It also was used in the videotape, the *ABCs of Eligibility for the College-Bound Student Athlete,* marketed by the College Board.)

FORM 48-H AND THE CLEARINGHOUSE

HIGH SCHOOL PROCEDURE:

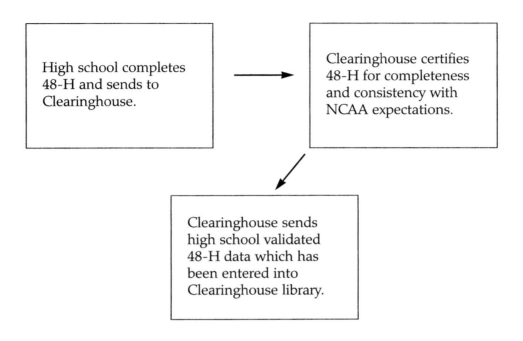

STUDENT ATHLETE PROCEDURE:

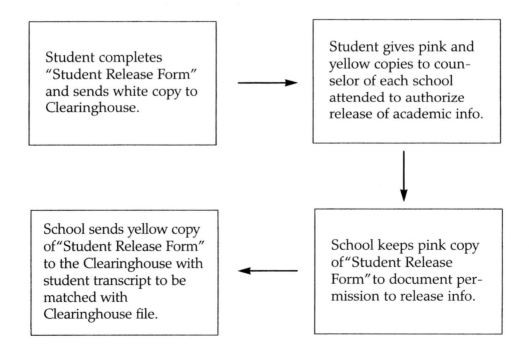

FINANCIAL AID AT A GLANCE

Student athletes and parents: Use the following information to give you a better idea of financial aid in college. If you have questions, call your counselor.

- *Student-Expense Budget*—In essence, this is the cost of attending a given college for one academic year. It includes both the direct and indirect expenses of attendance.
- *The Direct Expenses*—These expenses involve tuition and fees, room and board.
- *The Indirect Expenses*—These expenses normally involve the purchase of books and supplies, incidental expenses, and transportation to and from the campus.
- *Family Contribution*—This is the amount of money the family is expected to pay to meet the student's total college expenses, which are a combination of the direct and indirect expenses. It will be the same at any college to which the student applies, regardless of the variability of the costs of different colleges.

Student-expense budgets vary, depending on the tuition and room and board rates of different colleges. The student's financial need, therefore, as determined by the federal need-analysis formula, is the difference between the total costs of attending a given college and the family's expected contribution. This financial need becomes the basis for the family's search for financial aid.

- *Financial Aid*—This is any type of assistance used to help a student meet college costs. It is divided into two categories:
  - *Gift Aid*—normally consists of scholarships, grants, and/or athletic grants-in-aid
  - *Self-Help Aid*—normally involves loans and/or work assistance
- *Financial Aid Package*—A financial aid package is offered to students who evidence a financial need and consists of some combination of gift aid and self-help aid.

	COLLEGE		
	A	**B**	**C**
TUITION	$ 5,000	$ 9,200	$12,000
R&B	4,100	3,300	4,400
BOOKS	550	480	500
PERSONAL	600	600	600
TRAVEL	300	550	150
TOTAL	$10,550	$14,130	$17,650

(The above constitutes three different student-expense budgets, each consisting of direct and indirect expenses.)

Assume a family contribution of $7,000.

	COLLEGE	
A	**B**	**C**
$10,550	$14,130	$17,650
− 7,000	− 7,000	− 7,000
$ 3,550	$ 7,130	$10,650

This, too, can vary:

	COLLEGE		
	A	**B**	**C**
GRANT:	$2,000	$2,500	$2,000
LOAN:	1,000	4,000	3,200
WORK:	550	550	550
	$3,550	$7,050	$5,750

The above constitutes three different packages, only one of which meets all the needs.

SEE YOUR COUNSELOR FOR MORE INFORMATION

Used with permission from Joe Russo, Director of Financial Aid, University of Notre Dame.

THOUGHTS ABOUT NAIA
AND NCAA DIVISION III SCHOOLS

High school student athletes who are interested in playing a sport in college need to know a little bit about the NCAA's Division III schools. These generally are the smaller schools that don't receive national coverage by the media but that have every bit as much tradition and history as the major colleges—sometimes more. They are not allowed to award athletic scholarships, but more young athletes play in Division III schools than any other, and they generally receive among the finest educations in the country. Think about these facts:

- Division III and NAIA colleges and universities constitute some of the best schools in the country. They are among the most prestigious and provide some of the best educational programs.

- Division III and NAIA schools provide some of the best placement opportunities in the nation after graduation—for both jobs and graduate schools.

- Most Division III and NAIA schools provide informal and personalized educations. Students usually get to know their professors quite well.

- Division III and NAIA schools provide increased contact with professors and fewer contacts with graduate assistants.

- Student athletes who are not being recruited by major college programs may still have the chance to play their sports in Division III or NAIA colleges.

- Division III and NAIA schools tend to be extremely competitive both academically and athletically. They have some of the finest athletes in the nation.

- Student athletes often receive preferential treatment regarding admission. *If you are competitive academically*—maybe not quite as competitive as other applicants—your involvement in sports will help you get into Division III and NAIA schools.

SEE YOUR COACH AND YOUR COUNSELOR
ABOUT THE POSSIBILITY OF A GOOD DIVISION III OR NAIA SCHOOL
IF YOU HAVE THE ACADEMIC CREDENTIALS.
THEY ARE EXCELLENT OPTIONS TO GOOD *STUDENT* ATHLETES.

THOUGHTS ABOUT JUNIOR COLLEGES

A junior college may be your best bet for college next year! Junior colleges are schools that generally offer two kinds of programs for students who are interested in higher education. The first is called the transfer program. It enables you to enter the school as a college freshman, complete one or two years at the school, and transfer your credits to a four-year school. The second program is called a terminal program. It results in an associate's degree after two years and provides the qualifications for you to then find a job in your field of specialization. Certain junior colleges may award scholarships to recruited athletes. They provide excellent educations. Think about these facts:

- If you haven't done as well academically as you wanted, a junior college may provide an additional opportunity for you to improve your grade point average, then apply to a four-year school. Remember, you will be gaining college credits while you are improving your GPA!

- Junior colleges provide valuable educational and career experiences in their own right! They have some excellent programs that might meet your career interests.

- If you have failed to meet the provisions of the NCAA's bylaw 14.3 (Prop 48), a junior college may provide the opportunity for you to continue to play your sport in college and ultimately to transfer to a four-year school. If you are in this situation, be sure to see your coach and counselor for additional information about attending a junior college to satisfy the NCAA's requirements.

- Junior colleges generally offer an open-door admissions policy. You probably don't have to worry about acceptance. You *do* have to plan on working hard in each of your classes!

- If you have been contacted by coaches at one or more four-year schools but must attend a junior college, meet with counseling personnel at the junior college to make sure you meet admissions requirements and to guarantee that the courses you take at the junior college will transfer to the four-year school(s).

- Junior colleges often provide academic help to students. You may benefit from such help. Check with your high school counselor to be sure that any junior colleges you apply to have the kind of help you may need.

SEE YOUR COUNSELOR OR COACH FOR MORE INFORMATION.
A JUNIOR COLLEGE MAY BE JUST WHAT YOU NEED!

© 1996 by Michael D. Koehler

LETTER TO COACH FROM PARENTS
The Unrecruited Athlete

Date

(Coach's Name
Address
City, State Zip)

Dear (Coach's Name):

Now that the season has concluded, we'd like to meet with you to thank you for all you have done for (student's name) and to discuss some of her/his future plans. Although (student's name) had a great season and really enjoyed playing for you, we feel fairly confident that he/she probably won't receive a scholarship to continue the sport in college. We know how competitive they can be.

He/she has, however, explored the whole college issue and has developed a list of schools that meet his/her academic and career interests. Maybe she/he can continue playing for one of the schools, or for another that might provide the same opportunities. Because of your years of experience dealing with these issues, we would like to meet to discuss what, if anything, can be done to help (student's name) continue with the sport next year. He/she has even considered walking on.

We realize that you are busy and promise not to take too much of your time. Please check your calendar and give us a call regarding the particulars of a meeting. We would like to bring (student's name) with us, if that meets with your approval.

In advance, thanks for your help, and we look forward to seeing you in the near future.

Sincerely,

(Parents' Name)

PLAYER INFORMATION SHEET

The accompanying videotape illustrates the performance of:

Player Name: _____. The video is a:

    highlight tape _____

    tape of a game/contest _____ against (Opponent): _____

RELEVANT INFORMATION: (AS APPROPRIATE)

    Player's Position: _____

    Player's Number: Offense: _____ Defense: _____

    Color of jersey: _____

    Player Size:

        Height _____

        Weight _____

RELEVANT GAME/CONTEST STATISTICS:

ACADEMIC/CAREER INFORMATION:

    ACT score(s): _____

    SAT score(s): _____

    Class rank: No. _____ of _____ No. in class

    Cumulative grade point average on a 4.0 scale: _____

    Educational and career goals:

If you require additional information regarding this athlete, feel free to contact me at your convenience. When you have completed your review of the tape, please return it to:

(Coach's name, address, and phone number)

Thanks for your interest, and I look forward to talking to you.

(Signed)

RESUME

Student Athlete's Name: _____

NAME   GPA:

ADDRESS   CLASS RANK

CITY, STATE ZIP   ACT SCORE

PHONE NUMBER, INCLUDING AREA CODE   SAT SCORE

SOCIAL SECURITY NUMBER   HT. ____ WT. ____

DATE OF BIRTH   CONFERENCE _____

NAME OF HIGH SCHOOL:

HIGH SCHOOL COACH:

COACH'S HOME PHONE:

GUIDANCE COUNSELOR:

COUNSELOR'S SCHOOL PHONE:

SCHOOL FAX NUMBER:

ACADEMIC INTEREST IN COLLEGE:

   1.

   2.

   3.

HONORS AND AWARDS:

WORK EXPERIENCE:

ATHLETIC STATISTICS/PERFORMANCES: (If appropriate)

SO YOU WANT TO WALK ON?

A high school athlete who has not received a scholarship but wants to play a sport in college may be given the opportunity to "walk on" at one or more schools. "Walking on" means that he or she becomes an unscholarshipped member of the team, is allowed to try to earn a position on the team, and is given the opportunity to earn a scholarship at some time in the future. "Walking on" can be an excellent opportunity for a good athlete who is serious about his or her sport, but it requires careful planning with your counselor and your coach. If you are interested in "walking on," follow this advice:

WITH YOUR COUNSELOR:

- Be sure you satisfy the eligibility requirements of the NCAA. "Walk-on" athletes are subject to the same rules and regulations as scholarshipped athletes.
- Do all the preliminary planning needed to identify a possible career. You may not settle on one, but look into it anyway. The experience is helpful.
- Find the colleges that provide programs in your career area. Develop a list of them. If you have found no career areas, identify the schools that provide a broad range of programs.
- Discuss the list. Be sure to bring your parents to this meeting.
- Select your top three or four schools from the list.

WITH YOUR COACH:

- Discuss your ability to participate on the college level. Be open-minded during this meeting. Remember, your coach has only your best interests in mind.
- Identify any additional schools at which you may have the chance to play. Be sure they, too, satisfy your career and educational goals.
- Contact the school(s) to secure the college coach's permission to "walk on."
- Mail applications, being sure to follow the admissions procedures specified by the college coach.

BE SURE THE SCHOOL(S) ARE RIGHT FOR YOU.
DON'T ATTEND A SCHOOL JUST TO PLAY A SPORT!

WATCHING OUT FOR IMPROPER RECRUITING

High school athletes being recruited by one or more colleges must always be alert to improper tactics used by some recruiters. Most college coaches are honest men and women who are interested in you as a total person. Some few, however, are interested in you only if you can help their athletic programs. Such coaches are to be avoided. Fortunately, they are pretty easy to spot. If you are being contacted by one or more college coaches, keep these pointers in mind:

WATCH OUT FOR:

- The coach who "bum raps" other schools and coaches. Some coaches try to make their own light shine brighter by blowing out everyone else's. When they resort to this tactic, their own light isn't very bright in the first place. You want to know this.

- The coach who talks only about how great his or her program is. It may be a good one, but if that's the only thing he or she talks about, you are being recruited only to *keep* it good. College for you is much more than helping someone else maintain his or her reputation.

- The coach who promises you a starting position right away. Obviously, there are some entering freshmen who are good enough to be first string right away, but they are few and far between. Listen to the recruiter who is honest with you now, because only then will he or she be honest later.

- The coach who doesn't give an oral commitment to a four- or five-year scholarship. The NCAA allows only a one-year, renewable scholarship, but honest recruiters can promise more than one year. Make sure the recruiter makes such a verbal commitment to you, your parents, and your coach.

- The coach who puts you in contact with a "booster" from the college. The NCAA permits *no* contact with boosters. If you even talk to one, you jeopardize your future.

- The coach who promises easy admission, easy professors, or an easy schedule. He or she has no interest in you as a student.

- The coach who says that his or her school's academic program in your field of study is the best in the nation. Have your counselor check this out for you.

- The coach who promises to let your best friend "walk on" with the team. Rarely is such a coach concerned with the best interests of your friend. He or she is using your friend only to get to you.

There are other tactics to watch out for. Whenever you have a question or a concern, be sure to talk to your coach.

CONTACTS AND VISITS

High school athletes are as bound by NCAA rules and regulations as any college player. Your ignorance of these requirements could jeopardize your athletic future. Read the following NCAA rules carefully and share them with your parents. Be sure to talk with your counselor or coach if you have questions or need explanations.

CONTACTS WITH COLLEGE COACHES

- High school athletes can be contacted by a college coach only after the completion of their junior year. A contact is a any face-to-face meeting involving even a simple "hello."
- High school athletes can receive letters from college coaches, faculty members, and students, but not until after September 1 of the junior year.
- "Contacts" are prohibited with university boosters at any time.
- College coaches may contact you at home or at school but as restricted by NCAA rules. Refer to the *NCAA Guide for the College-Bound Student Athlete* for specific information.
- During any contact, you may not receive T-shirts, college mementos, or financial inducements to sign with a particular university.

VISITS TO COLLEGE CAMPUSES

- The NCAA allows "prospective student athletes" one expenses-paid visit to five different universities. Select your visits very carefully; you are allowed only five of them. Remember, this restriction applies even if you are being recruited in more than one sport.
- You may not receive an official visit until you provide the college authorities with an official high school transcript and a score from the PSAT, PACT, plus SAT, or ACT taken on a national test date. See your counselor for information about the Clearinghouse and the Student Release Form.
- Each visit may not last more than 48 hours.
- You may visit any campus at any time beyond your five official visits if *you* pay all the expenses for each visit.

SEE YOUR COACH OR COUNSELOR FOR COPIES OF QUESTIONS TO ASK DURING AND AFTER YOUR CAMPUS VISITS. THEY ARE VERY HELPFUL.

QUESTIONS TO ASK *DURING* YOUR VISIT

Before you decide to make your first visit, it's a good idea to think carefully about the kind of information you are going to need to eventually make a decision. Once you do, you'll be able to ask the right kinds of questions. Following are some good ones to get you started.

ASK THE RECRUITER:

1. What position (event) do you want me to play (perform), and how many others are you recruiting for the same position?
2. What is your philosophy of offense? Defense? Are you considering any changes?
3. Will I be red-shirted?
4. If I need a fifth year, will you finance it?
5. What happens to my scholarship if I'm injured or ineligible?
6. Whom do I see if I have academic problems?
7. Has drug use been an issue at your school? Athletic program?
8. Are all injuries handled by a team insurance policy?
9. If injured, may I use my family doctor? Who determines my fitness to compete after an injury?
10. What is expected of players during the off-season?

ASK OF THE PLAYERS AT THE SCHOOL:

1. What does your typical daily schedule look like? In-season? Off-season?
2. Approximately how many hours a night do you study?
3. What generally are the attitudes of professors in different fields of study? In my field of study? Toward athletes?
4. How do you like the living arrangements?
5. Do you have an academic advisor? Is he/she any good?
6. Are the coaches available to help if you have academic problems?

ASK OF NONATHLETES AT THE SCHOOL:

1. What do you think of the quality of the education you are receiving at this school?
2. If you had to do it all over again, would you choose this school to attend? Why or why not?
3. What is the general opinion of athletes on this campus?

ASK OF SCHOOL OFFICIALS/ADMISSIONS OFFICERS:

1. What are the different graduation rates for athletes? In my sport?
2. About how long does it take someone in my sport to earn a degree from this school?
3. What is the placement rate and the average starting salary for graduates in (your field of study)?
4. What is my eligibility for additional financial aid?

LET'S TALK! BRING YOUR PARENTS IN!

QUESTIONS TO ASK *AFTER* THE VISIT

You will have to ask yourself several important questions *after* you have visited your schools in order to decide ultimately on the right school. These questions will provide a good start. Take the time to think about your answers, and be sure to talk to me, your counselor, and your parents about answers that may be difficult for you. Remember, you want the right athletic *and* academic experience, so *all* these questions are important.

1. Did any of the recruiters have bad things to say about the other schools that are recruiting me?

2. Did any of the recruiters promise that I'd compete right away, even be a starter? (If they did, they may have been less than honest.)

3. Would I attend this school if I had no intention of competing in my sport?

4. Do the coaches and players seem to care genuinely about each other?

5. Will I be successful academically in this school? Athletically? How do I measure up to everyone else?

6. Were the coaches and players I met honest, available to me and others, friendly, genuinely interested, or did they seem phony?

7. Were the coaches interested in academics? Did they ask me about my educational and career interests? Were they knowledgeable about my intended program of study? If not, did they introduce me to someone who might answer my questions?

8. Will I fit in with the rest of the student body at this particular school? Will I be comfortable associating with them for four or more years?

9. How will I feel if one or more of the coaches leaves? Will I still be happy with the school? My sports participation?

10. Does the school satisfy all the requirements that I identified earlier with my parents and counselor? *This probably is the most important question.* Give it a lot of thought, and be sure to talk it over with me, your counselor, and your parents.

TALK TO ME *ANYTIME*—ABOUT *ANY* OF THESE QUESTIONS.

THANK-YOU NOTE

Date

(Coach's Name
Address
City, State Zip)

Dear (Coach's Name):

I want to take just a minute of your time to thank you for the recent visit to your campus. I enjoyed having the opportunity to meet the coaches and several of your players, to walk the campus, and to accept your hospitality. The trip was everything I expected it to be—and more. I'm not surprised that your school and athletic program enjoy such widely recognized reputations. My coach is right; your program is classy.

My parents asked me to thank you, too. They say they enjoyed a weekend of peace and quiet, and they appreciate your generosity!

Thanks again for the time you spent with me. I will be getting back to you soon regarding my decisions for the future. In the meantime, if you have any questions, please call me or my coach at your convenience.

Sincerely yours,

(Student's Name)

SELECTING YOUR ONE, *BEST* COLLEGE

Now that you've taken the time to study a range of colleges for the academic program and setting that's right for you, the time has come to make a decision. Because there are so many excellent schools "out there," you and your family probably will need help making such a decision. This form should help. It asks that you respond to a series of questions involving different aspects of your decision with the name of the college that is the single best answer. Obviously, academic considerations are the most important, so they receive the highest numerical value. Be honest as you complete this form, and be sure to discuss areas of disagreement with your parents, explaining your reasons with as much objective information as you can find.

1. (Worth 10 pts.) Which college meets all the program requirements I developed earlier with my counselor and parents? College: _____

2. (Worth 9 pts.) Which school meets all the other characteristics I desire in a school, such as geographical location, size, etc.? College: _____

3. (Worth 8 pts.) Which school would I attend if I had no intention of playing a sport? College: _____

4. (Worth 7 pts.) Which school had the best graduation rate and job placement possibilities after graduation? College: _____

5. (Worth 6 pts.) Which school satisfies my playing needs best: offensive philosophy, position, likelihood of playing, etc.? College: _____

6. (Worth 5 pts.) Will my schedule of sports activities provide enough time to do well in my academic program? College: _____

7. (Worth 4 pts.) Which school offers the best financial package? College: _____

8. (Worth 3 pts.) Are the professors accepting of athletes, and are relationships among teammates and coaches positive? College: _____

9. (Worth 2 pts.) Are the living arrangements to my liking? Will they promote study? College: _____

10. (Worth 1 pt.) Are injuries handled appropriately, insurance costs met? College: _____

Now add up the numerical value for each college.
The one with the highest number *may be* your one, best school.
At any rate, this process has given you something to think about
and discuss at home. Contact your coach and counselor
if you need more help.

GOOD LUCK!

LETTER OF ACCEPTANCE

Date

(Coach's Name
Address
City, State Zip)

Dear (Coach's Name):

Writing this letter gives me a great deal of pleasure because it enables me to confirm my decision to attend your school next year and to be a member of your (name of sport) program. Everyone involved in the decision, including my parents, my coach, and my counselor, agrees with me that the academic and athletic programs at your school satisfy all my needs as a student athlete. You have been particularly helpful throughout the process; I want to thank you for your help and understanding.

I am forwarding a copy of this letter to my high school coach for her/his records and would appreciate hearing from you at some time in the future regarding the next steps.

I know I've made the right decision, and, believe me, I'll do what I can to justify your confidence in me. Again, thanks for your help, and I look forward to hearing from you.

Sincerely,

(Student's Name)

cc: (High School Coach's Name)

STAYING IN COLLEGE

Getting into college is one thing; staying is another! Obviously, high school counselors give a lot of attention to college admissions requirements, SAT and ACT test results, recommendations, interviews, personal essays, and student resumes. We should also take a moment to mention what it takes to *stay* in college—not to shake you up or to apply any more pressure for your senior year but to make sure you don't get any surprises when you leave for college next year.

Good Academic Standing

Students in good academic standing generally maintain at least a C average (2.0 on a 4.0 scale) while in college. That means that for every D they might receive in one subject, they have to receive at least a B in another. Those students who fall below a cumulative C average after a semester or two are put on academic probation by the university. In essence, they are required to get their cumulative grade point back up to a C average, or they subject themselves to dismissal from the university for academic reasons.

Graduating from College

Think about it. If you maintain a C average throughout college, you will graduate at the bottom of your class. Obviously, this isn't all bad. Thousands of students do it every year. The point is, if you want to graduate in the middle or near the top of your class, you will have to maintain at least a B or a B+ average in college. And if you plan to keep a scholarship while in school, you will have to satisfy the academic requirements of the university to maintain "good academic standing."

The best way to earn the required grade point average in college is to maintain good academic standing is to develop the necessary study habits in high school. If you develop the right study habits now, you won't have any problems in college. Talk to your teachers, counselor, or coach if you need some help in this area.

SOME POINTERS FOR ACADEMIC SUCCESS

Student Athletes: The following pointers have been well researched by Dr. Roger Grooters, one of the nation's foremost directors of academic advisement, and have been proven to contribute to academic success in college. Read them carefully and apply them throughout college but especially during your freshman year. With use, they will become habits, the kind that carry over into everything you do in life.

1. *Organization*—Get organized! Read and periodically refer to the syllabuses your professors distribute in your classes. Also use the attached daily/weekly planner to provide regular reminders of work to be completed.

2. *Reading Materials in Advance*—Read assignments before class meets. Sometimes it's even a good idea to read the summaries of chapters before you read the chapters. That will give you a good idea of what is to come. As you read, list questions about confusing material, then be sure to ask about it in class.

3. *Class Attendance*—Go to class! This sounds pretty obvious, but you're about to discover that college provides more free time than some high school kids can handle. The freedom you experience in college can provoke some bad habits, so maintain the good habit of going to class regularly. And when you get there, you might as well participate. That's why you jot down all those questions when you read class assignments.

4. *Take Good Notes*—Learn good note-taking skills and record much of what you hear in class. That's why you have to be there! Then take your notes back to the dorm or the library and break down the key concepts, so you understand how everything fits together. Talk to your high school teachers about this skill before going to college and get pointers from them.

5. *Develop Exam Strategies*—Find some exams used previously in your courses and study them, even try to take them. They are usually available in department offices, in fraternities, or directly from the professor. Scan each exam before you take it to determine where you should put your priorities.

6. *Review and Rehearse*—Take just a few moments to review class notes on a daily basis. Overlearn the material before quizzes and exams! Look at your notes until you know what you're about to read before you turn the page. You'll be surprised how helpful this can be.

7. *Develop Your Writing Skills*—Understand what the professor wants in the paper and develop an outline. Then write the first draft on a word processor and look it over very carefully for changes. Write the final draft and have someone look it over for you, preferably someone in the academic advisement program.

8. *Get to Know Your Professors*—Visit them periodically so they know you. See them in their offices to ask about clarification of class materials and to let them know how serious you are about succeeding. You may feel funny saying such things, but they like to hear it!

**SEE YOUR COUNSELOR AND TEACHERS FOR MORE POINTERS.
GOOD LUCK IN COLLEGE!**

SOME POINTERS FOR ACADEMIC SUCCESS *(continued)*

DAILY/WEEKLY PLANNER

DIRECTIONS: Use the following calendar to record assignments and their completion dates. Each time you receive an assignment in class, write down the due date on this calendar, then indicate those times during the day when you will work on it. Include tests and quizzes and the amount of time you plan to devote to each one. Make approximately 50 extra copies of this form before going to college. You'll want to develop one each week.

For the Week of: _____

HOUR	MONDAY	TUESDAY	WEDNESDAY	THURSDAY	FRIDAY	SATURDAY	SUNDAY
8							
9							
10							
11							
12							
1							
2							
3							
4							
5							
6							
7							
8							
9							
10							

Especially important tasks for this week:

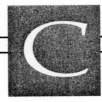

LOOKING FOR AN ATHLETIC SCHOLARSHIP TO COLLEGE?

If you are a female high school athlete,
you need this booklet!

HOW TO USE THIS BOOKLET

It's unfortunate but true that female high school athletes often experience a recruiting process that is much different from that for male athletes. This happens for a variety of reasons, most of which relate to the simple fact that women's college programs lack the funds to engage in widespread recruiting. A result is that female high school athletes, their parents, and their coaches have to be a bit more aggressive than males when seeking athletic scholarships.

This is not to say that girls have to be combative, just more enterprising and, maybe, more energetic than boys. This booklet will help. It provides the tools you need to open the door to the recruiting process and ultimately sell yourself to one or more colleges. If selling yourself is not an issue, it also provides a needed emphasis on academics, your primary reason for going to college.

Remember, college is, first of all, an experience that prepares you for the world of work and that is educationally, socially, and personally fulfilling in its own right. It can be one of the happiest times of your life and should not be restricted to athletic competition. Certainly, athletics will play a large part in your decision. That's one of the reasons for this booklet. But, as you will see when you complete this booklet, your selection of a particular college involves several considerations, only one of which involves sports.

Read the following discussion and refer to the forms that are mentioned. Use or modify them to suit your purposes. Some require that you meet with your counselor or coach to gather the right information. Make these appointments as necessary. You probably already know that these two people can provide some very important answers for you.

Additional answers can be found in the book, *Advising the Student Athlete,* published by Prentice Hall, Englewood Cliffs, NJ 07632 or the videotape, the *ABCs of Eligibility for the College-Bound Student Athlete,* marketed by the College Board, 45 Columbus Ave, New York, NY 10023.

A DISCUSSION OF THE FORMS

The first form, "My Did I List," is one of the most important because it outlines the important steps you must take to identify and ultimately choose the right college. It suggests the process you must follow in your junior year and provides a checklist so you can mark your progress through your last two years in high school. Once you have completed this list, you will be prepared to make a college decision for the right reasons.

The second form, "Form 48-H and the Clearinghouse," explains what happens when you fill out the Student Release Form to secure permission to be recruited and ultimately to receive an athletic scholarship to college. This is an important step to take early in your senior year, so be sure to see your counselor for more information.

The next two pages, "The Total Sports Picture," provides a look at scholarship availability for women athletes in college. We have selected a few representative sports to emphasize the fact that scholarships aren't as widely available as many people believe. This is not intended to discourage you—just prepare you for reality. Notice particularly the pie charts on the second page of the form. In the population of high school girls who play volleyball, for example, only the darkened wedge receive scholarships to college. Keep in mind as well that the NCAA Division III programs—those with the greatest number of sports programs—don't give athletic scholarships.

That's where the two forms, "Thoughts About NAIA and NCAA Division III Schools" and "Thoughts About Junior Colleges," come in. Read them very carefully. Each provides different, sometimes very appealing alternatives to schools that offer athletic scholarships.

To start the whole process, however, refer to the form, "Financial Aid at a Glance," to give you an idea of how to compute your college expenses. You may discover that you and your family have less financial need than you originally suspected. Or you may discover that an athletic scholarship would help considerably. Whatever the case, use the next form, "Letter from Junior Athlete to College Coach," as a model for the development of your own letter. You can change the form letter to reflect your situation; just be sure to include similar kinds of information.

As you approach your senior year, you will want to intensify your efforts to impress college coaches. You and your coach might send videotapes of your performance during your junior year to those coaches who don't have the kinds of travel budgets that enable them to watch you in action. Include the form, "Player Information Sheet," with each mailing. You might also at this time include a copy of your resume as prescribed in the form "Resume."

During or after your senior year season, share the "Sample Letter to College Coach" with your high school coach to promote his or her help with another contact at this time. You probably also will want to send more videotapes, including "skill tapes" that reveal your ability to handle a stick, to field a grounder and throw to first, kick a soccer ball, high jump, or shoot a free throw. Such tapes need not be long; they need only provide brief evidence of your ability to compete on the college level. Also consider the development of one tape that combines the highlights of your entire senior year. Again, keep it relatively short. College coaches don't want to spend all day watching tapes.

The point is, you might need to sell yourself to one or more college programs. Videotapes can be very helpful in this regard. Be sure, however, to have your high school coach call each college before sending such tapes. College coaches may be more inclined to watch them at certain times of the year and only after having spoken with the high school coach.

Once the recruiting process has started for you, the next two forms will be helpful. "Watching Out for Improper Recruiting" and "Contacts and Visits" provide important considerations about recruiting and NCAA requirements. Read both forms carefully. If, for some reason, you violate an NCAA requirement, even mistakenly, you can jeopardize your eligibility to play a sport in college. Discuss these two forms at home and with your coach and counselor. They can provide additional information.

The next two forms, "Questions to Ask During Your Visit" and "Questions to Ask After Your Visit" are extremely important and should be read very carefully before you visit a college campus. Notice that each of the forms addresses issues that go well beyond athletics, the kind that can influence the quality of your college experience. The answers to the questions on these two forms will be among the most important elements in your eventual decision to attend a particular college.

Write something similar to the "Thank-you Note" every time you return from a college visit. Such a note impresses coaches with your sincerity and basic consideration.

If after all is said and done, nothing much gets done, you may need the form, "Selecting Your One, Best College." You hope to be able to choose from among a number of great colleges. Although this can be a wonderful advantage, it can also interfere with your ability to make a final decision. If you are having a problem making a decision or narrowing down your list, use this form. It provides the objectivity you may need to complete the process.

Once you have made a decision, write something similar to the form "Letter of Acceptance." Then be sure to write or call the other schools that have recruited you. It's only fair that you let them know of your decision. Be sure, however, that both your commitment and your acceptance to your number-one school have been finalized. You don't want to be discouraging others if your chosen school hasn't yet finalized your admission or financial aid package.

Finally, read the last two forms, "Staying in College" and "Some Pointers for Academic Success," to orient yourself to the world of college. The expectations and opportunities are considerably different from those you experienced in high school. These two forms are designed to give you a head start before you arrive on a college campus. You'll find some very helpful information in them.

When you review these materials, you will be well on your way to one of the most enjoyable and rewarding experiences of your life. It can also be one of the most successful, if you recognize that athletics is only part of your total college experience. Consider every aspect of college before you make your final decision and discuss it with your parents, your high school coach, and your counselor. Their input can identify elements that you may have forgotten. Good luck with the process and best wishes for several years of memorable experiences!

MY "DID I" LIST

Use the following checklist to remind yourself through the year of the tasks you need to perform to find the "right" college experience.

Pre-Season

DID I:

_____ Meet with my counselor in the spring of the junior year to discuss my college plans?

_____ Take the ACT and/or the SAT near the end of my junior year?

_____ See my counselor about a career inventory to find potential college majors?

_____ Meet with my counselor to make sure my senior year courses comply with NCAA rules and regulations?

_____ Review my transcript at the end of my junior year to be sure I am in compliance with bylaw 14.3?

_____ Develop a list of colleges with my counselor?

_____ Visit a representative sample of college campuses?

_____ Identify a school or schools I can apply to that meet my academic and career needs in the event I don't play a sport in college?

In-Season

DID I:

_____ Apply to at least one school that will meet my needs if I don't play a sport?

_____ Double-check with my counselor to assure compliance with the NCAA?

_____ Maintain good academic standing?

_____ If highly recruited, meet with my coach to deal with persistent recruiters?

Post-Season

DID I:

_____ Meet with my coach to assess my potential to play in college?

_____ Meet with my coach to deal with persistent recruiters?

_____ Review the NCAA rules regarding recruiting?

_____ Make college visits?

_____ Assure the right program of study in the schools that have expressed an interest in me?

_____ Meet with my counselor, coach, and parents to make a final decision?

_____ Discuss the proper application procedure with college coaches?

(This form is reprinted from Mike Koehler's *Football Coach's Survival Guide,* published by Prentice Hall. It also was used in the videotape, the *ABCs of Eligibility for the College-Bound Student Athlete,* marketed by the College Board.)

FORM 48-H AND THE CLEARINGHOUSE

HIGH SCHOOL PROCEDURE:

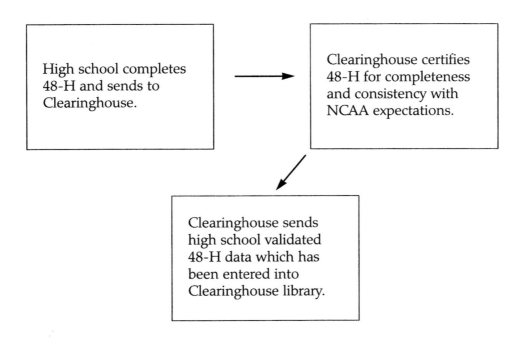

STUDENT ATHLETE PROCEDURE:

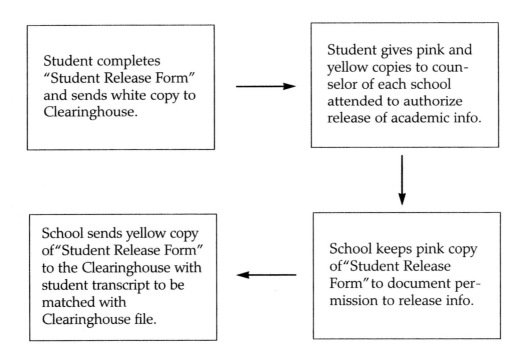

THE TOTAL SPORTS PICTURE
WOMEN AND NCAA SPORTS

SPORT	DIVISION I	DIVISION II	DIVISION III
Volleyball	270	200	290
Soccer	90	60	200
Field Hockey	75	13	125
Softball	170	160	240
Swimming	160	50	180

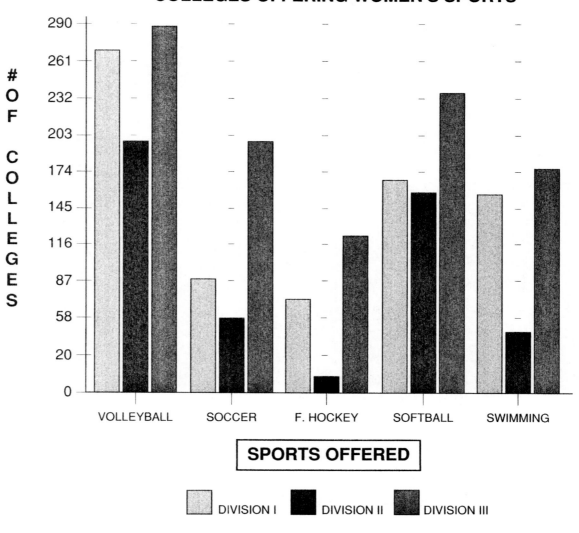

COLLEGES OFFERING WOMEN'S SPORTS

OF COLLEGES

290 · 261 · 232 · 203 · 174 · 145 · 116 · 87 · 58 · 20 · 0

VOLLEYBALL   SOCCER   F. HOCKEY   SOFTBALL   SWIMMING

SPORTS OFFERED

DIVISION I   DIVISION II   DIVISION III

THE TOTAL SPORTS PICTURE
DIVISION I SCHOLARSHIPS FOR WOMEN

SPORT	NCAA DIV I COLLEGES	H.S. SENIORS IN SPORT	FRESHMEN SCHOLARSHIPS AWARDED	TEAM SCHOLARSHIPS [TOTAL]	ODDS OF RECEIVING SCHOLARSHIP
Volleyball	270	85,000	3	10	1:105
Soccer	90	37,500	3-4	11	1:119
F. Hockey	75	13,000	3	11	1:58
Softball	170	56,250	3	11	1:110
Swimming	160	23,375	3-4	14	1:42

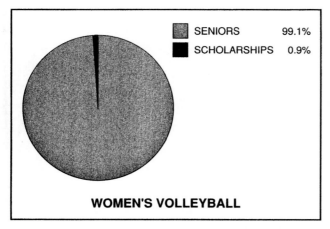

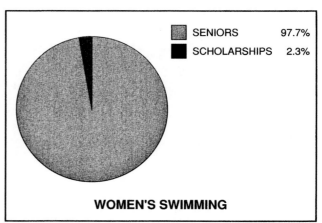

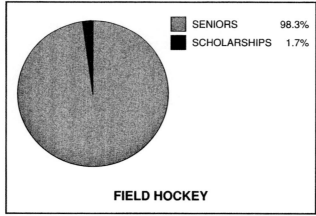

THOUGHTS ABOUT NAIA
AND NCAA DIVISION III SCHOOLS

High school student athletes who are interested in playing a sport in college need to know a little bit about the NCAA's Division III schools. These generally are the smaller schools that don't receive national coverage by the media but that have every bit as much tradition and history as the major colleges—sometimes more. They are not allowed to award athletic scholarships, but more young athletes play in Division III schools than any other, and they generally receive among the finest educations in the country. Think about these facts:

- Division III and NAIA colleges and universities constitute some of the best schools in the country. They are among the most prestigious and provide some of the best educational programs.

- Division III and NAIA schools provide some of the best placement opportunities in the nation after graduation—for both jobs and graduate schools.

- Most Division III and NAIA schools provide informal and personalized educations. Students usually get to know their professors quite well.

- Division III and NAIA schools provide increased contact with professors and fewer contacts with graduate assistants.

- Student athletes who are not being recruited by major college programs may still have the chance to play their sports in Division III or NAIA colleges.

- Division III and NAIA schools tend to be extremely competitive both academically and athletically. They have some of the finest athletes in the nation.

- Student athletes often receive preferential treatment regarding admission. *If you are competitive academically*—maybe not quite as competitive as other applicants—your involvement in sports will help you get into Division III and NAIA schools.

SEE YOUR COACH AND YOUR COUNSELOR
ABOUT THE POSSIBILITY OF A GOOD DIVISION III OR NAIA SCHOOL
IF YOU HAVE THE ACADEMIC CREDENTIALS.
THEY ARE EXCELLENT OPTIONS TO GOOD *STUDENT* ATHLETES.

THOUGHTS ABOUT JUNIOR COLLEGES

A junior college may be your best bet for college next year! Junior colleges are schools that generally offer two kinds of programs for students who are interested in higher education. The first is called the transfer program. It enables you to enter the school as a college freshman, complete one or two years at the school, and transfer your credits to a four-year school. The second program is called a terminal program. It results in an associate's degree after two years and provides the qualifications for you to then find a job in your field of specialization. Certain junior colleges may award scholarships to recruited athletes. They provide excellent educations. Think about these facts:

- If you haven't done as well academically as you wanted, a junior college may provide an additional opportunity for you to improve your grade point average, then apply to a four-year school. Remember, you will be gaining college credits while you are improving your GPA!

- Junior colleges provide valuable educational and career experiences in their own right! They have some excellent programs that might meet your career interests.

- If you have failed to meet the provisions of the NCAA's bylaw 14.3 (Prop 48), a junior college may provide the opportunity for you to continue to play your sport in college and ultimately to transfer to a four-year school. If you are in this situation, be sure to see your coach and counselor for additional information about attending a junior college to satisfy the NCAA's requirements.

- Junior colleges generally offer an open-door admissions policy. You probably don't have to worry about acceptance. You *do* have to plan on working hard in each of your classes!

- If you have been contacted by coaches at one or more four-year schools but must attend a junior college, be sure to meet with counseling personnel at the junior college to make sure you meet admissions requirements and to guarantee that the courses you take at the junior college will transfer to the four-year school(s).

- Junior colleges often provide academic help to students. You may benefit from such help. Check with your high school counselor to be sure that any junior colleges you apply to have the kind of help you may need.

SEE YOUR COUNSELOR OR COACH FOR MORE INFORMATION. A JUNIOR COLLEGE MAY BE JUST WHAT YOU NEED!

FINANCIAL AID AT A GLANCE

Student athletes and parents: Use the following information to give you a better idea of financial aid in college. If you have questions, call your counselor.

- *Student-Expense Budget*—In essence, this is the cost of attending a given college for one academic year. It includes both the direct and indirect expenses of attendance.
- *The Direct Expenses*—These expenses involve tuition and fees, room and board.
- *The Indirect Expenses*—These expenses normally involve the purchase of books and supplies, incidental expenses, and transportation to and from the campus.
- *Family Contribution*—This is the amount of money the family is expected to pay to meet the student's total college expenses, which are a combination of the direct and indirect expenses. It will be the same at any college to which the student applies, regardless of the variability of the costs of different colleges.

Student-expense budgets vary, depending on the tuition and room and board rates of different colleges. The student's financial need, therefore, as determined by the federal need-analysis formula, is the difference between the total costs of attending a given college and the family's expected contribution. This financial need becomes the basis for the family's search for financial aid.

- *Financial Aid*—This is any type of assistance used to help a student meet college costs. It is divided into two categories:
  - *Gift Aid*—normally consists of scholarships, grants, and/or athletic grants-in-aid
  - *Self-Help Aid*—normally involves loans and/or work assistance
- *Financial Aid Package*—A financial aid package is offered to students who evidence a financial need and consists of some combination of gift aid and self-help aid.

	COLLEGE		
	A	**B**	**C**
TUITION	$ 5,000	$ 9,200	$12,000
R&B	4,100	3,300	4,400
BOOKS	550	480	500
PERSONAL	600	600	600
TRAVEL	300	550	150
TOTAL	$10,550	$14,130	$17,650

(The above constitutes three different student-expense budgets, each consisting of direct and indirect expenses.)

Assume a family contribution of $7,000.

COLLEGE		
A	**B**	**C**
$10,550	$14,130	$17,650
− 7,000	− 7,000	− 7,000
$ 3,550	$ 7,130	$10,650

This, too, can vary:

	COLLEGE		
	A	**B**	**C**
GRANT:	$2,000	$2,500	$2,000
LOAN:	1,000	4,000	3,200
WORK:	550	550	550
	$3,550	$7,050	$5,750

The above constitutes three different packages, only one of which meets all the needs.

SEE YOUR COUNSELOR FOR MORE INFORMATION.

Used with permission from Joe Russo, Director of Financial Aid, University of Notre Dame.

LETTER FROM JUNIOR ATHLETE
TO COLLEGE COACH

Date

(Coach's Name
Address
City, State Zip)

Dear (Coach's Name):

I would like to take this opportunity to introduce myself to you. I am currently a junior at (name of high school) and, with the completion of this current season, have played softball for three years, starting at shortstop for the last two. I am 5'9" and weigh 145 pounds and can also play first base and catcher. I have been All-Conference for the past two years and was recently selected to the All-Area team.

My coach's name is Sandra Miller; she has encouraged me to write this letter. She indicates that she plans to write one as well. Regarding my statistics: I committed only two errors this season and batted .425, with 23 triples and 19 home runs. I currently own five school records in softball and also play basketball and field hockey.

I rank 23 in a class of 389 and have a 3.4 grade point average on a 4.0 scale. My career goals are as yet undefined, but I am interested in math and science, so I probably will want to go into engineering. I am looking forward to college as an opportunity to pursue my educational and career goals and would love to continue playing softball on the college level, especially with your program.

I hope to hear from you and am available in the event you are interested in additional information. Please forward whatever materials I need at this point to further express my interest in your program.

Thanks for the time, and I look forward to hearing from you.

Sincerely yours,

(Student Athlete's Name)

PLAYER INFORMATION SHEET

The accompanying videotape illustrates the performance of:

Player Name: _____. The video is a:

    highlight tape _____

    tape of a game/contest _____ against (Opponent): _____

RELEVANT INFORMATION: (AS APPROPRIATE)

    Player's Position: _____

    Player's Number: Offense: _____ Defense: _____

    Color of jersey: _____

    Player Size:

        Height _____

        Weight _____

RELEVANT GAME/CONTEST STATISTICS:

ACADEMIC/CAREER INFORMATION:

    ACT score(s): _____

    SAT score(s): _____

    Class rank: No. _____ of _____ No. in class

    Cumulative grade point average on a 4.0 scale: _____

    Educational and career goals:

If you require additional information regarding this athlete, feel free to contact me at your convenience. When you have completed your review of the tape, please return it to:

(Coach's name, address, and phone number)

Thanks for your interest, and I look forward to talking to you.

(Signed)

RESUME

Student Athlete's Name: _____

NAME	GPA:
ADDRESS	CLASS RANK
CITY, STATE ZIP	ACT SCORE
PHONE NUMBER, INCLUDING AREA CODE	SAT SCORE
SOCIAL SECURITY NUMBER	HT. ____ WT. ____
DATE OF BIRTH	CONFERENCE _____

NAME OF HIGH SCHOOL:

HIGH SCHOOL COACH:

COACH'S HOME PHONE:

GUIDANCE COUNSELOR:

COUNSELOR'S SCHOOL PHONE:

SCHOOL FAX NUMBER:

ACADEMIC INTEREST IN COLLEGE:

    1.

    2.

    3.

HONORS AND AWARDS:

WORK EXPERIENCE:

ATHLETIC STATISTICS/PERFORMANCES: (If appropriate)

C–15

SAMPLE LETTER TO COLLEGE COACHES
REGARDING RECRUITING

Date

(Coach's Name
Address
City, State Zip)

Dear (Coach):

Just a quick note to introduce you to Jessica Smith, one of the finest basketball players I have had the pleasure to coach within the past several years. Jessica was the center on this year's regional championship team, helped lead us to the second conference championship in her career, and distinguished herself and her teammates in the process. The team has the reputation of being one of the best in the school's history, and Jessica earned All-Conference, All-Area, and All-State honors.

Jessica is 6'2" and, although she has played with her back to the basket throughout much of her high school career, she has the ability to play any position other than point guard on the court. She has an excellent jump shot (averaging 22.3 points per game this season), can rebound as well as anyone in the area, and has the kind of court sense that results in assists and breakaway opportunities in every game she plays.

I have been coaching high school basketball for 25 years and am pleased to say that this is one of the best players I have ever coached. She will be a standout in college because of her basketball ability, leadership skills, and strong academic performance. Jessica will be with you for all four years and is likely to mature into an even better player than she is now. She already is an excellent student. She has earned a 3.4 GPA in a college prep program, a 25 composite on her ACT, and academic honors throughout her four years of high school.

I am certain that you will like Jessica. Call me at your convenience for additional information. I will be pleased to send videotapes for your evaluation. I look forward to hearing from you. Thanks for your time.

Sincerely,

(Coach's Name)

WATCHING OUT FOR IMPROPER RECRUITING

High school athletes being recruited by one or more colleges must always be alert to improper tactics used by some recruiters. Most college coaches are honest men and women who are interested in you as a total person. Some few, however, are interested in you only if you can help their athletic programs. Such coaches are to be avoided. Fortunately, they are pretty easy to spot. If you are being contacted by one or more college coaches, keep these pointers in mind:

WATCH OUT FOR:

- The coach who "bum raps" other schools and coaches. Some coaches try to make their own light shine brighter by blowing out everyone else's. When they resort to this tactic, their own light isn't very bright in the first place. You want to know this.

- The coach who talks only about how great his or her program is. It may be a good one, but if that's the only thing he or she talks about, you are being recruited only to *keep* it good. College for you is much more than helping someone else maintain his or her reputation.

- The coach who promises you a starting position right away. Obviously, there are some entering freshmen who are good enough to be first string right away, but they are few and far between. Listen to the recruiter who is honest with you now, because only then will he or she be honest later.

- The coach who doesn't give an oral commitment to a four-or five-year scholarship. The NCAA allows only a one-year, renewable scholarship, but honest recruiters can promise more than one year. Make sure the recruiter makes such a verbal commitment to you, your parents, and your coach.

- The coach who puts you in contact with a "booster" from the college. The NCAA permits *no* contact with boosters. If you even talk to one, you jeopardize your future.

- The coach who promises easy admission, easy professors, or an easy schedule. He or she has no interest in you as a student.

- The coach who says that his or her school's academic program in your field of study is the best in the nation. Have your counselor check this out for you.

- The coach who promises to let your best friend "walk on" with the team. Rarely is such a coach concerned with the best interests of your friend. He or she is using your friend only to get to you.

There are other tactics to watch out for. Whenever you have a question or a concern, be sure to talk to your coach.

CONTACTS AND VISITS

High school athletes are as bound by NCAA rules and regulations as any college player. Your ignorance of these requirements could jeopardize your athletic future. Read the following NCAA rules carefully and share them with your parents. Be sure to talk with your counselor or coach if you have questions or need explanations.

CONTACTS WITH COLLEGE COACHES

- High school athletes can be contacted by a college coach only after the completion of their junior year. A contact is a any face-to-face meeting involving even a simple "hello."
- High school athletes can receive letters from college coaches, faculty members, and students, but not until after September 1 of the junior year.
- "Contacts" are prohibited with university boosters at any time.
- College coaches may contact you at home or at school but as restricted by NCAA rules. Refer to the *NCAA Guide for the College-Bound Student Athlete* for specific information.
- During any contact, you may not receive T-shirts, college mementos, or financial inducements to sign with a particular university.

VISITS TO COLLEGE CAMPUSES

- The NCAA allows "prospective student athletes" one expenses-paid visit to five different universities. Select your visits very carefully; you are allowed only five of them. Remember, this restriction applies even if you are being recruited in more than one sport.
- You may not receive an official visit until you provide the college authorities with an official high school transcript and a score from the PSAT, PACT, plus SAT, or ACT taken on a national test date. See your counselor for information about the Clearinghouse and the Student Release Form.
- Each visit may not last more than 48 hours.
- You may visit any campus at any time beyond your five official visits if *you* pay all the expenses for each visit.

SEE YOUR COACH OR COUNSELOR FOR COPIES OF QUESTIONS TO ASK DURING AND AFTER YOUR CAMPUS VISITS. THEY ARE VERY HELPFUL.

QUESTIONS TO ASK *DURING* YOUR VISIT

Before you decide to make your first visit, it's a good idea to think carefully about the kind of information you are going to need to eventually make a decision. Once you do, you'll be able to ask the right kinds of questions. Following are some good ones to get you started.

ASK THE RECRUITER:

1. What position (event) do you want me to play (perform), and how many others are you recruiting for the same position?
2. What is your philosophy of offense? Defense? Are you considering any changes?
3. Will I be red-shirted?
4. If I need a fifth year, will you finance it?
5. What happens to my scholarship if I'm injured or ineligible?
6. Whom do I see if I have academic problems?
7. Has drug use been an issue at your school? Athletic program?
8. Are all injuries handled by a team insurance policy?
9. If injured, may I use my family doctor? Who determines my fitness to compete after an injury?
10. What is expected of players during the off-season?

ASK OF THE PLAYERS AT THE SCHOOL:

1. What does your typical daily schedule look like? In-season? Off-season?
2. Approximately how many hours a night do you study?
3. What generally are the attitudes of professors in different fields of study? In my field of study? Toward athletes?
4. How do you like the living arrangements?
5. Do you have an academic advisor? Is he/she any good?
6. Are the coaches available to help if you have academic problems?

ASK OF NONATHLETES AT THE SCHOOL:

1. What do you think of the quality of the education you are receiving at this school?
2. If you had to do it all over again, would you choose this school to attend? Why or why not?
3. What is the general opinion of athletes on this campus?

ASK OF SCHOOL OFFICIALS/ADMISSIONS OFFICERS:

1. What are the different graduation rates for athletes? In my sport?
2. About how long does it take someone in my sport to earn a degree from this school?
3. What is the placement rate and the average starting salary for graduates in (your field of study)?
4. What is my eligibility for additional financial aid?

LET'S TALK! BRING YOUR PARENTS IN!

QUESTIONS TO ASK *AFTER* THE VISIT

You will have to ask yourself several important questions *after* you have visited your schools to decide ultimately on the right school. These questions will provide a good start. Take the time to think about your answers, and be sure to talk to me, your counselor, and your parents about answers that may be difficult for you. Remember, you want the right athletic *and* academic experience, so *all* these questions are important.

1. Did any of the recruiters have bad things to say about the other schools that are recruiting me?

2. Did any of the recruiters promise that I'd compete right away, even be a starter? (If they did, they may have been less than honest.)

3. Would I attend this school if I had no intention of competing in my sport?

4. Do the coaches and players seem to care genuinely about each other?

5. Will I be successful academically in this school? Athletically? How do I measure up to everyone else?

6. Were the coaches and players I met honest, available to me and others, friendly, genuinely interested, or did they seem phony?

7. Were the coaches interested in academics? Did they ask me about my educational and career interests? Were they knowledgeable about my intended program of study? If not, did they introduce me to someone who might answer my questions?

8. Will I fit in with the rest of the student body at this particular school? Will I be comfortable associating with them for four or more years?

9. How will I feel if one or more of the coaches leaves? Will I still be happy with the school? My sports participation?

10. Does the school satisfy all the requirements that I identified earlier with my parents and counselor? *This probably is the most important question.* Give it a lot of thought, and be sure to talk it over with me, your counselor, and your parents.

TALK TO ME *ANYTIME*—ABOUT *ANY* OF THESE QUESTIONS.

THANK-YOU NOTE

Date

(Coach's Name
Address
City, State Zip)

Dear (Coach's Name):

I want to take just a minute of your time to thank you for the recent visit to your campus. I enjoyed having the opportunity to meet the coaches and several of your players, to walk the campus, and to accept your hospitality. The trip was everything I expected it to be—and more. I'm not surprised that your school and athletic program enjoy such widely recognized reputations. My coach is right; your program is classy.

My parents asked me to thank you, too. They say they enjoyed a weekend of peace and quiet, and they appreciate your generosity!

Thanks again for the time you spent with me. I will be getting back to you soon regarding my decisions for the future. In the meantime, if you have any questions, please call me or my coach at your convenience.

Sincerely yours,

(Student's Name)

SELECTING YOUR ONE, *BEST* COLLEGE

Now that you've taken the time to study a range of colleges for the academic program and setting that's right for you, the time has come to make a decision. Because there are so many excellent schools "out there," you and your family probably will need help making such a decision. This form should help. It asks that you respond to a series of questions involving different aspects of your decision with the name of the college that is the single best answer. Obviously, academic considerations are the most important, so they receive the highest numerical value. Be honest as you complete this form, and be sure to discuss areas of disagreement with your parents, explaining your reasons with as much objective information as you can find.

1. (Worth 10 pts.) Which college meets all the program requirements I developed earlier with my counselor and parents? College: _____

2. (Worth 9 pts.) Which school meets all the other characteristics I desire in a school, such as geographical location, size, etc.? College: _____

3. (Worth 8 pts.) Which school would I attend if I had no intention of playing a sport? College: _____

4. (Worth 7 pts.) Which school had the best graduation rate and job placement possibilities after graduation? College: _____

5. (Worth 6 pts.) Which school satisfies my playing needs best: offensive philosophy, position, likelihood of playing, etc.? College: _____

6. (Worth 5 pts.) Will my schedule of sports activities provide enough time to do well in my academic program? College: _____

7. (Worth 4 pts.) Which school offers the best financial package? College: _____

8. (Worth 3 pts.) Are the professors accepting of athletes, and are relationships among teammates and coaches positive? College: _____

9. (Worth 2 pts.) Are the living arrangements to my liking? Will they promote study? College: _____

10. (Worth 1 pt.) Are injuries handled appropriately, insurance costs met? College: _____

Now add up the numerical value for each college.
The one with the highest number *may be* your one, best school.
At any rate, this process has given you something to think about
and discuss at home. Contact your coach and counselor
if you need more help.

GOOD LUCK!

LETTER OF ACCEPTANCE

Date

(Coach's Name
Address
City, State Zip)

Dear (Coach's Name):

Writing this letter gives me a great deal of pleasure because it enables me to confirm my decision to attend your school next year and to be a member of your (name of sport) program. Everyone involved in the decision, including my parents, my coach, and my counselor, agrees with me that the academic and athletic programs at your school satisfy all my needs as a student athlete. You have been particularly helpful throughout the process; I want to thank you for your help and understanding.

I am forwarding a copy of this letter to my high school coach for her/his records and would appreciate hearing from you at some time in the future regarding the next steps.

I know I've made the right decision, and, believe me, I'll do what I can to justify your confidence in me. Again, thanks for your help, and I look forward to hearing from you.

Sincerely,

(Student's Name)

cc: (High School Coach's Name)

STAYING IN COLLEGE

Getting into college is one thing; staying is another! Obviously, high school counselors give a lot of attention to college admissions requirements, SAT and ACT test results, recommendations, interviews, personal essays, and student resumes. We should also take a moment to mention what it takes to *stay* in college—not to shake you up or to apply any more pressure for your senior year but to make sure you don't get any surprises when you leave for college next year.

Good Academic Standing

Students in good academic standing generally maintain at least a C average (2.0 on a 4.0 scale) while in college. That means that for every D they might receive in one subject, they have to receive at least a B in another. Those students who fall below a cumulative C average after a semester or two are put on academic probation by the university. In essence, they are required to get their cumulative grade point back up to a C average, or they subject themselves to dismissal from the university for academic reasons.

Graduating from College

Think about it. If you maintain a C average throughout college, you will graduate at the bottom of your class. Obviously, this isn't all bad. Thousands of students do it every year. The point is, if you want to graduate in the middle or near the top of your class, you will have to maintain at least a B or a B+ average in college. And if you plan to keep a scholarship while in school, you will have to satisfy the academic requirements of the university to maintain "good academic standing."

The best way to earn the required grade point average in college to maintain good academic standing is to develop the necessary study habits in high school. If you develop the right study habits now, you won't have any problems in college. Talk to your teachers, counselor, or coach if you need some help in this area.

SOME POINTERS FOR ACADEMIC SUCCESS

Student Athletes: The following pointers have been well researched by Dr. Roger Grooters, one of the nation's foremost directors of academic advisement, and have been proven to contribute to academic success in college. Read them carefully and apply them throughout college but especially during your freshman year. With use, they will become habits, the kind that carry over into everything you do in life.

1. *Organization*—Get organized! Read and periodically refer to the syllabuses your professors distribute in your classes. Also use the attached daily/weekly planner to provide regular reminders of work to be completed.

2. *Reading Materials in Advance*—Read assignments before class meets. Sometimes it's even a good idea to read the summaries of chapters before you read the chapters. That will give you a good idea of what is to come. As you read, list questions about confusing material, then be sure to ask about it in class.

3. *Class Attendance*—Go to class! This sounds pretty obvious, but you're about to discover that college provides more free time than some high school kids can handle. The freedom you experience in college can provoke some bad habits, so maintain the good habit of going to class regularly. And when you get there, you might as well participate. That's why you jot down all those questions when you read class assignments.

4. *Take Good Notes*—Learn good note-taking skills and record much of what you hear in class. That's why you have to be there! Then take your notes back to the dorm or the library and break down the key concepts, so you understand how everything fits together. Talk to your high school teachers about this skill before going to college and get pointers from them.

5. *Develop Exam Strategies*—Find some exams used previously in your courses and study them, even try to take them. They are usually available in department offices, in fraternities, or directly from the professor. Scan each exam before you take it to determine where you should put your priorities.

6. *Review and Rehearse*—Take just a few moments to review class notes on a daily basis. Overlearn the material before quizzes and exams! Look at your notes until you know what you're about to read before you turn the page. You'll be surprised how helpful this can be.

7. *Develop Your Writing Skills*—Understand what the professor wants in the paper and develop an outline. Then write the first draft on a word processor and look it over very carefully for changes. Write the final draft and have someone look it over for you, preferably someone in the academic advisement program.

8. *Get to Know Your Professors*—Visit them periodically so they know you. See them in their offices to ask about clarification of class materials and to let them know how serious you are about succeeding. You may feel funny saying such things, but they like to hear it!

SEE YOUR COUNSELOR AND TEACHERS FOR MORE POINTERS.
GOOD LUCK IN COLLEGE!

SOME POINTERS FOR ACADEMIC SUCCESS (*continued*)

DAILY/WEEKLY PLANNER

DIRECTIONS: Use the following calendar to record assignments and their completion dates. Each time you receive an assignment in class, write down the due date on this calendar, then indicate those times during the day when you will work on it. Include tests and quizzes and the amount of time you plan to devote to each one. Make approximately 50 extra copies of this form before going to college. You'll want to develop one each week.

For the Week of: _____

HOUR	MONDAY	TUESDAY	WEDNESDAY	THURSDAY	FRIDAY	SATURDAY	SUNDAY
8							
9							
10							
11							
12							
1							
2							
3							
4							
5							
6							
7							
8							
9							
10							

Especially important tasks for this week:

LOOKING FOR AN ATHLETIC SCHOLARSHIP TO COLLEGE?

If you are currently
a high school underclassman,
you need this booklet!

HOW TO USE THIS BOOKLET

As an underclassman in high school and someone who hopes to play a sport in college, you—and your parents—are in need of a lot of information. To play a sport in college, you must meet certain academic eligibility requirements as specified by the NCAA and other regulatory organizations. If you don't meet them, you won't play or practice or qualify for an athletic scholarship. Your first job in high school, then, is to hit the books to be eligible and take advantage of everything college has to offer.

College is, first of all, an experience that prepares you for the world of work and that is educationally, socially, and personally fulfilling in its own right. It can be one of the happiest times of your life—just as high school can be—and should not be restricted to athletic competition. Certainly, athletics will play a large part in your life in high school, and possibly in college.

Read the following discussion and refer to the forms that are mentioned. Use or modify them to suit your purposes. Some require that you meet with your counselor or coach to gather the right information, especially those involving NCAA requirements. Make these appointments as necessary. You probably already know that these two people can provide some very important answers for you.

Additional answers can be found in the book, *Advising the Student Athlete*, published by Prentice Hall, Englewood Cliffs, NJ 07632 or the videotape, the *ABCs of Eligibility for the College-Bound Student Athlete*, marketed by the College Board, 45 Columbus Ave, New York, NY 10023.

A DISCUSSION OF THE FORMS

The first form, "From the Counseling Department," encourages you and, maybe your parents, to meet with your counselor to discuss the pressures of athletic competition and the steps you will have to take to assure progress toward your goal. One of the most important steps is compliance with the NCAA's eligibility requirements. Your counselor is one of the only people in the school who can guide you in the right direction. Meet with your counselor now to talk about the right procedures to follow.

The next form, "Important Terms," is a glossary of sports terminology. You and your parents will find it very helpful during discussions with coaches and counselors or whenever you encounter unfamiliar terms. Read this form now as time permits, and be sure to keep it handy during the next couple of years.

"Eligibility Requirements for Intercollegiate Sports" provides a basic form you can use to write down the specifics of the NCAA's and the NAIA's requirements. The form avoids specific reference to the NCAA bylaws because they have changed so much within the past few years. It does provide space for you to include the specifics during discussions with coaches or counselors. Once you identify these specific requirements, keep the form to refer to it periodically to assure compliance with the NCAA.

"A Glance at the Core Curriculum" provides an indication of what the basic NCAA's core curriculum looks like. It indicates how a student can satisfy the requirements of bylaw 14.3 and still leave room for other, nonacademic courses. It also, however, encourages any college-bound student to take as many academic courses as possible to prepare for the rigors of a college education.

The following form, the "Educational Profile," enables you and your parents to record the completion of required courses and to make an assessment of your readiness to handle the academic challenge of college. We suggest that you update this form every time you receive a semester report card. That way, you will know what kind of progress you are making toward meeting the expectations of the NCAA and achieving your own personal goals to prepare for an eventual college program.

The next form, "A Word of Advice to Student Athletes," provides a general overview of preparation for college and identifies the steps you will want to take before you eventually select a particular college. Read the form carefully and be sure to follow the year-by-year suggestions. When you follow them, you will discover that the college identification and selection processes are enjoyable.

Next, "The World of College Sports," takes a closer look at the extraordinary talents of college athletes. This form is not intended to discourage you from planning on a sport in college, just to look at such competition as realistically as possible—and to reemphasize the importance of academics *now* and *later* in college.

"Is College in Your Future?" is most appropriate for high school juniors. You might also use the form if you plan to start your college search process late in your sophomore year. This form is appropriate even for the highly recruited student athlete.

If you want to start notifying colleges of your interest to play a sport intercollegiately, you might use the form "Letter from Junior Athlete to College Coach" as a model for any letter you write. Such a letter will represent your first big step toward a college and the recruiting process. Be sure to discuss this whole process with your counselor and your coach.

Finally, "Staying in College" gives you a preliminary indication of what is required of college students to stay academically eligible for graduation. Because most high school graduation requirements are different from the requirements of most colleges, it's important that you read this form. You'll notice, for example, that maintaining good academic standing is more difficult in college than in high school. This is just another reason to prepare yourself *now* for what is awaiting you on a college campus.

Look over these materials very carefully and use the references mentioned in this booklet. And always remember that the harder you work—in sports and in the classroom—the luckier you get! Have a wonderful high school career and good luck with finding the right college for you. Most of all, enjoy both experiences. They are among the most rewarding in your life.

FROM THE COUNSELING DEPARTMENT

A Complementary Perspective

Our school's coaches and counselors enjoy a shared responsibility with young athletes. We realize that the benefits of sports are maximized when young athletes develop the right attitude about their participation. We are concerned that our school's athletes guard against overidentifying with their sports and failing to realize the primary importance of academics. We recognize the realities of competitive stress and want to provide ways for young athletes and their parents to deal with it. We also acknowledge the challenges that parents face when assuming the sometimes conflicting roles of "cheerleader" and family leader. Counselors are available to meet with young athletes and their parents to complement the significant relationship that coaches have with them.

Academics and Athletics

Counselors are also available to oversee the academic progress that all students must make to realize the educational and career goals they will establish for themselves. Counselors are also familiar with the provisions of the NCAA's bylaw 14.3, which requires a specific academic program and grade point average of all high school student athletes who plan to play a sport in college. Periodic meetings with counselors are important to assure compliance with the NCAA.

This aspect of counselor involvement is particularly important because most young athletes and many parents are unfamiliar with the extraordinary competition for athletic scholarships. An athletic scholarship certainly is a worthwhile goal, but it is often unrealizable. Hard work in the classroom involves bigger, more realizable benefits. It must never take a back seat to sports.

Stay in contact, therefore, with your counselor *and* your coach. Both are committed to our young people as *student* athletes and are available to parents whenever they have questions or concerns. Let's be sure to work together during the next few years to guarantee your student a valuable sports experience.

IMPORTANT TERMS FOR ATHLETES
AND THEIR PARENTS

If you are involved in the transition from high school to college sports or you assist student athletes with that transition, you may encounter some unfamiliar terms. It is important that you understand these terms in order to promote the transition and to avoid possible violations of NCAA requirements. Read the following list to familiarize yourself with significant terms and review it as appropriate before meetings or phone conversations. For more detailed information, refer to the *NCAA Guide for the College-Bound Student Athlete*. Copies are available in the Athletic and Guidance Offices.

1. *Agents*—High school and college athletes are in violation of NCAA rules if they agree (orally or in writing) to be represented by an agent while in high school or college.

2. *All-Star games*—High school athletes are permitted to participate in only two all-star games per sport.

3. *Blue-chipper*—A "blue-chipper" is any exceptionally gifted high school athlete who is being recruited by a significant number of major colleges.

4. *Booster*—High school athletes may not be contacted by boosters (persons who represent a school's athletic interests) or alumni for purposes of promoting their selection of certain schools. This restriction does not apply, however, to alumni who contact students as part of the college's regular admission program for all prospective students.

5. *Bylaw 14.3*—The NCAA legislation for Division I and II colleges (formerly Proposition 48) that requires high school student athletes to satisfy the provisions of a specific core curriculum, a minimum grade point average, and minimum ACT or SAT scores in order to participate in college sports. Bylaw 14.3 also specifies graduation from high school. Refer to other terms in this glossary for specific information.

6. *Clearinghouse*—The Clearinghouse is an extension of the NCAA coordinated by ACT to determine the eligibility of high school student athletes to be recruited and ultimately scholarshipped by athletic programs in Division I and II colleges and universities.

7. *Contacts*—Any face-to-face meetings between a college coach and you or your parents. High school athletes may not be contacted off the college campus on or before July 1 following the completion of their junior year. Refer to the *NCAA Guide for the College-Bound Student Athlete* for information regarding the number of contacts permitted.

8. *Core Curriculum*—A provision of bylaw 14.3 that requires student athletes to complete an academic program of at least 13 academic units, consisting of at least 3 years of English, 2 of mathematics, 2 of social studies, 2 of natural or physical science (including at least 1 lab class, if offered by the high school), 2 additional academic courses, and 2 more from the above or foreign language, computer science, philosophy, or nondoctrinal religion. Effective August 1, 1996, students first entering college will be expected to complete a core curriculum of 13 academic units, including 4 years of English. In addition, the 2 years of math must involve algebra and geometry.

IMPORTANT TERMS FOR ATHLETES
AND THEIR PARENTS *(continued)*

9. *Drug policies*—Each academic year, student athletes are required to sign a drug-testing consent form at the time of reporting for practice or prior to the Monday of the college's fourth week of classes, whichever occurs earlier. Anyone who tests positive during routine testing is ineligible for further participation, subject to appeal for reinstatement.

10. *Financial aid*—Student athletes who have met the requirements of Bylaw 14.3 may receive financial aid from the college that includes tuition and fees, room and board, and books. See the *NCAA Guide for the College-Bound Student Athlete* regarding the specifics of aid in other circumstances.

11. *Letter of Intent*—The National Letter of Intent is administered by the Collegiate Commissioners Association and involves a commitment from the student athlete to attend a specific school. For detailed information, contact the conference offices of the colleges of interest. It also is important not to sign an institutional or conference letter of intent prior to the National Letter of Intent signing date.

12. *Minimum College Admissions Scores*—Bylaw 14.3 requires that all student athletes score a minimum composite of 17 on the ACT and combined 700 on the SAT with a grade point average of 2.0 on a 4.0 scale. Effective August 1, 1995, these minimum scores will require a grade point average of 2.5 on a 4.0 scale. See "Sliding Scale" in this glossary.

13. *NAIA*—the National Association of Intercollegiate Athletics normally represents smaller schools but does provide financial aid for athletic purposes. Student athletes must meet two of the following three requirements: achieve an 18 on the ACT or a 740 on the SAT; earn an overall grade point average of 2.0 on a 4.0 scale; graduate in the top half of the class.

14. *NCAA*—The National Collegiate Athletic Association is the primary regulatory organization for intercollegiate athletics. Information can be secured from them by writing NCAA, 6201 College Blvd., Overland Park, Kansas 66211-2422, or by calling 913-339-1906.

15. *NCAA Divisions*—The NCAA is composed of three divisions. Division I is normally considered the "major college" division, the big schools that attract considerable media attention. These are the schools that give full scholarships and engage in widespread recruiting. Division I-AA schools are somewhat smaller, recruit on a smaller scale, and give fewer full scholarships but a sizable number of partial scholarships. Division II schools are similar to Division I-AA schools in their recruiting practices and the allocation of scholarships but on a somewhat smaller scale. Division III schools give no athletic scholarships, tend to recruit locally, and represent some of the most prestigious colleges in the country.

16. *Professionalism*—High school and college athletes are considered professionals if they are paid to compete in an athletic contest; commit in writing or orally to an agent or a professional sports organization; request that their names be placed on a draft list; use their athletic skills for pay in any form (TV commercials, etc.); play on a professional sports team; or play on an amateur team and receive any payment or gratuity.

IMPORTANT TERMS FOR ATHLETES
AND THEIR PARENTS *(continued)*

17. *Prospective Student Athlete*—A player is a "prospective student athlete" once he or she starts the ninth grade of school. Prior to the completion of the junior year, high school student athletes may meet with college coaches, but only on the coach's campus. Refer to the definition of a "contact" regarding meetings anywhere else.

18. *Recruited Prospective Student Athlete*—A player is a "recruited prospective student athlete" when a coach or a representative of a particular school's athletic interests encourages the student to play for that school. Such encouragement normally occurs when the coach or booster provides transportation to the school or some kind of entertainment such as complimentary tickets to a game, calls the player's home, or visits the player anywhere other than the college campus. Be sure to review the definitions of "Boosters" and "Contacts" when discussing the whole issue of recruitment.

19. *Red-shirt*—An athlete is "red-shirted" when (s)he is withheld from actual competition for one year. The athlete may practice with the team during that time but, because of injury or coach's decision, (s)he will not play in games. Be advised that the athlete must complete his or her athletic eligibility within a six-year period once matriculated at the college. The red-shirt year must occur within this time frame.

20. *Sliding Scale*—The most recent provisions of bylaw 14.3 provide a sliding scale for equating grade point average with ACT or SAT scores. Please refer to the *NCAA Guide for the College-Bound Student Athlete* for specifics.

21. *Student Release Form*—The "Student Release Form" is the document used by high school student athletes and high school counselors to verify the academic eligibility of the athletes to be recruited and ultimately accepted to compete in Division I and II athletic programs.

22. *Visits*—Prospective student athletes are permitted by NCAA requirements only one expenses-paid visit to a particular college. Subsequent visits to that college must be paid for by the athlete. Student athletes are allowed a maximum of five such visits. In essence, they can visit only five schools during the senior year, regardless of the number of sports they may play.

23. *Waiver of bylaw 14.3 requirements*—Bylaw 14.3 requirements may be waived based on documented evidence demonstrating student achievement that warrants something other than the normal application of the bylaw. All appeals must be made by a member institution that has officially admitted the student as a regular student. Athletes, coaches, or counselors should contact the college or university in question for more information about the waiver process.

MORE QUESTIONS?
CONTACT THE ATHLETIC DEPARTMENT.

ELIGIBILITY REQUIREMENTS FOR *INTERCOLLEGIATE* SPORTS

DIRECTIONS: The following discussion contains very important information. You *must* abide by it if you plan to play a sport in college. ***The Bad News:*** If you fall short in any area, you will not be eligible to receive a scholarship, practice, or play in an NCAA Division I or II school during your first year. For that matter, you may *never* play a sport in college if you are declared academically ineligible. ***The Good News:*** The rules are not hard to follow. If you maintain a decent college-prep program in high school and study to the best of your ability, you will have no problem with the following requirements.

Be sure to write them down as we go along, and ask questions at any time. We're here to make sure you understand the rules.

The NCAA's Bylaw 14.3 (Proposition 48)

1. Graduate from high school.
2. Maintain a grade point average of _____ on a 4.0 scale and earn a composite score of _____ on the ACT or a _____ on the SAT or earn a lower grade point average but a higher ACT/SAT score. Ask your counselor or coach to see the NCAA "Sliding Scale." It shows the relationship between test scores and grade point average.
3. Maintain a program of at least _____ academic units (full-year courses), including the following:
   - English—4 years
   - Math—2 years
   - Social Studies—2 years
   - Science—2 years
   - Other:

NOTES:

NAIA REQUIREMENTS

The requirements of the National Association of Intercollegiate Athletics (NAIA) are similar to those of the NCAA. The NAIA also awards athletic scholarships and has its own set of eligibility requirements. Write them down as they are mentioned.

YOU MUST MEET ANY TWO OF THE FOLLOWING THREE REQUIREMENTS:

1. Graduate from the upper half of your high school class.
2. Earn a grade point average of _____ on a 4.0 scale.
3. Receive a composite score of _____ on the ACT or a score of _____ on the SAT.

For further explanations of some of the specifics of test scores and academic program, see your coach and counselor. You may have a unique situation that requires special consideration. Talk to your coach and counselor anyway, if only to make sure that you are meeting the requirements of either organization.

NOTES:

A GLANCE AT THE CORE CURRICULUM

What 13 Academic Units Look Like

Following is a sample high school program that contains 13 academic units (they are underlined in each column). It also contains room for additional academic courses (they are listed in italics). This program is required if you plan to play a sport in college. In fact, if you are serious about college, you'll take more academic courses than those mentioned in this sample. This is just a sample program; other variations are possible.

FRESHMAN

English 1, 2
Algebra 1,2
Physical Science 1, 2
Intro to Computers 1/Art 1
Physical Education
Social Studies Intro 1, 2

SOPHOMORE

English 3, 4
Geometry 1, 2
Biology 1, 2
Art 3, 4
PE/Health
Cons. Ec. 1/*Computer 2*

JUNIOR

English 5, 6
Algebra 3, 4
United States History 1, 2
Art 5, 6
Physical Education
  Business Course or (Language?)

SENIOR

English 7, 8
Chemistry 1, 2
Study and Work Program or (Language and Sci?)
Physical Education
Metal Shop 1, 2

THINK ABOUT:

- A foreign language; many colleges want it. (2 years)
- More academic courses (pay me now or pay me later!)

SEE YOUR COACH OR COUNSELOR IF YOU HAVE QUESTIONS!

EDUCATIONAL PROFILE

To the Student Athlete:

Use this profile to keep track of your academic progress through school. It will help during future planning activities.

NAME: _____

ACT:

Composite: _____

Subtest Scores: _____ _____ _____ _____

SAT:

Composite: _____

Subtest Scores: _____ _____

CLASS RANK:

_____ of _____   _____ of _____   _____ of _____
(5th sem.)   (6th sem.)   (7th sem.)

GPA IN CORE COURSES:

	5TH SEM.	6TH SEM.	7TH SEM.
MATH	_____	_____	_____
SCIENCE	_____	_____	_____
SOCIAL STUD.	_____	_____	_____
ENGLISH	_____	_____	_____

ASSESSMENT OF ACADEMIC STRENGTHS:

	JUNIOR YEAR	SENIOR YEAR
ACADEMIC COMMITMENT	_____	_____
SOCIAL MATURITY	_____	_____
COMMUNICATION SKILLS	_____	_____
ORGANIZATION SKILLS	_____	_____

Rate the above skills "High," "Medium," or "Low," then discuss your rating with your parents and counselor. This will give you an idea of a few things you might do between now and the time you leave for college. The above information will also be important when you make decisions about the program of study you will pursue in college.

A Word of Advice
to
Student Athletes

... and Their
Parents

The Counselor
and Coach Commitment

Your counselor and coach(es) are committed to providing the assistance you will need to realize your academic and athletic goals. As much as we would like to—we can't guarantee you an athletic scholarship to college, but we can assure you and your parents that we will help you plan, work, and search for an appropriate college experience.

This brochure identifies for you and your parents the process and the people who will help you prepare for your goals.

Save it and refer to it each year to assure yourself that you are doing everything necessary to plan for your future college experience.

Sports may or may not be in that future. Ultimately, that is up to you. We are here to help.

So Stay in Contact
with the 4 C's:

Coach
Counselor
Career Consultant
College Consultant

The World
of College Sports

The world of college sports is as competitive as any activity in the United States. Players every year are getting bigger, smarter, and stronger. In football alone, the average lineman is 6′4″ and bench presses over 400 pounds. Such athletes represent the finest in the world. High school athletes, therefore, are encouraged to remember the statistics mentioned in this brochure and to seek a college primarily as an *academic* experience.

What you do *now* in high school will determine in large measure what you will do in college, both on the court or the playing field and in the classroom. The success you realize in both areas will be the direct result of how hard you are willing to work now.

Sports requires an enormous amount of time. Now is the time to develop the right habits!

Hit
the
Books!

Do You Need to Plan Carefully for High School and College Sports?

Consider these facts:

- Only 3% of high school football players receive a scholarship to play in college; most of those are partials.

- Only 1½% of high school basketball players receive scholarships to play in college; also mostly partials.

- Only 38% of Division I (major college) football players graduate at the end of five years. The percentage is lower for basketball.

- Tennis, swimming, and other kinds of scholarships are necessarily limited because of financial restrictions in many colleges.

- If you receive a questionnaire from a major college expressing interest in you as a football player, the odds are still as high a 320:1 that you'll ever receive a scholarship.

- If our school had started when our nation did, we would still have to wait a quarter of a century to have a graduate play professional basketball.

Academics Is The Answer!

How Do You Plan Carefully?

Your Freshman Year ...

- Sign an athletic code and get doctor's permission to participate. This must be done every year.

- Meet with your counselor to discuss your four-year plan as a roadmap to college. (Early December)

- Meet again with your counselor before registration for the sophomore year to discuss college entrance requirements and to assure compliance with the NCAA eligibility rules. (Early February)

Your Sophomore Year ...

- Take the PACT to practice for the ACT.

- Meet again with your counselor before registration for the junior year to assure compliance with the NCAA eligibility requirements.

- View the videotape the *ABC's of Eligiblity for the College-Bound Student Athlete.* It is available in the library and the Guidance Office.

Your Junior Year ...

- Take the PSAT in October to practice for the SAT.

- Meet with your counselor before registration for your senior year to be sure to meet

college admission requirements and to assure compliance with the NCAA eligibility rules.

- Secure a copy of the NCAA *Guide for the College-Bound Athlete* from your coach or the Athletic Director. Specifically read the section on athletic eligibility. Discuss it with your parents and coach.

- Sign up for a *Career Search* and a *College Search.*

- Meet with your counselor and the appropriate consultant to discuss the results.

- Take the SAT and ACT in the winter or spring of the year.

- Inform your coach of your interest in playing a sport in college.

- Visit potential colleges.

Your Senior Year ...

- Retake the ACT and/or the SAT as needed.

- Meet with your counselor early in the fall to review your transcript to assure compliance with the NCAA eligibility requirements.

- Meet with your coach to discuss your potential to play for certain colleges.

- Mail college applications.

- Review the NCAA *Guide for the College-Bound Athlete* and the videotape the *ABC's of Eligibility for the College-Bound Student Athlete.*

THE WORLD OF COLLEGE SPORTS

Athletics in College

College sports has changed considerably within the past five to ten years. Most significantly, Title IX has provided a wide range of opportunities for women to play competitive sports in high school and college. Women's facilities have improved; the range of sports has expanded; and the number of college scholarships has increased. Of equal significance, the competition for those scholarships has intensified, for both men and women.

Atypical just ten years ago, a 300-pound lineman in football and a 6'5" woman in basketball are commonplace today. Even more surprising is the fact that both are stronger and quicker than their smaller counterparts of 10 years ago. Recently, the tallest player for a major university was the center on the *women's* basketball team. She was 6'10".

It is no longer uncommon for linemen in football to bench press 500 pounds or for backs to run 4.3 forties, nor is it surprising to find a variety of 7"0" men's basketball players or 6'3" women's volleyball players. College athletes in the United States are as gifted as any in the world, *and* they are good students.

Academics in College

The average graduation rate for college athletes is higher than the rate for nonathletes, especially for women. Whereas approximately half of all nonathletes graduate in five years, almost two-thirds of women athletes graduate. The average is lower for male athletes but still higher than for nonathletes. When college recruiters visit our school, therefore, one of the first questions they ask coaches about players is "What kind of student is she/he?" They have learned that poor students, no matter how good they are as athletes, don't stay in college long enough to help their teams.

The Challenge to You

If you want to play a sport in college, exercise your muscles and your brain *right now.* You'll benefit from both, even if you don't play a sport in college. Few athletes get to play a sport in college, so enjoy your high school participation. College is in your future; high school is now. Your coaches are here to help you with both. Let's work together to help you become the best *student athlete* you can be.

IS COLLEGE IN YOUR FUTURE?

To Student Athletes and Their Parents:

Many high school athletes look forward to a continuation of their sports in college. In many instances, these expectations can be very realistic; in others, they are not. When the time comes, be sure to talk to your coach about college sports. He or she will be able to give you all the help you need to make that important transition in your life. In the meantime, if a college sport is what you want, keep the following pointers in mind:

1. *Search out the right academic program.* Talk to your counselor about interest inventories, career searches, and the college exploration process. You may not end up with a definite career focus, but the process will introduce you to several very important considerations about your future. It will also provide the academic orientation you need when you go to college to hit the books and to realize success in your studies.

2. *Find the best schools for you.* When you have completed the process, you probably will have developed a list of colleges that meet your academic, career, and personal requirements. You'll be surprised at some of the things your counselor tells you about the college selection process. It's an eye-opening experience!

3. *Visit several schools.* After you have developed a list of schools that are just right for you, visit several of them. Everything else being equal, a visit to a college campus is the best way to determine if that school is what you want. If it doesn't result in a decision, at least it will give you the information you need to eventually make that decision.

4. *Apply to two or three schools early in your senior year.* We don't want to jinx you with this memo, but sports in college is not a sure thing for you. You may get injured between now and then, or you may discover a sudden disinterest from college recruiters next year. Even if you are highly recruited, the work you do to select the right college program will make the recruiting process a whole lot easier next year.

**SEE YOUR COUNSELOR AND YOUR COACH
FOR ADDITIONAL INFORMATION
ABOUT THIS BIG STEP YOU ARE PLANNING!**

LETTER FROM JUNIOR ATHLETE
TO COLLEGE COACH

Date

(Coach's Name
Address
City, State Zip)

Dear (Coach's Name):

I would like to take this opportunity to introduce myself to you. I am currently a junior at (name of high school) and, with the completion of this current season, have played softball for three years, starting at shortstop for the last two. I am 5'9" and weigh 145 pounds and can also play first base and catcher. I have been All-Conference for the past two years and was recently selected to the All-Area team.

My coach's name is Sandra Miller; she has encouraged me to write this letter. She indicates that she plans to write one as well. Regarding my statistics: I committed only two errors this season and batted .425, with 23 triples and 19 home runs. I currently own five school records in softball and also play basketball and field hockey.

I rank 23 in a class of 389 and have a 3.4 grade point average on a 4.0 scale. My career goals are as yet undefined, but I am interested in math and science, so I probably will want to go into engineering. I am looking forward to college as an opportunity to pursue my educational and career goals and would love to continue playing softball on the college level, especially with your program.

I hope to hear from you and am available in the event you are interested in additional information. Please forward whatever materials I need at this point to further express my interest in your program.

Thanks for the time, and I look forward to hearing from you.

Sincerely yours,

(Student Athlete's Name)

STAYING IN COLLEGE

Getting into college is one thing; staying is another! Obviously, high school counselors give a lot of attention to college admissions requirements, SAT and ACT test results, recommendations, interviews, personal essays, and student resumes. We should also take a moment to mention what it takes to *stay* in college—not to shake you up or to apply any more pressure for your senior year but to make sure you don't get any surprises when you leave for college next year.

Good Academic Standing

Students in good academic standing generally maintain at least a C average (2.0 on a 4.0 scale) while in college. That means that for every D they might receive in one subject, they have to receive at least a B in another. Those students who fall below a cumulative C average after a semester or two are put on academic probation by the university. In essence, they are required to get their cumulative grade point back up to a C average, or they subject themselves to dismissal from the university for academic reasons.

Graduating from College

Think about it. If you maintain a C average throughout college, you will graduate at the bottom of your class. Obviously, this isn't all bad. Thousands of students do it every year. The point is, if you want to graduate in the middle or near the top of your class, you will have to maintain at least a B or a B+ average in college. And if you plan to keep a scholarship while in school, you will have to satisfy the academic requirements of the university to maintain "good academic standing."

The best way to earn the required grade point average in college to maintain good academic standing is to develop the necessary study habits in high school. If you develop the right study habits now, you won't have any problems in college. Talk to your teachers, counselor, or coach if you need some help in this area.